Youth and sustainable peacebuilding

Edited by

Helen Berents, Catherine Bolten and
Siobhán McEvoy-Levy

MANCHESTER UNIVERSITY PRESS

Published by Manchester University Press
Oxford Road, Manchester, M13 9PL

www.manchesteruniversitypress.co.uk

British Library Cataloguing-in-Publication Data
A catalogue record for this book is available from the British Library

ISBN 978 1 5261 7620 2 hardback
ISBN 978 1 5261 7787 2 paperback

First published 2024

Typeset
by Cheshire Typesetting Ltd, Cuddington, Cheshire

Contents

Figures

Notes on contributors

Ali Altiok is a Doctoral Student in Peace Studies and Political Science at the Kroc Institute for International Peace Studies at the University of Notre Dame, USA. He co-authored the policy paper *We Are Here: An Integrated Approach to Youth Inclusive Peace Processes*, and served as researcher to *The Missing Peace: Independent Progress Study on YPS*, mandated by UN Security Council Resolution 2250.

Helen Berents is an Australian Research Council DECRA Fellow with the Griffith Asia Institute, and a Senior Lecturer in the School of Government and International Relations at Griffith University, Australia. Her research, which is interested in the politics of children and youth in international conflict and peacebuilding, has been published in journals including *International Affairs*, *International Political Sociology* and the *International Feminist Journal of Politics*. She is the author of *Young People and Everyday Peace: Exclusion, Insecurity and Peacebuilding in Colombia* (Routledge, 2018).

Jordan Bighorn has been working at CEDA for the past ten years as Program Manager of the CEDA Pathways Program, Co-Director Intern, and most recently as the Co-Director of Operations. Prior to his employment at CEDA, Jordan worked with the National Spiritual Assembly of the Baha'ís of Canada with their Urban Indigenous Youth Program, and at Southeast Collegiate as a guidance counsellor and lodge manager. He is an active member of the Winnipeg Baha'í community and cherishes the opportunities to work for the betterment of his community, or wherever he finds himself.

Catherine E. Bolten is Professor of Anthropology and Peace Studies at the Kroc Institute for International Peace Studies at the University of Notre Dame, USA. She is the author of *I Did It to Save My Life: Love and Survival in Sierra Leone* (University of California Press, 2012) and *Serious*

Youth in Sierra Leone (Oxford University Press, 2020). She has published widely on issues of youth, education, work and child rights in postwar Sierra Leone.

Bush Buse Laki is a South Sudanese activist and founding member of Take Tea Together (TTT). He works for Whitaker Peace and Development Initiative as a programme co-ordinator. Bush holds a bachelor's degree in Economics with first class honors from Kampala University – Uganda and is currently pursuing a master's degree programme in peace and development studies in the University of Juba.

Justin de Leon PhD is an Assistant Professor of Ethnic Studies at Chapman University and a Senior Adviser to the Mediation Program at University of Notre Dame's Kroc Institute for International Peace Studies, USA. His research and community work focuses on story-telling and Indigenous sovereignty, working with Indigenous youth throughout North America. De Leon has published works on relation-ality, Indigenous international relations, militarisation and Indigenous filmmaking.

Prashan de Visser founded Sri Lanka Unites, a youth movement bringing people together in the wake of the country's civil war, in 2009. The movement is now Global Unites, with chapters across dozens of countries around the Global South. Prashan holds an MA in Peace Studies from the University of Notre Dame, USA.

Netra Eng is the Director of Research and Director of the Center for Governance and Inclusive Society at Cambodia Development Resource Institute (CDRI). She leads and co-lead a number of research projects examining the impacts of youth on Cambodia's economic development and governance reforms, and the impacts of Covid-19 on social protection and work for youth in Cambodia.

Anna Fett is a Rosenwald Postdoctoral Fellow in US Foreign Policy and International Security at Dartmouth's John Sloan Dickey Center for International Understanding for the 2023–2024 academic year. She received her PhD in Peace Studies and History from the Kroc Institute for International Peace Studies at the University of Notre Dame, USA. She has published in the journals *Diplomatic History* and *Peace and Change*. Her areas of interest include the history of the US in the world, and youth and peacebuilding.

Caroline Hughes is Rev. Theodore M. Hesburgh CSC Professor of Peace Studies at the Kroc Institute for International Peace Studies at the University of Notre Dame, USA. She is co-author of *International Intervention and Local Politics* (Oxford University Press, 2017) and *The Politics of Accountability in South East Asia* (Cambridge University Press, 2014).

Emmily Koiti is a medical doctor as well as a peace and human rights activist. Alongside her medical career, she has participated as youth representative and signatory in track 1 peace negotiations that culminated in the signing of the South Sudan's Revitalised Agreement on the Resolution of Conflict in South Sudan. She is Executive Director of South Sudanese In Medicine (SSWIM) and also currently practises medicine in Kenya.

Angela J. Lederach is Assistant Professor of Peace Studies at Chapman University, USA. She is co-author of *When Blood and Bones Cry Out: Journeys through the Soundscape of Healing and Reconciliation* (Oxford University Press, 2010). Her most recent book, *Feel the Grass Grow: Ecologies of Slow Peace in Colombia* (Stanford University Press, 2023) examines the temporal politics of peacebuilding at the intersection of environmental and political violence in Colombia.

Katrina Lee-Koo is a Professor of International Relations at Monash University, Melbourne, Australia. She recently co-edited *Gender Politics: Navigating Political Leadership in Australia* (with Zareh Ghazarian, 2021) and is the co-author of *Young Women and Leadership* (with Lesley Pruitt, 2020).

Jaimarsin Lewis is from Indianapolis, Indiana, USA, where he works at the Martin Luther King Community Center and as a visiting youth researcher with the Desmond Tutu Peace Peace Lab at Butler University.

Patrícia Martuscelli is a Lecturer in International Relations at the University of Sheffield, UK. She has a MA in International Relations (University of Brasília) and a PhD in Political Science (University of São Paulo). Her research interests involve asylum and migration politics in Latin America and children in international relations.

Siobhán McEvoy-Levy is Professor of Political Science and Peace & Conflict Studies at Butler University and Director of the Desmond Tutu Peace Lab in Indianapolis, Indiana, USA. Her publications include *Peace and Resistance in Youth Cultures* (Palgrave, 2018), and (as editor)

Troublemakers or Peacemakers? Youth and Post-accord Peace Building (Notre Dame, 2006).

Caitlin Mollica is a Lecturer of Politics in the Business School at the University of Newcastle, Australia. Her book *Agency and Ownership in Reconciliation: Young People and the Practice of Transitional Justice* will be published by SUNY University Press in 2024. She has also published work in leading journals including *Cooperation and Conflict*, *Pacific Review*, *Human Rights Quarterly* and the *Australian Journal of International Affairs*. Her current research focuses on human rights approaches to donor funding for the realisation of youth-led peacebuilding practices.

Chara Nyaura currently works with one of South Sudan's security mechanisms that monitors the implementation of the 2018 peace agreement. She is a Gender adviser to Ceasefire & Transitional Security Arrangement Monitoring & Verification Mechanism (CTSAMVM). CTSAMVM ensures that monitoring, verifying and reporting on the gender dimensions of the Permanent Ceasefire & Transitional Security Arrangement (PCTSA) of the chapter 2 of the 2018 ARCSS and the overall mainstreaming are prioritised throughout all its activities.

Obasesam Okoi is Assistant Professor of Justice and Peace Studies at the University of St Thomas, Minnesota, USA, Associate Editor of *African Security Journal* and Charles E. Scheidt Faculty Fellow in Atrocity Prevention at the Institute for Genocide and Mass Atrocity Prevention (I-GMAP), Binghamton University, New York. He is author of *Punctuated Peace in Nigeria's Oil Region: Oil Insurgency and the Challenges of Post-Conflict Peace* (Palgrave, 2021).

Karaijus Perry is from Indianapolis, Indiana, USA, where he works at the Martin Luther King Community Center and as a visiting youth researcher with the Desmond Tutu Peace Peace Lab at Butler University.

Trinity Perry is from Indianapolis, Indiana, USA, where he works at the Martin Luther King Community Center and as a visiting youth researcher with the Desmond Tutu Peace Peace Lab at Butler University.

Lesley Pruitt is Senior Lecturer in the School of Social and Political Sciences at the University of Melbourne. Lesley is author of *Youth Peacebuilding: Music, Gender and Change* (State University of New York Press, 2013) and co-author of *Dancing through the Dissonance: Creative Movement and Peacebuilding* (Manchester University Press, 2020).

Julio Trujillo is the C2C Pathways to Success Facilitator at the Martin Luther King Community Center in Indianapolis, USA. A first-generation college student, he graduated from Butler University in 2019 with a BA in Criminology and Political Science. He was the Neighborhood Youth Liaison Intern for the Desmond Tutu Peace Lab between 2018 and 2019. He is currently a Children's Law Fellow at Loyola Law School, Chicago.

Acknowledgements

Many people made this book possible. Firstly, we are exceedingly grateful for the enthusiasm and persistence of our chapter authors, who came together across time zones, experiences, interests and passions to contribute to this remarkable book. We started this work prior to the Covid-19 pandemic, and we are truly indebted to our authors for their patience in sticking with the project, participating in online workshops in lieu of in-person meetings, and for being responsive to deadlines and requests for updates. Thank you all for making this volume the rich contribution that it is. It has also been a true joy for the three editors working together across time zones, making this an enjoyable and easy collaboration. We are also grateful to Rob Byron and Humairaa Dudhwala at Manchester University Press and to the three anonymous reviewers whose comments helpfully enhanced the volume.

Catherine Bolten would also like to thank her collaborators in Sierra Leone, without whom her chapter would not have been possible. Of special note are Martin and Emma Bamin, Father Joe Turay and the staff of the University of Makeni, and her research assistants, Mohamed Kallon and AbuBakkar Taylor-Kamara, with whom she has had the pleasure of working for almost two decades.

Siobhán McEvoy-Levy thanks her coauthors and other collaborators at the Martin Luther King Center in Indianapolis, colleagues at Butler University, and friends and family, particularly Andy and Aedan, and Ginnis the dog.

Helen Berents's work on this volume was enabled by an Australian Research Council DECRA Fellowship (DE200100937). She is thankful to her research interlocutors in the global YPS community for their openness and enthusiasm for this research, as well as for the support of loved ones, in particular Brendan and Harry the dog.

Introduction: Youth and sustainable peace

Helen Berents, Catherine E. Bolten and Siobhán McEvoy-Levy

Scholarly and policy consideration of young people and the challenges of conflict resolution and peacebuilding have expanded in recent decades. However, as we examine in the chapters of this book, young people's roles in peacebuilding continue to be viewed through the lenses of pre-existing assumptions about their competencies and dangerousness. Furthermore, narrow ideas about what peacebuilding is and where it takes place fail to notice and closely address the myriad ways in which young people already work on peace in their communities. Sustainable peace, we argue, involves more than simply including youth in official peacebuilding mechanisms or recognising their local peacebuilding work; it requires a transformation in thinking about youth as actors in the world of security and peace.

The context for such new thinking is ripe. As a policy issue youth and peacebuilding reached a new phase and level of acceptance with the establishment of the United Nations-initiated global Youth, Peace and Security (YPS) agenda in 2015 and there have been three related UN Security Council Resolutions. UN Security Council Resolution 2250 (2015) was the first thematic resolution recognising the 'positive' role of youth in peacebuilding and calls for 'integrated mechanisms for meaningful participation of youth in peace processes and dispute-resolution'. Three of the Resolution's five pillars for action focus on violence – its prevention, protection of youth from violence, and disengagement and reintegration of armed actors. Two of the five YPS pillars (Participation and Partnership) address involvement of youth in decision-making. The two further UN Security Council Resolutions have developed the YPS framework. Resolution 2419 (2018) calls for 'inclusive representation of youth for the prevention and resolution of conflict, including when negotiating and implementing peace agreements, to take into account the meaningful participation and views of youth, recognizing that their marginalization is detrimental to building sustainable peace and countering violent extremism as and when conducive to terrorism' (S/RES/2419 (2018) 18–09198). Resolution 2535 (2020) is focused on provisions aimed at the 'mainstreaming' of YPS into the work of the UN secretariat. As a whole this YPS agenda emerged from more than a decade of global advocacy by civil society, youth-led organisations, NGOs, governments and IGOs (Berents 2022). Beyond the resolutions a range of programmatic responses and interventions are evolving. In the United States a YPS bill was introduced to Congress in March 2020. In June 2020, after several years of development and institutionalisation, the African Union's Peace and Security Council adopted the 'Continental Framework on Youth, Peace and Security'. As implementation efforts are under way through a range of National Action Plans and other efforts (UNSC 2022), the time is ripe to consider exactly how youth are or are not 'inclusively represented', do and do not undertake 'meaningful participation', and are recognised – or fail to be recognised – in the process of building sustainable peace.

This book is aimed both at those who are new to the consideration of youth in peacebuilding (and who may be coming to the issue via attention to the YPS agenda) and at those who have been working on youth issues for many years. This latter group may find themselves ambivalent about YPS: on the one hand, pleased to see the recognition of youth as agentic peacebuilders, and, on the other, justifiably concerned about the impact that YPS may have in the lives of young people, especially as translated to the national and local level. On the one hand, the moment seems promising for a transformation of institutional understandings of peacebuilding, through a close engagement with lessons from how young people define and seek to produce sustainable peace. However, as the interests of multiple actors continue to shape this agenda, key ongoing challenges include concerns about how young people are being included in YPS (Berents 2022; Berents and Mollica 2022), and how are they are being further securitised by the agenda (Sukarieh and Tannock 2018; Ensor 2021).

A further practical challenge relates to resourcing and supporting youth peacebuilding work through the YPS agenda framework. While there has been significant rhetorical support from UN Member States, regional bodies and NGOS/CSOs, the work of young peacebuilders remains chronically underfunded and under-resourced. A 2017 survey of youth peacebuilders by UNOY Peacebuilders and Search for Common Ground found that 49 per cent of youth organisations operate on less than US $5000 a year, and 97 per cent of the work carried out occurs on a volunteer basis (UNOY and Search for Common Ground 2017). In his periodic report on YPS the UN Secretary-General noted that 'inadequate resourcing remains a central challenge to implementation' of the agenda (UNSC 2020). Competing framings of youth and practical obstacles pose challenges to how youth can build peace and how institutional support might be provided to youth peacebuilders. However, it is important not only to critique but to offer constructive ways forward, and this volume takes on both tasks.

The authors in this volume contribute to critical questioning and problem-identifying around these novel efforts by highlighting three interrelated issues that emerge at this juncture. First, whose security does YPS promote? Is it security for youth or security from them? The YPS agenda replicates old and persistent discourses about both the peril and promise of youth. While 'protection' of youth is a key pillar, the agenda continues to 'securitise' young people by labelling them as risks for violent extremism. We argue that this dynamic persists as an extension of states' interests, perceptions, and often misconceptions of who youth are, what they want, and how prone they are to challenging state power. Fear of youth produces policies that construct the threat they were designed to prevent while idealising a subset of 'peaceful' youth as being diametrically opposed to their violent counterparts. The reality is more complex and fluid as contributions demonstrate – for example, young peacebuilders face great dangers and are often ambivalent about the 'peace' label – and this complicates the engagement of young peacebuilders with official institutions.

Second, does a UN agenda of including youth in peacebuilding solve these problems of securitisation and stereotyping of youth, and/or does it create new problems? We argue that the new emphasis on high-level inclusion of youth in peacebuilding fails to solve the issues of marginalisation, idealisation, securitisation and the power relations that are inherent in youth 'participation' in official processes, and creates different ideological and symbolic problems for the youth involved. At many levels of social and political engagement young people are not taken seriously and are conditioned to not take themselves seriously. When they do insist on their inclusion they are forced to use existing tools and methods of engagement that both disadvantage them and tend towards status-quo outcomes. Their representativeness is questionable and contingent upon compliance. YPS is vigorously promoted by countries with strong interests in counter-terrorism, but creating substantial, 'meaningful' roles for youth in peace processes entails dismantling certain norms and beliefs about youth as dangers. Contributors to this volume show that young people are participating in different ways in formal peace and security spaces, even when these structures limit or obfuscate their contributions. They are also participating though informal processes, and their experiences in both settings provide important lessons.

Third, in what ways are youth conceptualising and building peace outside of both institutional discourses of inclusion and narratives of securitisation? Official youth inclusion initiatives have difficulty acknowledging and embracing the creative, dynamic, practical and pluralistic peacebuilding efforts that youth have generated on their own around the world, most often outside of official peace processes. What we argue, however, is that it is precisely these efforts that offer the greatest insights for sustainable peace-building. In highlighting the varied approaches young people have taken to generating peace on their own terms in different parts of the world, the volume shows how youth are also finding their own spaces and innovative models, and inviting older allies to join them, in efforts that offer new ways of conceptualising and building sustainable peace.

The three parts of this volume address each of these arguments in turn as they take on the core puzzle of how young people are participating in building sustainable peace and how youth may be most effectively supported and accompanied in these efforts. The rest of this introduction previews the sections and chapters to come and contextualises them within the existing literatures related to youth and sustainable peacebuilding.

Sustainable peace and youth

For peace to be sustainable, we must understand it as interconnected in multi-scalar and multi-temporal dimensions. This means taking seriously the local and the global, as well as the links between; it means paying attention to how the conditions for violence and insecurity are fostered through problematic policy frameworks, historic and cultural framings of social worlds and the complex landscapes of conflict and rebuilding from violence. With this more comprehensive perspective of where peace happens, it is logical to consider youth as integral to an understanding of what sustainable peace might look like – youth are omnipresent in these spaces, whether as the perceived danger in policy agendas, on the frontlines of conflict or in the myriad ways they build and maintain peaceful homes, communities and futures.

We take as our starting point the definition of sustainable peace by John Paul Lederach, who argued that it requires 'a comprehensive approach to the transformation of conflict that addresses structural issues, social dynamics of relationship building and the development of a supportive infrastructure for peace' (1997, 22). As Lederach has cautioned, sustainable peacebuilding involves more than attention to 'mechanical tasks, process and solutions': 'To be at all germane to contemporary conflict, peacebuilding must be rooted in and responsive to the experiential and subjective realities shaping people's perspectives and needs' (1997, 24). In this vein our exploration of sustainable peace in this volume is grounded in the lived experiences of youth. We consider these lived experiences in turn in relation to the subjective realities of their elders, the states in which they live and peacebuilding organisations operating there.

As a concept, sustainable peace has been debated by scholars and practitioners, and this volume contributes to ongoing conversations about the activities, actors and spaces that are part of sustainable peacebuilding. A lot of focus has been placed on activities in 'post-conflict' contexts with a strong bias towards top-down implementation of peace accords and large-scale reconstruction efforts (e.g. Darby and Mac Ginty 2008; Paris 2004; and for a systematic review of peacebuilding literature since 1990 see Simangan 2022). For example, the existing literature on sustainable peacebuilding notes that it involves numerous intersecting tasks and dynamics:

> disarming warring parties, decommissioning, destroying weapons, de-mining, repatriating refugees, restoring law and order, creating or rebuilding justice systems, training police forces and custom agents, providing technical assistance, advancing efforts to protect human rights, strengthening civil society institutions and reforming and strengthening institutions of governance – including assistance in monitoring and supervising electoral processes and promoting formal and informal participation in the political process. (Keating and Knight 2004, xxxiii)

Previous research has shown that young people's interests, needs and roles in conflict zones intersect with all of these and other post-conflict peacebuilding issues and sectors (McEvoy-Levy 2001, 2006; Borer, Darby and McEvoy-Levy 2006; Özerderm and Podder 2011; Özerderm and Podder 2015; Schwartz 2010; Schnabel and Tabyshalieva 2013) and that young people are directly participating in technical assistance, as well as observing negotiations and ceasefire monitoring (Altiok and Grizelj 2019; Grizelj 2019). The contributions in this volume span the spectrum of peacebuilding concerns including addressing issues of ex-combatant reintegration and transitional justice, but they also widen the lens to take a broader view of the spaces and activities involved in sustainable peace.

Attention to the local, the everyday and hybrid forms of peace in scholarship has offered a corrective to the ahistorical, universalising and dehumanised approaches of top-down liberal peace frameworks (e.g. Randazzo 2017; Richmond and Mitchell 2011; Mac Ginty 2010, 2021; Mac Ginty and Richmond 2013; Sylvester 1994). Locally grounded studies of youth peacebuilding and the literature on youth and everyday peace have helped expand understandings of the alternative, often quiet, spaces and modes of activism through which young people seek to understand and transform their worlds toward more justice and peace. Studies have documented this work through, for example, the arts, pop culture, caretaking, friendship groups and hustling (e.g. Berents 2018; Berents and McEvoy-Levy 2015; Bolten 2020; Dizdaroğlu 2023; Kurze 2019; Lederach 2020; McEvoy-Levy 2018; McMullin, 2022; Oosterom 2022; Podder 2022; Pruitt

2013; Pruitt and Jeffrey 2020; Thorne 2022). The contributions in this volume build on these insights and connect them to the challenges, tensions and opportunities of the current era's issue-based social movements and global policy frameworks. The volume straddles attention to the local and the global, and between the everyday and the institutional.

This connectionist thinking across levels is necessary (Lederach and Appleby 2010) because sustainable peace, according to psychological theory and research, requires common global bonds and understanding, social rejection of violence, 'a strong sense of positive interdependence' and 'fair recourse' (Deutsch and Coleman 2012, 5–6). Leadership for sustainable peace requires 'multimodal and multi-level systems thinkers' who recognise blockages in relations and processes that are preventing peace (Almadalas and Byrne 2018). But critical, decolonial, feminist and peace-geographies approaches to peacebuilding foreground how established dominance and governance logics make little room for consideration of the plurality of spaces and methods for peace that exist, or for the multiplicity of voices and practices needed to understand deeply rooted violence and to pursue the necessary justice and healing (see Courtheyn 2018; Hudson 2016; McConnell, Megoran and Williams 2014; Suffla, Malherbe and Seedat 2020; Sabaratnam 2011; Fitzgerald 2021; Goete 2016). The plural forms of peace that these perspectives encounter are in tension with the 'standardising tendencies' of the multilateral system (Mac Ginty 2008).

While rooted in the aforementioned critical approaches, the volume bridges a gap between consideration of the informal or local peace work of youth and the efforts of youth activists to engage with high-level institutions through the new YPS framework. Continued critical engagement with the paradoxes and tensions involved in bridging the local and the global, and linking the everyday and the institutional is important (see Mac Ginty 2011; Richmond and Mitchell 2011; Richmond 2015) because what happens in terms of peacebuilding has very real significance for the lives of young people around the world. Over four hundred million young people aged fifteen to twenty-nine live in a state or province where armed conflict or other organised violence took place in 2016; 23 per cent of the global youth population are affected, in some way, by armed conflict or other organised violence (Hagerty 2017). Yet as previous interventions in the field have argued, hybrid processes of local and international peacebuilding are likely to reproduce the exclusionary patterns of the liberal peace even (perhaps especially) when there is an invitation to participate for subaltern groups (Nadarajah and Rampton 2015) and many youth are intersectionally sub-subaltern. The chapters in the volume all respond directly to this problem in different ways. Furthermore, addressing this problem is inherent to the three-part interconnecting structure of the book: first, we critically unpack how the securitisation of youth occurs; second, we interrogate where and why the blockages to youth participation in formal peacebuilding are exclusionary by design and where this happens by accident (i.e. due to unexamined bias); third, we respond to these securitising and exclusionary dynamics with recommendations that are rooted in active agency of youth as pluralistic peacebuilders in various phases, geographic locations and states of 'conflict'.

Following Lederach, we see sustainable peacebuilding beginning where there is latent conflict, occurring while armed conflict is ongoing, and continuing long after agreements happen or wars end. We also perceive that, today, understanding sustainable peacebuilding involves moving beyond so-called 'post-conflict' or 'transitioning' societies to address the root causes of violence and injustice and modes of peacebuilding wherever they appear, including in post-post-conflict settings and also in supposedly 'at peace' countries. This makes possible a pluriversal approach (Escobar 2018) to understanding peace rooted in young people's lived experience. As Garrett Fitzgerald argues: 'scholars and practitioners of peacebuilding hoping to engage with pluriversal re-imaginings of peace must also be attentive to the risks of privilege that attend decolonial critique abstracted from the lived struggles of Indigenous and other racialized and colonized peoples' (2021, 5). Chapters in our volume closely engage with the understandings and work of Black, Indigenous and People of Colour (BIPOC) youth, and the volume bridges between attention to youth in the Global South and the Global North, challenging constructions of the Other to be securitised and have peace built upon them, and recognising the interdependence of young people's futures across borders and cultures.

In exploring the challenge of sustainable peacebuilding, this volume uses a critical youth studies approach that emphasises young people's knowledge and agency, based in locally lived experience, and shaped within historical, socio-economic and political structures (e.g. Best 2007; Ibrahim and Steinberg 2014; Kelly and Kamp 2015). This approach resists 'deficit' models of youth and community development (Tuck and Yang 2014). Thus the volume attends to the new thinking needed in overcoming millennia-old problems of hegemonic gerontocracy, where the assumption is always that youth, because they will 'age out' of their liminal state, can be treated perpetually as 'future' leaders and works-in-progress, rather than fully formed agents of change, for better or worse. As explained further below, we strive to take seriously, but not romanticise, youth and their roles in relation to three key parts of sustainable peacebuilding – security, participation and peace leadership.

Youth and security

An important 'precondition' of 'sustainable peace' is 'objective and subjective security' (Reychler 2001) which we see as equally belonging to youth as being acquired from them. While UNSC Resolution 2250 may have been a watershed moment in elevating 'youth and peacebuilding' on the international policy stage, it also continues a drama of youth being considered in relation to war, violence and security in quite narrow ways (Berents 2022). Indeed both scholarly and policy interest in youth and peacebuilding over the last three decades has unfolded in overlapping trends related to war and security concerns. In the early 1990s attention to so-called 'new wars' brought a focus to young people's roles as combatants and/or victims of armed conflict as an adjunct to the literature on child soldiers (e.g. Machel 1996; Brett and Specht 2004; Boyden and de Berry 2004; Byrne 1997; Özerderm and Podder 2011; Shepler 2010). The complex pathways of young people into armed roles in conflicts are deeply contextual and these roles blur with the other non-violent political and cultural roles and economic imperatives of youth. A related focus on youth as 'post-conflict' actors, including as participants in peace processes, postwar disarmament, demobilisation, reintegration (DDR) and reconstruction, and transitional justice and reconciliation, surfaces how young people have interests in, and are already shaping, the post-conflict landscapes of their countries but at the same time are excluded from many official mechanisms and processes (see Berents and Mollica 2020a, 2020b; Borer, Darby and McEvoy-Levy 2006; Bolten 2012; Justino 2018; Heykoop and Adoch 2017; Kemper 2005; Ladisch 2017; McEvoy-Levy 2001, 2006, 2013; Martuscelli and Villa 2018; Mollica 2017; Özerderm and Podder 2015; Schnabel and Tabyshalieva 2013; Schwartz 2010). As these literatures have highlighted, young people have been harmed by conflict, and have played important roles in conflict both as reproducers of conflict and as conflict transformers, but their active roles tend to be discounted, simplified and depoliticised. Furthermore the literature has until now not gone beyond 'post-conflict' to 'post-post conflict'; youth have never been included in discussions of long-term sustainable peace.

At the same time research on 'youth bulges' spurs concern about overly large numbers of young people in societies by identifying a relationship between significant-sized youth populations and the likelihood of civil war, political violence, social unrest and crime (Urdal 2004, 2006; Ebata et al. 2006). In security policy youth are seen as present and future dangers to national and world orders. In development policy youth are often viewed in binary terms as neoliberal assets and resources to be 'harnessed' and invested in for economic growth and stability (Distler 2017). Limited economic frames exclude understandings of youth as active agents of change in multiple social spheres (Altiok et al. 2020) and lead to policies to prevent armed conflict such as job creation despite conflicting evidence of its effectiveness in all settings (Walton 2010). Scholars document that globally, but on the African continent in particular, many youth are 'stuck' and experiencing 'waithood' due to conflict, poor governance and neoliberal economic structures, but at the same time they are innovating entrepreneurial and other survival strategies (Honwana 2012; Sommers 2012). But problematic policy discourses emerged in which youth were blamed for these conditions and conceptualised as destabilisers, demographic disasters, even 'tsunamis', that needed to be contained, eliminated, distracted and/or re-educated further, casting youth as a risk and male youth in the Global South as particularly dangerous (for documentation and critiques see McEvoy-Levy 2009, 2023; Pruitt et al. 2018; Pruitt 2020).

Deepened and expanded interest in youth as a security threat accompanied the 'global war on terror' and saw the introduction of programming to Prevent and Counter Violent Extremism (P/CVE) that implicitly as well as explicitly targets Muslim youth and youth of colour as a 'radicalisation' risk. As the young 'drivers of extremism' became the focus of policy, the linkage of youth and radicalisation has been increasingly studied (Lombardi et al. 2014; Sommers 2018; Venhaus 2010) and critiqued (Maira 2016; Pruitt 2020; Simpson 2018; Sommers 2018). As Simpson explains: 'The political urgency for governments to respond to the threat of global terrorism has contributed to a discourse in which sweeping characterizations of youth as fundamentally at risk of violent extremism have produced un-nuanced, counterproductive policy responses' (2018, 46). Although most youth do not opt for violence to repair their economic, social, cultural and political exclusions and grievances, they are stereotyped as an always latent danger. The roles of young people in uprisings against their governments in the Middle East and North Africa region since around 2011, as well as movements such as Occupy and the Indignados, demonstrated young people's collective change-making power (Riemer 2012; Sonay 2017) posing further concern for states concerned primarily with maintaining status-quo order. These events and discourses provide the context for the global YPS agenda and they indicate a strong trend of securitising youth: seeing them as dangers to be controlled.

The first challenge to sustainable peacebuilding that we identify in Part I of this volume relates to this persistent framing of youth as threats to security. The editors' introduction to Part I highlights how states historically and around the world have targeted youth as problems to be feared or solved. Drawing parallels between negative scholarly or policy framings of African and Black US youth, the editors' introduction sets the scene for the three chapters in this section, and argues that states construct their own youth 'problems' both at home and abroad. The first chapter by Netra Eng and Caroline Hughes examines how the Cambodian government is narrating, defining and addressing its postwar 'youth problem', even as the problems articulated by the government bear little resemblance to the actual orientations and practices of young people. Imagining its youth to be radical, the official strategy includes co-option and surveillance. But, as the authors unpack by reflecting on a large survey of Cambodian youth attitudes, youth are less liberal, and their parents are more liberal, than the official framing anticipates. Cambodia's 'youth problem' is 'a series of elite ideological fantasies' which is substituted for real engagement with youth and obscures the widespread frustrations of the general population.

Chapter 2 by Obasesam Okoi addresses the challenges of ex-combatants and their reintegration in Nigeria's oil region, highlighting the ways in which state interventions as part of the peace process have created alienation among youth and economic incentives for continued violence. Here the Nigerian government, in collaboration with liberal peacebuilders and multinational oil companies, has created a youth problem by focusing on some ex-combatants and neglecting the needs of the wider community of youth. On the basis of a survey of thousands of ex-insurgent youth, Okoi argues that sustainable peace is hampered by the peacebuilding programme in the region which has become an 'anti-peace machine', creating incentives for marginalised youth to rearm in order to negotiate their survival needs.

In Chapter 3 Anna Fett turns to framings of youth in US Cold War foreign policy which she considers in the context of the contemporary YPS agenda. Examining an earlier period of concern about a 'too large' global youth population during the Kennedy administration, Fett unpacks how the US government identified certain 'youth leaders' in the Global South for surveillance and co-option. She argues that the YPS agenda is likely to be implemented by powerful states following similar patterns of focusing on strategic foreign youth to be moulded in the United States' own image. Fett notes the exclusion of youth in the Global North from consideration for YPS-related funding, despite the continued securitisation of US youth in the war on terror. On these terms the 'realignment of US foreign policy' in relation to YPS that some envision cannot support sustainable peace.

The chapters in this section show how youth are selectively framed as threats to security in different forms, despite most not being involved in violence. They also highlight how young people are in fact facing multiple forms of marginalisation that contribute to their insecurity. This insecurity is a result of direct state violence as well as exclusion from access to education, employment and healthcare, factors which were further compounded by the Covid-19 pandemic (Search for Common Ground 2020;

Compact 2020). States' fear of youth leads them to minimise the needs and interests of non-combatant youth, who by and large form the majority of the young population, and to focus overmuch on the actions of a few, hampering the building of sustainable peace. In considering if YPS can help support sustainable peace by providing security for youth, the current policy context of the YPS agenda offers an opportunity to re-evaluate which youth are engaged and how they are included. However, it is possible that its potential impact will be overshadowed by a continued emphasis on providing states with security from their exaggerated youth threats. With this in mind we turn next to the question of youth participation in spaces of peace and security.

Youth and 'meaningful' participation

Existing literature argues that sustainable peace requires institutions and mechanisms that address the root causes of conflict, promote constructive conflict resolution and provide procedural and distributive justice (e.g. Lederach 1997; Reychler 2001; Peck 1998). The inclusion of youth in peacebuilding and transitional justice institutions and processes has been hailed both as a right and as a means of introducing new and more accurate analyses of youth needs to peace processes (McEvoy-Levy, ed. 2006; Mollica 2023). Globally, youth consultation efforts are being powered by a combination of top-down domestic elite initiatives, international advocacy and norm diffusion (Belschner 2021; Berents 2022), and by pressure from youth civil society groups (see European Youth Forum 2020). The latter pressure indicates a significant youth-led interest in being part of high-level decision-making institutions. Yet barriers to youth inclusion and to their 'meaningful' participation, as it is termed in the YPS agenda, are significant. The time and availability of youth for institutional consultation and involvement are inhibited by the different forms of insecurity that youth face, as described above, and they also face lack of interest and scepticism when they do participate on their own terms. For example, young people participated in pandemic response, including distributing food, tests and medicine and implementing efforts to combat misinformation and to respond to the mental health impact of isolation (Search for Common Ground 2020; Compact 2020). Yet media, political and educational discourses minimised these contributions and scapegoated youth for the pandemic's spread in certain areas. Similarly, we show that pervasive and powerful interests and stereotypes structure and condition young people's presence and participation in formal spaces of peace and security.

Recent studies suggest that many youth perceive themselves as necessary stakeholders in peace negotiations (Grizelj 2019; Altiok and Grizelj 2019;

Ozcelik et al. 2021; Spalding et al. 2021). They have direct roles as witnesses and observers to negotiations, providing research and technical support, and monitoring ceasefires (Altiok and Grizelj 2019) and they also see protest outside the system as an important form of participation (see Altiok and Grizelj 2019; Spalding et al. 2021). Reports suggest that participation of youth adds longevity and legitimacy to peace processes (Simpson 2018), produces 'more inclusive and representative governance structures that build the basis for more peaceful societies' (Altiok and Grizelj 2019, 8) and supports the multilateral system (Berents and Prelis 2020). Yet, with the multiplicity of institutions, actors, processes and forms of engagement involved in peacebuilding efforts (Philpott and Powers 2010; Zelizer 2013), it is perhaps not surprising that youth face practical and ideological barriers to involvement on their own terms.

Youth continue to be seen as pre-citizens. A still powerful view of even older youth is that they lack understanding and may endanger vital peacebuilding processes (Simpson 2018), and that they must be taught the 'necessary skills and knowledge to enable them to become active members of their society' (European Youth Forum 2020, 4). Policy documents emphasise the need for preparation of youth for participation through training in skills and 'quality citizenship education' (European Youth Forum 2020, 4). Less common is the argument that older stakeholders and policy-makers need to have preparation and training for effectively working alongside younger people. Practically, youth leaders and activists change in every generational cohort, which makes long-term connections and influence with elite decision-makers in government and the multilateral system more difficult to maintain (Altiok et al. 2020) and this slows the changing of norms around youth capabilities. At the local level, getting adults to see young people as positive for peacebuilding has necessitated 'significant awareness raising and sensitization' (McGill et al. 2015, 17) but remains an unfortunately rare procedure.

Therefore, the second challenge to sustainable peacebuilding that this volume unpacks relates to the challenges of youth participation within existing power hierarchies. The editors' introduction to Part II of the volume sets the scene by drawing on Audre Lorde's ideas about the institutional obstacles to radical transformation (Lorde 1984) and reviews findings that underscore the existing and long-standing political marginalisation of young people from formal institutions. As 'participation' is 'a facet of liberal, multicultural ideology' (Dhillon 2017, 13), the invitation to participate in the YPS agenda can be viewed as the deployment of a youth-governing mechanism by elite actors. Nevertheless, we must take seriously the efforts of young activists from around the world who are insisting on their recognition and inclusion within these spaces of peace and security.

The chapters in this section help us better understand who is participating and who is not and why; and they also provide nuanced analyses of what 'meaningful' participation requires.

The first chapter in this section underscores how the visibility of youth as potential participants does not necessarily lead to transformative outcomes. Patrícia Nabuco Martuscelli notes that in many peace processes young people are excluded from the very beginning because they are not mentioned in foundational transitional justice documents. But simply being named as actors is not enough to guarantee substantive participation for young people either. In her chapter Martuscelli shows that children and youth *are* included in the documents of the Colombian Truth Commission and Special Jurisdiction for Peace. However, these documents construct only certain categories of the young as stakeholders in the peace process. The Special Jurisdiction for Peace identifies only children who were victims of armed conflict as peacebuilders and does not recognise youth. It defines victimhood in specific ways and creates a victim hierarchy. On the other hand, as Martuscelli carefully unpacks, the Colombian Truth Commission took a different approach that allowed for inclusion of a broader range of children's and youth voices.

Moving from visibility to consideration of the limited impact youth can have within established frameworks, Catherine Bolten's chapter on youth in Sierra Leone employs feminist theory to show how being taken seriously by adults requires youth to take themselves seriously, and vice versa. This challenging dynamic is structured and inhibited by layers of power relations and cultural values. Focusing on local dialogues organised to create a new university for marginalised youth and the work of a youth-led peace union, Bolten argues that some youth showing up to take seats at the table in planning discussions is 'not enough to be transformative'. Institutional practices of consultation and inclusion of youth are established by adult power holders and may be both well-meaning and (often unconsciously) driven by a desire for control. Existing research has remarked on a tendency for institutions to work with easy-to-reach young people and the elevation of the already-elite youth voice in peace and security circles (Simpson 2018; Sommers 2015; Pruitt 2015; Lee-Koo and Pruitt 2020). But as Bolten's analysis shows, a combination of factors conspire to underscore the symbolic violence that makes young people complicit in their own exclusion. Marginalised in everyday life, young people in Sierra Leone were predisposed to ignore youth leaders seeking to mobilise them because they saw the youth leaders as following the direction of adults who failed to take them and their efforts seriously.

These first two chapters in Part II establish that visibility and an invitation to participate do not necessarily lead to meaningful outcomes for youth.

The next two chapters turn to the efforts of young peacebuilders to be included in the YPS agenda. In Chapter 6 Ali Altiok begins by unpacking the divergent meanings that 'meaningful' participation has for states and for young peace activists. The language of *meaningfulness* attached to participation, he argues, is a performative move by states to pacify youth demands. At the same time Altiok argues that the YPS agenda is based on faulty assumptions around youth political inclusion as a means to get young people to reject violent extremism. He argues that governments championing YPS are fostering 'nepotism, elitism and tokenism' and romanticising nonviolent participation. For reasons which Altiok articulates, ambitious elite youth whose views on counter-terrorism align with that of their elders dominate the space. An uncritical feedback loop therefore exists between security actors and these unrepresentative youth voices. Furthermore Altiok is concerned that YPS will be used by governments to suppress youth protest and participation in civic spaces and will increase 'political alienation and exclusion of young people'. To really foster 'meaningful' youth participation, he argues, YPS has to be 'liberated' from counter-terrorism policy frameworks and measures.

While agreeing that YPS is potentially fraught with challenges of tokenism, nepotism, erasures, siloing and co-option, Helen Berents's chapter calls for the sustaining of the 'radical' potential of youth participation in this space. Berents argues that, within the prevailing liberal peace framework, YPS actually provides an emancipatory vision, because agreeing that youth may be collaborators and co-constitutors of knowledge and practice is a radical move in this context. Furthermore, youth activists have been able to bring radical sensibilities to the corridors of power to press claims for justice as part of these new processes. Nevertheless, maintaining the agenda's 'radical' beginning as it is further formalised will be challenging. Drawing on discourse analysis and interviews with key stakeholders involved in YPS, Berents surfaces tensions around what participation means, exclusions based on notions of who the right youth to participate are, and the trivialisation of the agenda by some states. She addresses the critique of youth inclusion in YPS as merely a neoliberal move to depoliticise and control youth by providing first-hand examples of both the silencing of youth representatives and their resistance and contestation within formal YPS meetings.

Caitlin Mollica's chapter builds on the theme of how the politics of transitional justice processes construct only some (young) people as peacebuilders and explores how these processes also limit and construct not only which youth get to speak but how they are able to participate. Mollica explores the examples of the South African Truth and Reconciliation Commission (TRC) and two youth-led art projects in Timor-Leste and Kenya to examine the contrasts between the youth stories that emerge through formal and informal mechanisms of transitional justice. While inclusion in formal processes increases youth visibility, 'their stories are often silenced or reappropriated to fit the desirable politicised narrative'. Mollica argues that, while well-meaning, youth inclusion in TRCs tends towards producing narratives that fail to support healing and restoration. Arts-based approaches provide opportunities for intergenerational dialogue, collective healing and the restoration of positive interpersonal relationships. Informal art-based processes create space for multiple voices and ways of understanding the impact of conflict, centring experiences of trauma and resilience to consideration of youth agency. Mollica's chapter creates a bridge between the chapters on participation and the final section of the book on youth-led local peacebuilding by showing how participation of youth in informal transitional justice mechanisms 'challenges the political hierarchies and agendas embedded in the stories that formal mechanisms construct'. A holistic approach to peacebuilding, she argues, should seek to support both formal and informal transitional justice approaches as synergistic and complementary.

The chapters in this section show how 'inclusion' of youth and 'meaningful participation' do not necessarily solve the problem of youth marginalisation when old ideas about the roles, dangers and competencies of youth are maintained and powerful interests in the status quo are in play. They show how security foci hamper broadly youth-inclusive and productive participation within and beyond the YPS agenda, but also how youth activists are resisting efforts to water down and co-opt their demands. These chapters suggest that sustainable peacebuilding entails a both/and approach to youth participation, struggling with, but also going beyond, a narrow emphasis on formal inclusion in peace negotiations and transitional justice.

Youth-led peacebuilding

Part III of the book turns to the ways in which youth seek to create peace outside of formal political structures. Young people participate at the forefront of intersectional social movements against racism, climate catastrophe, state violence, authoritarianism and other issues. At the same time iconic youth activists – such as Greta Thunberg and Malala Yousafzai – help perpetuate notions of activism led by exceptional, paradigmatic individuals. As noted earlier, the literature on youth peacebuilding has brought to wider attention the local and microlocal peace work of young people. This section of the volume addresses a gap in connecting the issue-based concerns and protests of youth with their less visible local roles in long-term formation of peaceful and just societies. It also links both change processes – issue-based protest and grassroots peace labour – with the challenges of securitisation and meaningful participation examined in the first two sections of the book. The chapters in this section are written by scholars and scholar-practitioners and include chapters written by young peacebuilders and others that are intergenerational collaborations.

The editors' introduction to Part III highlights the ways that young people are leading and creating in peacebuilding through efforts that are at best ignored or discounted by official organisations, and, at worst, stymied or co-opted. Raced, gendered, neoliberal and colonial dominance logics provide the context for young people's intersectional efforts not only to resist but also to generate new visions, practices and spaces of peace. This section of the book argues for looking closely at how diverse young people conceptualise and work for sustainable peace within their wider circles of friends, families, elders and communities; and using that as the basis for defining peace (building), as a spatially grounded and politically situated relational process, centring the issues and approaches that young people value in peacebuilding agendas.

Environmental caretaking practices are the focus of the first chapter in this section. Angela Lederach provides an ethnographic inquiry into how campesino youth understand and build sustainable peace in Montes de María, Colombia. Though many youth seek to leave their area for urban opportunities, the campesino Youth Peace Provokers undertook environmental caretaking work to reconcile with their land that held many marks and memories of violence. For example, the death of the avocado forest from fungal blight during the war provided a symbolic focal point for the young campesinos' desire to revive and re-celebrate their ancestral place. Drawing on indigenous theories of resurgence, Lederach shows how environmental caretaking practices are the young people's way not just of reviving the land and animals but also of renewing 'intergenerational relations of solidarity'. The youth helped repair the cost violence had wrought on the natural landscape and reclaimed dignity and sense of identity for themselves at the same time. 'Daily work of caretaking social and ecological relations that breathe life into the campo empower youth to reclaim stigmatised bodies and territories as beautiful,' Lederach argues. Crucially, the youth do not work alone but as part of a larger collective sharing knowledge about the land, culture and ancestral claims to place. Thus sustainable peace is understood in this chapter as a multi-species and multigenerational 'regenerative struggle'. In addition to placing an emphasis on ecological reconciliation, Lederach's chapter profoundly challenges assumptions that meaningful participation and real change happen in halls of governments or multilateral zoom meetings. Like Mollica's chapter on transitional justice spaces in Part II, this chapter centres intergenerational dialogue and the restoration of positive interpersonal relationships as key peacebuilding processes.

The second chapter in this section also rethinks the spaces, actors and processes involved in peacebuilding while responding to the 'racial silence within peace studies' (Azarmandi 2018). Focusing on the knowledge, practices and struggles of BIPOC youth in the United States, an intergenerational team of authors, Jaimarsin Lewis, Siobhán McEvoy-Levy, Karayjus Perry, Trinity Perry and Julio Trujillo report on a youth-led Participatory Action Research study conducted by the young co-authors of the chapter in a Midwestern US city. These authors emphasise the ways poverty, violence, structural racial inequalities and the carceral system exacerbate insecurity and obscure the positive contributions of youth of colour in the US. Out-of-school youth are particularly excluded from opportunities to have their ideas and experiences of peacebuilding recognised and supported. As the chapters earlier in the volume by Fett and Altiok have noted, YPS centres elite youth as participants and does not create space for marginalised youth in the US to participate as actors in peace and security. This chapter shows how BIPOC US youth are already peacebuilders in their homes, friendship groups and community centers and demonstrates their capacity and interest in being peace researchers and advocates. The chapter also shows that non-violence is not an easy choice to make or maintain for many youth, but that this does not preclude them from peacebuilding labour. From the basis of their own lived experience the young people engaged in this chapter prompt a reimagined peace praxis towards more inclusive and emancipatory forms that values practical needs, caretaking, knowledge production and non-formal educational dialogues as peacebuilding work and that makes it possible for youth on the margins in the Global North to enjoy sustained participation as thought-leaders for peace.

While ecological and racial justice are themes of the previous two chapters, the chapter by Katrina Lee-Koo and Lesley Pruitt centres gender justice, examining why taking young women seriously as peacebuilders is crucial for sustainable peace. Drawing from interviews conducted with young women leaders in Asia and the Pacific (India, Myanmar, Papua New Guinea and Bougainville, Sri Lanka, Solomon Islands), Lee-Koo and Pruitt's chapter documents young women's leadership in peacebuilding efforts. Linking with Bolten's earlier chapter on the difficulties of youth being taken seriously, the chapter highlights the exclusion of young women peacebuilders because of assumptions connected to the intersections of age *and* gender. Younger women, in particular, have difficulty being taken seriously as peacebuilders in militarist and patriarchal societies. Women's experiences in the region – such as early marriage, denial of education and gender-based violence (GBV) – and the issues that young female activists care about – e.g. raising awareness around GBV and trafficking, building leadership skills or sexual and reproductive health rights – are not recognised as peace issues or peacebuilding work. However, as Lee-Koo and Pruitt show, young women are insisting on the seriousness of their own expertise and describe peacebuilding as beginning in their homes, schools and churches – the spaces where they are most immediately affected by violence, discrimination and gender inequality. Collaborative, horizontal peer-networks such as informal community spaces and friendship groups are their preferred sites of peacebuilding. Thus the values and sites of young women's leadership for sustainable peace 'challenges the dominant models of leadership operating in most of the world today,' these authors argue. Among the recommendations in this chapter are safe spaces for women to speak about peace in the region, and community-based and externally supported leadership training to build intergenerational gender-inclusive leadership.

Like their peers in the Asia-Pacific, the South Sudan-based authors of our next chapter agree that youth, and young women in particular, are ignored by their elders and by external peacebuilders. Nevertheless, Emmily Koiti, Bush Buse Laki, and Chara Nyaura show how their practices of peacebuilding are innovative and effective. These practices include a series of encounters with former opponents called 'Taking Tea Together' and the inclusion of stigmatised amputees in designing peacebuilding initiatives. Their initiative to include amputees, whether or not their injuries were war-related, replaces narrow formal definitions of victims and peacebuilders with more inclusive forms (a problem that was also identified by Martuscelli in her chapter). Koiti, Laki and Nyaura note that peacebuilding for them is not a short-term exercise or 'project', like those of the visiting INGOs, but a matter of life and survival. Like other chapters in this section, this account raises the questions: if young people are creating innovative and effective peace processes outside of formal processes, why not leave them alone? What is the benefit of adults and external organisations getting involved? These authors directly address the role of adults and adult-led organisations in supporting their work as young peacebuilders in South Sudan, emphasising the need for flexibility and accompaniment rather than adult leadership to allow young people to lead the way in local peacebuilding efforts. Among their recommendations are that 'local peacebuilders should maintain the courage of their convictions and stick to what is working locally rather than what is told to them by outsiders'. They also provide guidance for how INGOs should show up, including 'embracing ambiguity' and 'giving things time to grow'. This chapter provides practical advice in decolonising peacebuilding with youth leading the way.

Continuing the exploration of possibilities for decolonising peace-building, Prashan de Visser, co-founder of the youth-led Global Unites movement that began in Sri Lanka, documents the spread of the movement and the contributions of its youth leaders to peacebuilding, including through social media campaigns against hate speech and toxic national-ism. Critiquing shortsighted top-down interventions that prioritise their own goals and timelines over the real needs of local peacebuilding, de Visser shows how Global South alliances of youth peacebuilders are over-coming these obstacles and effecting transgenerational change for peace. The chapter begins with the recollections of youth peacebuilders from Sri Lanka, Afghanistan and the Democratic Republic of Congo whose memories of traumatic violence shaped their commitments to peacebuild-ing. These stories are presented by de Visser to make the case that the commitment of young people to peacebuilding exceeds that of external organisations and institutions. Like the South Sudan-based authors of the previous chapter, they have an existential stake in peace. A young peacebuilder from Afghanistan notes that youth will still be there when the INGOs and government agencies leave. Highlighting the high cost, lack of organic grassroots connections, funding streams that drive harmful and unnecessary programmes, and ultimately fickle partners of the current peacebuilding system, de Visser argues for a re-evaluation. A new youth-led approach to peacebuilding is expressed in the Global Unites movement in at least four ways. First, Global Unites is a grassroots organissation that networks nationally and globally to promote non-violent conflict transfor-mation. It is locally engaged and globally connected. Second, and linking with the concern about securitisation of youth raised in earlier chapters, for Global Unites violent extremism is part of the conflict transformation puzzle, but peacebuilders are not idealised as the polar opposites of the agents of violence. They are peers who are able to understand the frustra-tion and grievances of youth who participate in political violence. Third, the Global Unites movement in Sri Lanka enjoys strong financial contri-butions from its former student participants who are now introducing their own children to the movement – its continuity appears to be locally guaranteed and transgenerational. Finally, the Global Unites movement has transnational influence, having spread from Sri Lanka to thirteen countries; and it is an example of Global South-rooted methodology that has disseminated to the Global North in the form of the USA Unites branch of the movement.

The decolonisation of knowledge production about peace is also the focus of the final chapter in the volume. Reflecting on peacebuilding from within the operations of the settler colonial and carceral states in the Global North, the intervention by Justin de Leon and Jordan Bighorn reflects on the role of youth in Indigenous perspectives on peacebuilding. These authors focus on the sacred and illuminative meaning that youth have in Native communities in North America, while acknowledging the weight of oppression that historical dispossession and ongoing violence continues to play in their lives. Sustainable peacebuilding in this context involves more than addressing the symptoms of exclusion and trauma, such as the disproportionate youth suicide rates in Native communities. De Leon and Bighorn envision sustainable peacebuilding towards a decolonial future as a ceremony to create 'a new lodge' or tipi – a Native housing structure built from poles that each represent spiritual and material principles. Reflecting on the significance of each pole that combines to produce the sheltering structure, the authors highlight ideas of the coexistence and inclusion of all things, spiritual connection, reverence for the cycle of life and processes of bridging, balancing, reciprocity, and transformation in place. Their chapter is an invitation to youth, and to scholars and practitioners working with youth, to risk moving beyond established frameworks to imagine new possibilities for peacebuilding rooted in spiritual practices and in appreciation for life in community together. Thus, the final chapter returns to the theme of peacebuilding as 'regenerative struggle' that was centred in Lederach's chapter that begins this section of the book.

The chapters in Part III of the volume all highlight the ways in which young people resist constraining structures to undertake peace work that is fundamentally embedded in place and in relational practices, and pursuing alternative possibilities built on notions of justice, reciprocity and intersectionality. While they offer plural expressions of peace and decolonial processes of peacebuilding, these chapters also raise questions of the obligations of adults to support, 'accompany', and make space for youth leadership in its diverse manifestations.

Conclusion

Collectively the contributions of this volume show that to support youth peacebuilders requires a transformation in thinking about them as actors in peace and security. It requires moving away from conceptualising them as risky pre-citizens to embracing them as equal co-contributors, learners and leaders in peacebuilding. It also necessitates rethinking the dimensions, locations and directions of peacebuilding. Outside of formal institutions and processes, youth use creativity and care to resist plural violences from local, national and global sources and to create multiple forms of peace including new peace movements. They also make claims on institutional spaces to recognise their leadership. The important contributions to peacebuilding that young people make need to be taken seriously. Obviously one volume cannot provide a comprehensive documentation of all of the diverse ways in which young people are conceptualising and building peace and this book is an invitation for future research and collaboration. In the concluding chapter to the volume we draw together the lessons of these chapters to create an agenda for research, action and advocacy around peace and security that is anchored in the practices and aspirations of diverse youth peacebuilders.

References

Almadalas, Stan, and Sean Byrne. 2018. 'Conclusion: Peace Leaders Leading for Peace'. In *Peace Leadership: The Quest for Connectedness*, edited by Stan Almadalas and Sean Byrne, pp. 212–20. Abingdon: Routledge.

Altiok, Ali, Helen Berents, Irena Grizelj and Siobhán McEvoy-Levy. 2020. 'Youth, Peace, and Security.' In *Routledge Handbook of Peace, Security and Development*, edited by Fen Osler Hampson, Alpaslan Özerdem and Jonathan Kent, pp. 433–47. Abingdon: Routledge.

Altiok, Ali, and Irena Grizelj. 2019. *We Are Here: An Integrated Approach to Youth Inclusive Peace Processes*. New York: Office of the Secretary General's Envoy on Youth.

Azarmandi, Mahdis. 2018. 'The Racial Silence within Peace Studies', *Peace Review* 30 (1): 69–77, https://doi.org/10.1080/10402659.2017.1418659.

Belschner, Jana. 2021. 'The Adoption of Youth Quotas after the Arab Uprisings.' *Politics, Groups, and Identities* 9 (1): 151–69.

Berents, Helen. 2018. *Young People and Everyday Peace: Exclusion, Insecurity and Peacebuilding in Colombia*. New York: Routledge.

Berents Helen. 2022. 'Power, Partnership, and Youth as Norm Entrepreneurs: Getting to UN Security Council Resolution 2250 on Youth, Peace, and Security.' *Global Studies Quarterly* 2: 1–11.

Berents, Helen, and Siobhán McEvoy-Levy. 2015. 'Theorising Youth and Everyday Peace(building).' *Peacebuilding* 3 (2): 1–14.

Berents, Helen, and Caitlin Mollica, 2020a. 'Youth and Peacebuilding.' In *The Palgrave Encyclopedia of Peace and Conflict Studies*, edited by Gëzim Visoka and Oliver Richmond, pp. 1–16. Cham: Palgrave Macmillan.

Berents, Helen, and Caitlin Mollica. 2020b. *Youth and Peace in the Indo-Pacific: Policy, Practice, Action: Report on the Academy of Social Science in Australia (ASSA) Workshop*. QUT Centre for Justice.

Berents, Helen, and Saji Prelis. 2020. *More than a Milestone: The Road to UN Security Council Resolution 2250*. Washington, DC: Search for Common Ground.

Berents, Helen, and Caitlin Mollica. 2022. 'Reciprocal Institutional Visibility: Youth, Peace and Security and "Inclusive" Agendas at the United Nations'. *Cooperation and Conflict* 57 (1): 65–83, https://doi.org/10.1177/00108367211007873.

Best, Amy L., ed. 2007. *Representing Youth: Methodological Issues in Critical Youth Studies*. New York: New York University Press.

Bolten, Catherine. 2012. *I Did It to Save My Life: Love and Survival in Sierra Leone*. Berkeley: University of California Press.

Bolten, Catherine. 2020. *Serious Youth in Sierra Leone: An Ethnography of Performance and Global Connection*. New York: Oxford University Press.

Borer, Tristan Anne, John Darby and Siobhán McEvoy-Levy. 2006. *Peacebuilding after Peace Accords: The Challenges of Violence, Truth and Youth*. South Bend: University of Notre Dame.

Boyden, Jo, and Joanna de Berry, eds. 2004. *Children and Youth on the Front Lines: Ethnography, Armed Conflict, and Displacement*. New York: Berghahn Books.

Brett, Rachel, and Irma Specht. 2004. *Young Soldiers: Why They Choose to Fight*. Boulder: Lynne Rienner.

Byrne, Sean. 1997. *Growing Up in a Divided Society: The Influence of Conflict on Belfast School Children*. Madison: Fairleigh Dickinson University Press.

Compact for Young People in Humanitarian Action. 2020. *Covid-19: Working with and for Young People*. New York and Geneva: United Nations Population Fund and International Federation of Red Cross and Red Crescent Societies. https://www.youthcompact.org/the-compact-response. Accessed 5 May 2021.

Courtheyn, Christopher. 2018. 'Peace Geographies: Expanding from Modern-Liberal Peace to Radical Trans-Relational Peace.' *Progress in Human Geography* 42 (5): 741–58.

Darby, John, and Mac Ginty, Roger. eds. 2008. *Contemporary Peacemaking: Conflict, Peace Processes and Post-war Reconstruction*. Second Edition. New York: Palgrave.

Deutsch, Morton, and Peter T. Coleman. 2012. 'Psychological Components of Sustainable Peace: An Introduction". In *Psychological Components of Sustainable Peace*, edited by Peter T. Coleman and Morton Deutsch, 1–15. New York: Springer.

Dhillon, Jaskiran K. 2017. *Prairie Rising: Indigenous Youth, Decolonization, and the Politics of Intervention*. Toronto: University of Toronto Press.

Distler, Werner. 2017. 'Dangerised Youth: the Politics of Security and Development in Timor-Leste.' *Third World Quarterly* 40 (4): 727–42.

Dizdaroğlu, Cihan. 2023. 'Understanding Cypriot Youth Views on Peace: Bottom-up Experiences of Everyday Peace.' *Southeast European and Black Sea Studies*, https://doi.org/10.1080/14683857.2023.2170722.

Ebata, Michi, Valeria Izzi, Alexandra Lenton, Eno Ngjela and Peter Sampson, with Jane Lowicki-Zuca and Jennifer MacNaughton. 2006. *Youth and Violent Conflict Society and Development in Crisis?* New York: United Nations Development Programme.

Ensor, Marisa O., ed. 2021. *Securitizing Youth: Young People's Role in the Global Peace and Security Agenda*. New Brunswick: Rutgers University Press.

Escobar, A. 2018. 'Transition Discourses and the Politics of Relationality: Towards Designs for the Pluriverse.' In B. Reiter (ed.), *Constructing the Pluriverse: The Geopolitics of Knowledge*. Durham, NC: Duke University Press.

European Youth Forum. 2020. *Policy Document on Quality Youth Participation and Representation in Institutions*. Online General Assembly, 20–2 November: 1–35. https://tools.youthforum.org/policy-library/wp-content/uploads/2021/04/0017-20_FINAL_Policy-Paper-on-Quality-Youth-Participation.pdf. Accessed 12 December 2023.

Fitzgerald, Garrett. 2021. 'Pluriversal Peacebuilding: Peace beyond Epistemic and Ontological Violence.' *E International Relations*, https://www.e-ir.info/2021/11/27/pluriversal-peacebuilding-peace-beyond-epistemic-and-ontological-violence/. Accessed 30 November 2023.

Goetze, Catherine. 2016. *The Distinction of Peace: A Social Analysis of Peacebuilding*. Ann Arbor: University of Michigan Press.

Grizelj, Irena. 2019. 'Engaging the Next Generation: A Field Perspective of Youth Inclusion in Myanmar's Peace Negotiations.' *International Negotiation* 24 (1): 164–88.

Hagerty, Talia. 2017. *Data for Youth, Peace and Security: A Summary of Research Findings*, Institute for Economics and Peace. https://www.youth4peace.info/system/files/2018–04/16.%20TP_Youth%20affected%20by%20violent%20conflict_IEP.pdf. Accessed 5 May 2021.

Heykoop, Cheryl, and Juliet Adoch. 2017. 'Our Stories, Our Own Ways: Exploring Alternatives for Young People's Engagement in Truth Commissions.' *Peace and Conflict: Journal of Peace Psychology* 23 (1): 14–22.

Honwana, Alcinda. 2012. *The Time of Youth: Work, Social Change, and Politics in Africa*. Boulder: Lynne Rienner Publishers.

Honwana, Alcinda. 2013. *Youth and Revolution in Tunisia*. London: Zed Books.

Hudson, Heidi. 2016. 'Decolonising Gender and Peacebuilding: Feminist Frontiers and Border Thinking in Africa.' *Peacebuilding* 4 (2): 194–209. https://doi.org/10.1080/21647259.2016.1192242.

Ibrahim, Awad, and Shirley R. Steinberg, eds. 2014. *Critical Youth Studies Reader*. New York: Peter Lang.

Justino, Patricia. 2018. 'Youth, Violent Conflict and Sustaining Peace: Quantitative Evidence and Future Directions.' *UNDP*, 1–122. https://www.youth4peace.info/system/files/2018–01/%5BDRAFT%5D%20UN%20Youth%20and%20Peacebuilding_Justino%20-%20Jan%202018.pdf. Accessed 5 May 2021.

Keating, Tom, and W. Andy Knight, eds. 2004. *Building Sustainable Peace*. Edmonton and Tokyo: Alberta Press and United Nations University Press.

Kelly, Peter, and Annelies Kamp, eds. 2015. *A Critical Youth Studies for the 21st Century*. Leiden: Brill.

Kemper, Yvonne. 2005. *Youth in War-to-Peace Transitions: Approaches of International Organizations*. Berghof Report, No. 10. Berlin: Berghof Research Center for Constructive Conflict Management.

Kurze, Arnaud. 2019. 'Youth Activism, Art and Transitional Justice: Emerging Spaces of Memory after the Jasmine Revolution.' In *New Critical Spaces in Transitional Justice: Gender, Art, and Memory*, edited by Arnaud Kurze and Christopher K. Lamont, pp. 63–86. Bloomington: Indiana University Press.

Ladisch, Virginie. 2017. *Engaging Youth in Transitional Justice*. New York: International Center for Transitional Justice.

Lederach, Angela J. 2020. 'Youth Provoking Peace: an Intersectional Approach to Territorial Peacebuilding in Colombia', *Peacebuilding* 8 (2): 198–217.

Lederach, John Paul. 1997. *Building Peace: Sustainable Reconciliation in Divide Societies*. Washington, DC: United States Institute of Peace Press.

Lederach, John Paul, and Scott Appleby. 2010. 'Strategic Peacebuilding: an Overview.' In *Strategies of Peace*, edited by Daniel Philpott and Gerard F. Powers, pp. 19–44. Oxford: Oxford University Press.

Lee-Koo, Katrina, and Lesley Pruitt, eds. 2020. *Young Women and Leadership.* New York: Routledge.

Lombardi, Marco, Eman Ragab, Vivienne Chin, Yvon Dandurand, Valerio de Divitiis and Alessandro Burato. 2014. *Countering Radicalisation and Violent Extremism among Youth to Prevent Terrorism*, NATO Science for Peace and Security Series 118. Amsterdam: IOS Press.

Lorde, Audre. 1984. 'The Master's Tools Will Never Dismantle the Master's House.' In *Sister Outsider: Essays and Speeches*, pp. 110–14. Berkeley: Crossing Press.

Mac Ginty, Roger. 2008. 'Indigenous Peace-Making versus the Liberal Peace.' *Cooperation and Conflict: Journal of the Nordic International Studies Association* 43 (2): 139–63.

Mac Ginty, Roger. 2010. 'Hybrid Peace: the Interaction between Top-down and Bottom-up Peace.' *Security Dialogue* 41 (4): 391–412.

Mac Ginty, Roger. 2011. *International Peacebuilding and Local Resistance: Hybrid Forms of Peace.* Rethinking Peace and Conflict Studies. New York and Basingstoke: Palgrave Macmillan.

Mac Ginty, Roger. 2021. *Everyday Peace: How So-called Ordinary People Can Disrupt Violent Conflict.* Oxford: Oxford University Press.

Mac Ginty, Roger, and Oliver Richmond. 2013. 'The Local Turn in Peace Building: a Critical Agenda for Peace.' *Third World Quarterly* 34 (5): 763–83. https://doi.org/10.1080/01436597.2013.800750.

Maira, Sunaina M. 2016. *The 9/11 Generation: Youth, Rights, and Solidarity in the War on Terror.* New York: NYU Press.

Martuscelli, Patrícia Nabuco, and Rafael Duarte Villa. 2018. 'Child Soldiers as Peace-builders in Colombian Peace Talks between the Government and the FARC–EP.' *Conflict, Security and Development* 18 (5): 387–408.

McConnell, Fiona, Nick Megoran and Phillipa Williams, eds. 2014. *Geographies of Peace.* New York: I.B. Tauris.

McEvoy-Levy, Siobhán. 2001. 'Youth as Social and Political Agents: Issues in Post-settlement Peace Building.' *Kroc Institute, Occasional Paper* 21 (2), December.

McEvoy-Levy, Siobhán, ed. 2006. *Troublemakers or Peacemakers? Youth and Post-accord Peace Building.* Notre Dame: University of Notre Dame Press.

McEvoy-Levy, Siobhán. 2013. 'Youth.' In *Routledge Handbook of Peacebuilding*, edited by Roger Mac Ginty, pp. 296–307. Abingdon: Routledge.

McEvoy-Levy, Siobhán. 2018. *Peace and Resistance in Youth Cultures: Reading the Politics of Peacebuilding from Harry Potter to The Hunger Games.* New York: Palgrave Macmillan.

McGill, Michael, Claire O'Kane, Bibhuti Bista, Nicolas Meslaoui and Sarah Zingg. 2015. *Evaluation of Child and Youth Participation in Peacebuilding: Nepal, Eastern Democratic Republic of Congo, Colombia.* No Location: Global Partnership for Children and Youth in Peacebuilding. https://reliefweb.int/report/world/evaluation-child-and-youth-participation-peacebuilding-nepal-eastern-democratic. Accessed 30 November 2023.

McMullin, Jaramey R. 2022. 'Hustling, Cycling, Peacebuilding: Narrating Postwar Reintegration through Livelihood in Liberia.' *Review of International Studies* 48 (1): 67–90.

Mollica, Caitlin. 2017. 'The Diversity of Identity: Youth Participation at the Solomon Islands Truth and Reconciliation Commission.' *Australian Journal of International Affairs* 71 (4): 371–88.

Mollica, Caitlin. 2024 (forthcoming). *Acknowledging Agency in Reconciliation: Young People and the Practice of Transitional Justice*, New York: SUNY Press.

Nadarajah, Suthaharan, and David Rampton. 2015. 'The Limits of Hybridity and the Crisis of Liberal Peace.' *International Studies Review* 41 (1): 49–72. https://doi.org/10.1017/S0260210514000060.

Oosterom, Marjoke. 2022. 'Youth and "Everyday Peace" in the City of Jos, Nigeria.' In *Youth and Non-Violence in Africa's Fragile Contexts*, edited by Akin Iwilade and Tarila Marclint Ebiede. Cham: Palgrave Macmillan. https://doi.org/10.1007/978-3-031-13165-3_3.

Ozcelik, Asli, Yulia Nesterova, Graeme Young and Alex Maxwell. 2021. 'Youth-Led Peace: the Role of Youth in Peace Processes.' University of Glasgow. http://eprints.gla.ac.uk/242178/. Accessed 30 November 2023.

Özerderm, Alpaslan, and Sukanya Podder. 2011. *Child Soldiers from Recruitment to Reintegration*. New York: Palgrave.

Özerdem, Alpaslan, and Sukanya Podder. 2015. *Youth in Conflict and Peacebuilding: Mobilization, Reintegration and Reconciliation*. Basingstoke: Palgrave Macmillan.

Paris, Roland, 2004. *At War's End: Building Peace after Civil Conflict*. Cambridge: Cambridge University Press. https://doi.org/10.1017/CBO9780511790836.

Peck, Connie. 1998. *Sustainable Peace: The Role of the UN and Regional Organizations in Preventing Conflict*. London: Rowman and Littlefield.

Philpott, Daniel, and Gerard F. Powers, eds. 2010. *Strategies of Peace*. Oxford: Oxford University Press.

Podder, Sukanya. 2022. *Peacebuilding Legacy: Programming for Change and Young People's Attitudes to Peace*. Oxford: Oxford University Press.

Pruitt, Lesley. 2013. *Youth Peacebuilding: Music, Gender, and Change*. Albany: State University of New York (SUNY) Press.

Pruitt, Lesley. 2015. 'Gendering the Study of Children and Youth in Peacebuilding.' *Peacebuilding* 3 (2): 157–70.

Pruitt, Lesley. 2020. 'Rethinking Youth Bulge Theory in Policy and Scholarship: Incorporating Critical Gender Analysis.' *International Affairs* 96 (3): 711–28.

Pruitt, Lesley, and Erica Rose Jeffrey. 2020. *Dancing through the Dissonance: Creative Movement and Peacebuilding*. Manchester: Manchester University Press.

Pruitt, L., H. Berents and G. Munro. 2018. 'Gender and Age in the Construction of Male Youth in the European Migration "Crisis".' *Signs* 43 (3): 687–709.

Randazzo, Elisa. 2017. *Beyond Liberal Peacebuilding: A Critical Exploration of the Local Turn*. London: Routledge.

Reychler, Luc. 2001. 'From Conflict to Sustainable Peacebuilding: Concepts and Analytical Tools.' In *Peace-building: A Field Guide*, edited by Luc Reychler and Thania Paffenholz, 3–16. Boulder: Lynne Rienner Press.

Richmond, Oliver. 2015. 'The Dilemmas of a Hybrid Peace: Negative or Positive?' *Cooperation and Conflict* 50 (1): 50–68. https://doi.org/10.1177/0010836714537053.

Richmond, Oliver, and Audra Mitchell, eds. 2011. *Hybrid Forms of Peace: From Everyday Agency to Post-Liberalism. Rethinking Peace and Conflict Studies*. London: Palgrave Macmillan.

Sabaratnam, M. 2011. 'IR in Dialogue . . . But Can We Change the Subjects? A Typology of Decolonising Strategies for the Study of World Politics.' *Millennium* 39 (3): 781–803.

Saud, Muhammad, and Hendro Margono. 2021. 'Indonesia's Rise in Digital Democracy and Youth's Political Participation.' *Journal of Information Technology and Politics* 18 (2): 1–12.

Schnabel, Albrecht, and Anara Tabyshalieva. 2013. *Escaping Victimhood: Children, Youth and Post-conflict Peacebuilding.* New York: United Nations Press.

Schwartz, Stephanie. 2010. *Youth and Post-conflict Reconstruction: Agents of Change.* Washington, DC: United States Institute of Peace Press.

Search for Common Ground. 2020. 'COVID-19 Discussion Paper: Youth & the COVID-19 Crisis in Conflict-Affected Contexts.' Policy Brief. https://www.sfcg. org/wp-content/uploads/2020/06/Youth_and_COVID-19_in_Conflict-Affected_ Areas_v2.pdf. Accessed 5 May 2021.

Shepler, Susan. 2010. *Childhood Deployed: Remaking Child Soldiers in Sierra Leone.* New York: New York University Press.

Simangan, Dahia. 2022. '"Peaces of the Puzzle": Mapping the Trajectories of Three Decades of Peacebuilding Scholarship.' In *Alternative Perspectives on Peacebuilding: Rethinking Peace and Conflict Studies*, edited by Mark Cogan and Hidekazu Sakai. Cham: Palgrave Macmillan. https://doi.org/10.1007/ 978-3-031-05756-4_3.

Simpson, Graeme. 2018. *The Missing Peace: Independent Progress Study on Youth and Peace and Security.* United Nations. https://www.youth4peace.info/system/ files/2018–10/youth-web-english.pdf. Accessed 5 May 2021.

Sommers, Marc. 2011. 'Governance, Security and Culture: Assessing Africa's Youth Bulge.' *International Journal of Conflict and Violence* 5 (2): 292–303.

Sommers, Marc. 2012. *Stuck: Rwandan Youth and the Struggle for Adulthood.* Athens: University of Georgia Press.

Sommers, Marc. 2015. *The Outcast Majority: War, Development, and Youth in Africa.* Athens: University of Georgia Press.

Sommers, Marc. 2018. *Youth and the Field of Countering Violent Extremism.* Washington, DC: Promundo-US.

Sonay, Ali. 2017. *Making Revolution in Egypt. The 6 April Youth Movement in a Global Context.* London: I.B. Tauris.

Spalding, Savannah, Casey Odgers-Jewell, Hayley Payne, Caitlin Mollica and Helen Berents. 2021. 'Making Noise and Getting Things Done: Youth Inclusion and Advocacy for Peace. Lessons from Afghanistan, South Sudan, and Myanmar.' QUT Centre for Justice. https://research.qut.edu.au/centre-for-justice/publications/ making-noise-and-getting-things-done-youth-inclusion-and-advocacy-for-peace-les sons-from-afghanistan-south-sudan-and-myanmar/. Accessed 30 November 2023.

Suffla, S., N. Malherbe, and M. Seedat, 2020. 'Recovering the Everyday within and for Decolonial Peacebuilding through Politico-Affective Space.' In *Researching Peace, Conflict and Power in the Field*, edited by Y.G. Acar, pp. 301–19. Cham: Springer.

Sukarieh, Mayssoun, and Stuart Tannock. 2018. 'The Global Securitisation of Youth.' *Third World Quarterly* 39 (5): 854–70.

Suwana, Fiona. 2020. 'What Motivates Digital Activism? The Case of the Save KPK Movement in Indonesia.' *Information, Communication and Society* 23 (9): 1295–310.

Sylvester, C. 1994. 'Empathetic Cooperation: a Feminist Method For IR.' *Millennium* 23 (2): 315–34.

Taft, Jessica K. 2011. *Rebel Girls: Youth Activism and Social Change across the Americas*, New York: New York University Press.

Thorne, Benjamin. 2022. 'The Art of Plurality: Participation, Voice, and Plural Memories of Community Peace.' *Conflict, Security & Development* 22 (5): 567–88. https://doi.org/10.1080/14678802.2022.2138697.

Tuck, Eve, and K. Wayne Yang, eds. 2014. *Youth Resistance Research and Theories of Change*. New York: Routledge.

United Nations Security Council. 2020. *Youth and Peace and Security: Report of the Secretary-General*. 2 March. S/2020/167. https://undocs.org/en/S/2020/167. Accessed 30 November 2023.

United Network of Young Peacebuilders (UNOY) and Search for Common Ground. 2017. *Mapping a Sector: Bridging the Evidence Gap on Youth-driven Peacebuilding*. The Hague: UNOY.

Urdal, Henrik. 2004. 'The Devil in the Demographics: the Effect of Youth Bulges on Domestic Armed Conflict, 1950–2000.' World Bank, *Social Development Papers: Conflict Prevention and Reconstruction* 14. Washington, DC: World Bank.

Urdal, Henrik. 2006. 'A Clash of Generations? Youth Bulges and Political Violence.' *International Studies Quarterly* 50 (3): 607–29.

Venhaus, John M. 2010. *Why Youth Join al-Qaeda*. USIP Report 236. Washington. DC: United States Institute of Peace.

Walton, Oliver. 2010. *Youth, Armed Violence and Job Creation Programmes: A Rapid Mapping Study*. https://core.ac.uk/download/pdf/103648.pdf. Accessed 5 May 2021.

Zelizer, Craig, ed. 2013. *Integrated Peacebuilding. Innovative Approaches to Transforming Conflict*. Boulder: Westview Press.

Part I

States and their 'youth problems'

Introduction to Part I

Helen Berents, Catherine E. Bolten and Siobhán McEvoy-Levy

In her early work in the favelas of Brazil and the townships of South Africa, Nancy Scheper-Hughes conceived of youth as simultaneously 'dangerous and endangered' (Scheper-Hughes 2004). Lawmakers in both of these places believed that young people's thoughts, activities and, most importantly, the presence of their bodies in public space were a threat to the social order and the state's ability to maintain its hegemony. This fear of youth generated policies that disproportionately targeted the bodies, minds and social worlds of the young for co-optation or destruction, ostensibly to protect the state and its citizens from the unidentified danger that young people, merely by virtue of their age, posed. Any public displays of organised youth deviance – whether public protests or novel subcultures – became the subject of moral panics, in essence, governmental-level fretting over danger that such deviance potentially posed to unproblematic social reproduction and, as a result, the safety of the existing state structure to challenges from within (Cohen 1980). Scheper-Hughes did not uncover anything unique in revealing this reality in Brazil and South Africa; rather, in capturing the duality of young people in public discourse, she revealed a larger issue present across states across time: that young people are, de facto, a 'problem' for the states they inhabit because of their potential non-conformation to the status quo. This perceived danger renders them vulnerable to state-level interventions, whether violent or policy-based. While violent interventions often occur extralegally – such as the police death squads that systematically killed street children in Brazil – legal interventions are policies designed to co-opt, contain and otherwise politically neutralise youth. In short, states around the world and throughout time have understood and managed their young people by securitising them.

Ostensible youthful deviance and divergent thinking were combined with population growth, resulting in a 'youth bulge' (Urdal 2006); the problem of youth refusing to conform was compounded by the possibility that, through their numbers, voices and potential actions, they might succeed in either overthrowing the status quo or at least mounting a substantial challenge to it. This could occur deliberately, through youth social movements that attract other marginalised people in large coalitions, or more spontaneously as chaotic violence. The latter was the argument made by Robert Kaplan warning of the 'loose molecules' of disaffected, unemployed youth that would overtake Africa in the 1990s, possibly presaging violence around the developing world from there, a situation he called 'the coming anarchy' (2000). Then-US-president Bill Clinton was so taken with the argument that these loose molecules needed to be contained, lest they start civil wars in every country with a youth bulge, that he sent Kaplan's article to every US embassy on the African continent. Fear of their numbers, creativity, energy and lack of investment in the status quo have driven youth policies around the world for over half a century. Many of these policies have been animated by the idea that youth must be placated, appeased and co-opted in order to avoid revolution at home; however they can be used productively to help rebellions within other states. If revolution had already been attempted, states seek to obtain their agreement to peace treaties, whether or not the leaders of such rebellions had themselves been young people (see Richards 1996). The divergence in these policies stemmed from ideological disagreements over whether it was only those young people who could be identified as possible leaders of change that should be targeted, or whether 'youth' as a whole demographic, however defined, needed to be addressed. The difference was animated by diverging perspectives on whether youth recognised and followed their own leaders, or whether their assumed anti-establishment tendencies extended to rejecting leadership in general; hence a fear of the connection between 'youth' and 'anarchy'. Nowhere was it recognised initially that youth might hold socially conservative or mainstream views; that their desires and goals conformed to those of their parents, but that it was situational dynamics – those generally created or reinforced by the state – that prevented this occurring. The state actively misinterpreting their energy and drive for deviance was what actually sparked youth protests (Harris 2017; Bolten 2020). That being the case, we must also examine how states in fact create and nurture their youth 'problems' by assuming their de facto existence. In essence it is a blanket state-level fear of youth that is the a priori youth 'problem', and not young people themselves.

States' fear of youth may be enhanced by other aspects of their social identities and meanings; for example, the current US mass incarceration system was built on 1970s predictions of the numbers of black youth in the population (Hinton 2016) which was in turn rooted in assumptions of black inferiority and danger to a white status quo. When white youth were affected by the punitive laws of the wars on poverty and crime in the 1970s, the laws were amended by Congress to decriminalise offences most associated with whites; these were framed by legislators as examples of the youthful 'mistakes'. The result was to reclassify white offenders as 'in trouble' and in need of social-welfare support, while black youth continued to be categorised as 'delinquent' and an issue for the Justice Department (Hinton 2016). In a perhaps cautionary tale for advocates of a domestic YPS act today, Hinton shows how bipartisan consensus and compromises passed the 1974 Juvenile Justice and Delinquency Act which was promoted by liberals and appeared progressive. Yet this Act was part of a history of policy that effectively re-secured white youth within the state while black youth were 'securitized'. The domestic US corollary to Kaplan's 'loose molecules' in Africa was the 'super-predator' – an idea popularised in the 1990s by the political scientist John DiIulio, then at Princeton, who later worked for the G.W. Bush administration. DiIulio's predictions of a black youth 'crime bomb' and 'the coming super-predators' was both racist and fear-mongering (Hendrixson 2004). By his own admission he drew his conclusions without close study of the population he was demonizing:

> [A] few years ago, I forswore research inside juvenile lock-ups. The buzz of impulsive violence, the vacant stares and smiles, and the remorseless eyes were at once too frightening and too depressing (my God, these are children!) for me to pretend to 'study' them. (DiIulio 1995)

Though his demographic projections proved wrong, enormous damage was done as these predictions are now recognised to have led to a range of punitive policies that led to massive increase in rates of incarceration that disproportionately affected people of colour. In the interim the widespread fear of young people of colour has led to a shift in ideas of who, exactly, comprises the demographic of 'black youth', with Americans perceiving black children as older, more dangerous and 'less innocent' than their white peers (American Psychological Association 2014). Thus, states' youth problems are complicated by the fact that, while all youth are potentially suspect, not all youth are feared equally. Perceptions of 'good' or 'bad' youth both at home and abroad are constructed in relation to the interests of states, which are themselves raced and gendered.

The chapters that animate this section offer an in-depth examination of how states construct, imagine, narrate and react to their ideas about who 'youth' are. In their policies states often replicate the securitszation of young people that they claim to overcome with each novel examination of their young. The authors take a close look at how states imagine the supposed differences between youth – in political thinking, in social networking and in exposure to novel ideas – and the adults who are meant to represent 'mainstream' political thought, the potential dangers they pose to the state and status quo, and the projects that unfold to understand, identify and potentially co-opt youth who have the capacity to lead in the present and future.

In the first chapter Netra Eng and Caroline Hughes reveal how the Cambodian government has nurtured a fear of a 'youth problem', imagining that their young electorate, who have no memories of the genocide or civil war, are growing critical of the ruling Cambodian People's Party and will agitate for democratic reform. In response, the government has recently adopted a strategy of simultaneous co-optation and surveillance to promote allegiance to the government among the young. However, a recent survey of the political attitudes of young people reveals instead that not only are young people more conservative and less prone to agitation than the government imagines, but the picture is rendered more complex by the increasingly liberal attitudes of their parents.

In the second chapter Obasesam Okoi writes on the aftermath of the peace accords in Nigeria's long-standing civil conflict over oil in the Delta region. Okoi examines the results of a large survey he conducted among youth in the area to assess the quality of that peace. In revealing that the accords paid too much attention to satisfying the demands of the leaders of the various factions at the expense of the training, education and betterment of the majority of the ex-insurgents, Okoi argues that the accords have turned into an *anti-peace machine*. In this case the young ex-insurgents who are dissatisfied by their continual marginalisation by the state utilise violence in an 'industry racket' to extract money from the state, which means that the accords themselves promote violence as a means to an end. In this case the 'youth problem' was generated by the Nigerian state's unwillingness to engage with the most marginal youth among the ex-combatants, and, in pandering to the desires of the elite leadership of the rebel organisations, created resentment and violence where it would not have taken root otherwise.

In Chapter 3 Anna Fett writes about the history of these youth narratives in the United States through her investigation of the 'emphasis on youth' that emerged during the Kennedy administration in its establishment of the Inter-Agency Youth Commission. She argues that this programme revealed a discourse of youth as *bifurcated*, where young leaders in developing countries were identified simultaneously as a threat to the status quo of US domination and the pursuit of expanding 'democracy' around the world, and the best hope for peace, as their ability to influence the next generation could also support US interests abroad. Fett argues that the Agency was designed to surveil, co-opt and influence young leaders to support American democracy, on the basis of the assumption that, without this influence, they would actively oppose the United States. Thus the narrative generated youth as a problem to be solved before they became the 'leaders' who would endanger US supremacy abroad.

The chapters in this section reveal that the 'problem' of youth is not their existence, their inherent radicalism or their propensity to agitate for change simply because of their age and lack of access to the reins of power. Instead, the problem of 'youth' is a creation of the state itself: in these cases states imagine young people writ large as a threat to the status quo, who are then created as these threats through the very programmes and policies meant to identify, suppress and ameliorate their activities.

References

American Psychological Association. 2014. 'Black Boys Viewed as Older, Less Innocent than Whites, Research Finds.' https://www.apa.org/news/press/releases/2014/03/black-boys-older. Accessed 30 November 2023.

Bolten, Catherine. 2020. *Serious Youth in Sierra Leone: An Ethnography of Performance and Global Connection*. New York: Oxford University Press.

Cohen, Stanley. 1980. *Folk Devils and Moral Panics: The Creation of the Mods and the Rockers* New York: St Martin's Press.

DiIulio, John. 1995. 'The Coming of the Superpredators.' *The Weekly Standard*, 27 November. https://www.washingtonexaminer.com/weekly-standard/the-coming-of-the-super-predators. Accessed 30 November 2023.

Harris, Malcolm. 2017. *Kids These Days: Human Capital and the Making of Millenials*. New York: Little, Brown.

Hendrixson, Anne. 2004. 'Angry Young Men and Veiled Young Women. Constructing a New Population Threat.' The Corner House Briefing 34. Sturminster Newton: The Corner House.

Hinton, Elizabeth. 2016. *From the War on Poverty to the War on Crime: The Making of Mass Incarceration in America*. Cambridge, MA: Harvard University Press.

Kaplan, Robert. 2000. *The Coming Anarchy: Shattering the Dreams of the Post Cold War*. New York: Random House.

Richards, Paul. 1996. *Fighting for the Rainforest: War, Youth, and Resources in Sierra Leone*. London: Heinemann.

Scheper-Hughes, Nancy. 2004. 'Dangerous and Endangered Youth: Social Structures and Determinants of Violence.' *Annals of the New York Academy of Science* 1036: 13–46.

Urdal, Henrik. 2006. 'A Clash of Generations? Youth Bulges and Political Violence.' *International Studies Quarterly* 50 (3): 607–29.

1

Challenging the construction and conceptualisation of Cambodia's young generation in the postwar order

Netra Eng and Caroline Hughes

Cambodia's young people can be viewed as early graduates of the post-Cold War liberal peace engineering experiment that their country experienced between 1991 and 1998. An early example of the impact of second-generation peacekeeping (Bellamy et al. 2010, 194–5) and fourth-wave democratisation (Doorenspleet 2005), Cambodia emerged from devastating civil war in 1998 following a United Nations peacekeeping intervention from 1991 to 1993, and has subsequently navigated twenty years of faltering democratisation and violently contested neoliberal development. Ideas of liberal peace and democracy have been championed within Cambodia over the past twenty-five years by a coalition of local civil society organisations, opposition politicians and international donors, but have been viewed with far more suspicion by the dominant ruling party, the Cambodian People's Party (CPP) and its allies in the military, business and the bureaucracy. Economic liberalisation prompted a development strategy based on accumulation by dispossession (Harvey 2007; Springer 2010), in which vast tracts of land have been enclosed and leased to foreign investors or well-connected Cambodian tycoons (Hughes 2008). The result has been high levels of economic growth combined with low-level violence against communities, increasing inequality and precarity of livelihoods and finally, in 2017, an outright political reversal that saw the major opposition party banned.

In this contested context, donors, analysts and the Cambodian government have conceptualised 'youth' as a category of political actors with special significance for Cambodia's future political trajectory. For the purposes of this chapter we define the young generation as aged between fifteen and thirty: the significance of this group is partly quantitative – 63 per cent of the population are aged below thirty (UNFPA 2016) – and partly reflects their status as the first post-Khmer Rouge generation, free of the brutalisation and trauma associated with the 'killing fields'. The current generation of young Cambodians are the first generation to leave the land and work in a regionally integrated manufacturing economy, where they face the logic of the neoliberal 'competition state' (Cerny 2010). This logic sits uneasily with the postwar ideological order propagated by the CPP, which promotes a nostalgic vision of Cambodia as a land of historical greatness, environmental bounty and rural rhythms. Young Cambodians working in poor conditions in factories and construction sites directly experience the disjuncture between this depiction and the realities of late export-oriented development. They are also the first generation to enjoy widespread literacy and easy access to information. Their economic dispossession, combined with better education, positions them, in theory, as an existential challenge to the legitimacy of the postwar order. As such they are perceived as co-optable by those who desire radical change, and as threatening to those who fear it. Cambodia's main political parties have responded to this through intense competition to secure the 'youth vote', while the government has increased efforts to co-opt youth groups and surveil youth political activity, particularly online.

However, a national academic survey conducted in 2018 suggests that generational effects on political attitudes are not as strong as might be expected. The data suggest that postwar Cambodian youth are not particularly liberal or particularly discontented compared to older Cambodians. However, the data also suggest that a quarter-century of postwar neoliberal economic reform, propagation of neo-traditionalist and neo-patrimonial ideologies of governance and selective political violence has produced an alienated society with few organised movements – among youth or otherwise – to press for political reform. Cambodia's 'youth problem' is less a real and present danger of widespread youth-led disorder or rebellion than a series of elite ideological fantasies, which disguise deeper and more widespread dissatisfaction with the postwar order amongst the general population.

Youth in Cambodia's economic transformation

Cambodia's civil war ended in a series of staged transitions: socialist planning was abandoned from 1989, while liberal political reform followed a peace agreement in 1991 and the war finally ended in 1998. Market reforms set in motion privatisation deals which cemented personal ties within the ruling party and between the party, the bureaucracy and the military. The ruling party dominated subsequent elections through campaigning funded by natural resource proceeds and donations from companies, domestic and foreign. Part of this funding was ploughed into politicised development projects benefiting the party's rural electoral base, and part into bolstering ties with the military and rewarding defecting insurgents. This strategy cemented systemic informal practice, militarisation and politicisation within Cambodian institutions (Hughes 2003; Cock 2016).

At the same time the ruling party's rhetoric evolved to blend a 1980s socialist vocabulary of solidarity with the poor with a new neo-traditionalism, expressed through structures of rural development governance, organised through a personalist and hierarchical party structure which linked top politicians with rural villages. The large-scale agro-industrial-plantation, mining and land deals brokered to fund this modus operandi have butted up against the needs of an expanding rural population, and ad hoc patronage-based strategies have not boosted productivity in the subsistence agricultural sector. Twenty years after the war the young generation occupies a particular place in this political economy. Young people missed the land distribution of the late 1980s and are now largely excluded from inflated land markets (SNEC 2007). However, manufacturing employment burgeoned in urban areas from the mid-1990s prompting large-scale youth rural–urban migration.

Young migrant workers operate as a safety valve in the Cambodian political economy, keeping the rural population financially afloat even while agriculture stagnates. Remittances from young urbanites boost rural household consumption by 10–12 per cent and reduce poverty incidence by 3–4 per cent on average (UNESCO 2017). However, urban work in factories or construction sites often means excessive hours for low wages in dangerous and unhealthy conditions with little social protection (Kawazu and Kim 2019; ILO 2018; UNESCO et al. 2017; Ministry of Planning 2012), in industries that are vulnerable to exogenous shocks.

Yet urban work does not employ all young Cambodians: 46.8 per cent of youth are unpaid workers in family businesses or farms (FAO and Humboldt University of Berlin 2019) and almost half work in agriculture (FAO and Humboldt University of Berlin 2019). This is precarious work, heavily reliant on uncertain rainfall, leaving rural youth vulnerable to poverty and hunger (ILO and ADB 2015). Furthermore, youth unemployment is high among the small but expanding middle class of university graduates (OECD 2017). Whereas waged young workers are pivotal to Cambodia's development strategy, rural agricultural and urban middle-class youth are largely excluded from it, and few civic or political organisations exist to press political claims by these groups. Thus the political and economic opportunities open to youth are severely constrained.

Cambodian youth values: results of a national survey

An academic survey of young Cambodians conducted in 2018 by a respected Cambodian non-governmental think tank suggests that the material circumstances of Cambodia's young generation has not prompted a generation gap in political views (CDRI 2019). The results of the survey agreed with other data sources that young Cambodians are better educated, more connected to social media, more likely to be waged and more mobile than older Cambodians. Asked if the older and younger generations were different, 81 per cent of Cambodians over thirty said that the younger generation was very different from their own generations; 66 per cent of Cambodians aged under thirty agreed.

However, this difference was not reflected in social attitudes, except on some gender issues, where young Cambodians were more egalitarian than older Cambodians. On other topics similarities were pronounced. For example both older and younger Cambodians agreed that younger Cambodians should make their own decisions about whom to vote for (95 per cent of youth and 93 per cent of adults); whom to marry (85 per cent of youth and 82 per cent of adults) and where to work (77 per cent of youth and 73 per cent of adults). This is somewhat unexpected given that, for example, arranged marriages were the norm in Cambodia only twenty years ago (Marcher 1999). More older Cambodians than youth believed it was acceptable for young Cambodians to disagree with their parents (60 per cent of older Cambodians, 55 per cent of younger Cambodians), suggesting a greater respect for age hierarchies among the younger generation than the older. Similarly, 87 per cent of youth, compared to 85 per cent of older Cambodians, disapproved of premarital relationships, suggesting that younger Cambodians are as conservative as their parents.

This conservatism was also demonstrated in rankings of life priorities. Of young Cambodians 75 per cent ranked 'family' as their top priority in life, followed by education and work, religion, politics, friends and leisure. Among older Cambodians 65 per cent ranked 'family' first, with religion in second place. Although asserting independence in voting decisions, young people ranked family as the strongest influence on those decisions. These findings suggest that family ties remain strong in the postwar era, but that the family has adapted to new political economic realities by increasing the freedoms of young people within the household. Kinship ties have long been central to Cambodian social organisation (Ovensen et al. 1993). The survey results suggest the significance for young Cambodians of household-level coping strategies and kin networks in ameliorating the precarity of life in the postwar economy.

The strength of intra-household relationships contrasts with the fragility of broader relationships. Only 43 per cent of youth and 42 per cent of adults 'trusted' or 'strongly trusted' their extended family, slightly fewer than reported trusting development workers. Politicians elicited more trust than friends, colleagues or neighbours, suggesting a persistent atomisation of everyday life in Cambodian society and an order in which horizontal community relationships appear less important than a disempowered form of attachment to vertical patronage relationships with state actors. Only 62 per cent of young people and 73 per cent of adults reported feeling attachment to their local community, and reported levels of care for the country were lower still – 50 per cent and 63 per cent respectively. Although, formally, local participatory governance is practised – 76 per cent of older Cambodians and 63 per cent of younger Cambodians surveyed had attended local government meetings – this is often cosmetic. In the survey, of those respondents who had ever attended a meeting, only one in three had ever spoken in one. Asked whether they were afraid to speak in such meetings, 69 per cent of respondents declined to answer.

Regarding the performance of the government and the direction of the country, there was little generational variance. The survey asked about government policy in three areas – helping the poor, providing job opportunities for youth and ensuring stability in the country. Fewer than 50 per cent of respondents praised the government's performance on the first two issues, but youth were slightly more positive than older Cambodians on both. With respect to stability, older people were slightly more positive (59 per cent approval) than younger Cambodians (57 per cent approval). Yet, asked more generally to rate the future of the country and their own future, young Cambodians were generally very optimistic – more so than older Cambodians.

The survey results suggest that among young Cambodians the postwar experience has intensified attachment to close-knit households. Households cope in a precarious economy through cultivating dependent relationships with local authorities and patrons, but sustain few horizontal links outside the family. Family structures may be changing to award young people more freedom. However, there is little evidence of the emergence of solidarity between young people beyond the household that might lay the foundation for a 'youth movement' or a youth-based civil society. There is also insufficient evidence of different political attitudes between younger and older people to justify attributing social malaise or recent electoral upsets exclusively to youth. A picture emerges of more generalised cross-generational discontent with government development policies, in a context where the atomisation of society precludes effective independent organisation for reform, and where households are instead co-opted into vertical structures of patronage-based development.

Imagining Cambodian youth

This analysis differs from the characterisations proffered in policy-related debates among government, NGOs and media, as this section will detail. Over the past twenty-five years, strong narratives have emerged depicting youth as radically different from previous generations, and consequently as a distinct threat or opportunity in relation to the existing political order. Four particular narratives align with the 'youth problem' framing discussed in this volume. The first narrative focuses on young factory workers, framed by the government, business and some donors as unruly disruptors of economic 'competitiveness', but by opposition politicians as a constituency for social justice. The second narrative constitutes a moral panic about 'damaged' youth, engaging in crime and antisocial behaviour. The third posits youth as social-media pioneers, democratisers and active voters for change, while the fourth casts youth as politically mobilisable by elite actors for political protest.

Each of these framings resonates somewhat with particular groups of youth, but none reflects the widespread family-oriented conservatism expressed in the youth survey, nor do these tropes capture the cross-generational alienation depicted in the survey results. Rather, as Fett describes in Chapter 3, these framings reflect politicised imaginings of youth by political elites who cast young people as either heroes or villains in the project of constructing a new social order. The distance between rhetoric and reality reflects the depoliticisation of elite visions for Cambodia's future, which have been imposed without offering young people themselves a voice. For elites presiding over the integration of Cambodia into a post-Cold War regional and global economy, building a more inclusive, negotiated political settlement which empowers young people appears risky. The location of youth in Cambodia's contemporary political economy places them in new relationships with the state that are not easily controlled through familiar means; yet economic integration is dependent upon the compliant labour of the young. Elites respond to this dilemma by invoking images of youth as both a threat to and hope for Cambodia's hard-won stability, substituting stifling ideological co-optation for political negotiation, disempowering not only youth but wider society also.

Youth as labour militants

Young manufacturing workers in the economically important garment industry have long been troublesome to government development strategies. Between 2010 and 2018 garment workers were responsible for more than a quarter of all protests in Cambodia (Bynum and Pfadt 2019). The government has regularly used armed police to disband pickets and protests, in support of factory owners, offering an opportunity to Cambodia's main opposition party, the Cambodia National Rescue Party (CNRP), which has organised successfully among workers since the 1990s. Garment workers have enthusiastically supported opposition rallies and protests, most notably in January 2014 when large CNRP protests challenging the integrity of the 2013 election were amplified by a garment industry strike for a higher minimum wage. At this election the tide of popularity appeared to turn against the ruling party, even though the party managed to remain in power, setting in motion events that led to the dissolution of CNRP in 2017. On this basis the CNRP claims the allegiance of the industrial young. However, young industrial workers, although organised, active and visible, do not comprise a majority of Cambodian youth and are disconnected from non-unionised young people outside the factories. This raises questions about how significant a role this constituency could play in promoting a transformative politics in Cambodia, or how adequately they represent the interests of 'youth'.

Youth as delinquents

A second framing of Cambodian youth, emerging from Cambodian NGOs and donors (UNICEF 1996 quoted in Hensengerth 2008; LICADHO 2001), has focused on concerns about gang membership and drug use. A spate of reports in the early 2000s documented gang membership and casual attitudes towards gang rape in the context of a newly emerging night entertainment scene in urban areas (Gender and Development 2003; Phnom Penh Post, 2 July 2004). As the debate continued, what began as a liberal concern about rights, equality and ongoing societal violence turned into a more paternalistic concern on the part of government about 'youth delinquency' as a problem to be managed (Hensengerth 2008).

Youth as reformers and influencers

A 2009 situation report on 'Youth in Cambodia' by UNDP interrupted this narrative, stating that 'young people are often feared or misunderstood', and noted the significant economic difficulties young Cambodians faced, while claiming that 'young people are Cambodia's greatest resource for the future' (UN 2009). Shortly afterwards, the government's youth ministry released a new strategy promoting civic education and volunteering work among youth (MOEYS 2011). The objective was:

to ensure that all Cambodian youths know their personal and national identity and the importance of knowledge by striving to develop their capacities, sense of responsibility, good morals, mutual assistance, vocational skills, science competency, information technology competency and positive attitudes, through the provision of good examples at work and in society, by possessing a deep understanding of evolution and social norms and by contributing equally to national development. (MOEYS 2011)

Within this positive reframing, a neoliberal approach commodifies youth as a development resource while simultaneously referencing a nostalgic nationalist ideal of the 'good Khmer youth' who conforms to 'norms' propagated by the party. The latter approach has extended into government-sponsored youth organisations, such as the Cambodian Boy Scout movement, which is funded from the national budget and chaired by the Prime Minister (Phok and Chen 2012). The party views the scout movement as training the young 'to become an *effective* and *loyal* next generation for the country' (Voun 2018, emphases added).

This paternalist and nationalist approach harks back to the socialist youth movements sponsored by the party in the 1980s (Kuch and Lewis 2013). Directed by older adults, they are seen primarily as training grounds for socialising youth, rather than as vehicles for youth politics (Mun 2022). Recently, pro-government youth organisations have launched initiatives to promote participation and pride amongst the young in specifically apolitical activities. These include successful attempts to capture Guinness world records for weaving the longest Khmer scarf (3,720 feet) and cooking the largest sticky-rice cake (8,900 lb) (New York Times, 23 January 2019). The stunts combined enrolment of youth in nostalgic re-enactments of traditional cultural activities with a claim for global prominence intended to showcase Cambodia's 'good culture' to the world (Phnom Penh Post, 13 April 2015).

The 2013 election gave new impetus to the framing of youth as a vehicle for reform. It was widely reported that youth voters were crucial in this electoral upset and in subsequent protests against electoral fraud (Seiff 2013; The Economist 2013; Reuters 2013; Everett 2013). OECD observers reported that young people had 'sent a clear message that the government had not done enough for them' (OECD 2017). Significant to this appraisal was the spectacle of crowds of youth greeting the return of the CNRP leader from temporary exile before the election, in gatherings organised on social media.

Social media access expanded rapidly between 2011 and 2013 in Cambodia, and its association with the young fuelled speculation that the opposition vote in the 2013 election was primarily a youth vote. Youth obsession with Facebook was exploited by the CNRP to circulate news and images critical of the government (Eng and Hughes 2017; Hughes and Eng 2019). In a narrative that differs sharply from the youth-as-delinquent or youth-as-loyal-nationalist tropes described above, opposition party activists and politicians have cast youth as confident, tech-savvy, politically sophisticated and pro-democratic. For example Mu Sochua, a leading opposition party figure, wrote in 2017, 'Two-thirds of Cambodians today are under 30 years of age. It is this generation that is hungry for the fundamental freedoms Hun Sen's government is intent on dismantling' (Mu 2017). However, the survey results reported earlier cast doubt on this account. Although young Cambodians are certainly better educated than older generations, there is less evidence to suggest that they are uniformly more desiring of political reform than older Cambodians, or that they have more political resources to effectively demand it.

The government responded to these developments with its own Facebook charm offensive. It also tightened internet control from 2014 (Hughes and Eng 2019). A series of laws restricted internet use and other media and expanded surveillance of telecommunications. Continued concern about the loyalties of young voters prompted the government to ban the CNRP in 2017, and to hold elections without them the following year.

Youth as street fighters and revolutionaries

This deterioration in Cambodian democracy illustrates the continued potential for confrontation between the ruling party and the opposition parties. Various political leaders have positioned youth as central in this confrontation. CNRP leader Sam Rainsy has repeatedly called for a 'people power' movement based on youth to combat the government's tightening control. In 2013 he compared Cambodia's situation to the Arab Spring: 'Contrary to the Arab Spring, youth there have no political party, and they were disorganised. But in Cambodia, especially in this election, youth are associated with the opposition' (The Nation 2023).

The CPP used the threat of 'colour revolution' to justify outlawing the CNRP in 2017 (MFA 2018), but the CPP has also seen youth as a bulwark against such a revolution. In a 2018 speech the Prime Minister called on Cambodian youth to 'contribute to protecting peace and political stability; to work together to support socio-economic development; and to prevent color revolution in Cambodia at all cost' (Fresh News Asia 2018). In fact the CPP has frequently been successful in mobilising groups of young people on to the streets as counter-protestors. From the late 1990s, for example, the CPP regularly mobilised 'Pagoda Boys' – young rural men lodging in Phnom Penh Buddhist temples while studying in the city – to engage in counter-protests against other youth groups, such as striking wage-earners or urban middle-class opposition supporters (Aun and Henderson 2013; US State Department Bureau of East Asian Affairs 2003; Yun 2004).

Youth and political participation in Cambodia

These inconsistent framings of Cambodian youth arguably reflect the inadequacies of Cambodia's postwar political settlement. The CPP entrenched its power over this period through a pragmatic, neo-traditionalist ideology of governance characterised by patron–client relationships of dependence, particularly in rural society. These relationships have been used to promote surveillance and co-optation and to assert values of loyalty, obedience and order as central to peace. These relationships were constructed through directing flows of resources, obtained from investors and donors, to key constituencies to maintain their allegiance.

The framings of young people described above reflect the ideological needs of this order. The young fit awkwardly into a neo-traditionalist, hierarchical ideology in which age is specifically equated with authority. Similarly, the literacy, connectedness, mobility and wage-earning capacities of many young Cambodians conflict with an order of patronage-based dependence and gratitude designed for subsistence farmers receiving basic development goods from benefactors. Some groups – Boy Scouts and Pagoda Boys, sponsored by party figures – fit into the CPP's social order, but striking factory workers visibly challenge it. Consequently the CPP routinely portrays youth *both* as a potential menace to be carefully controlled *and* as a political weapon, and adopts policies accordingly. Neither characterisation adequately captures the range of youth attitudes or aspirations, or offers opportunities for youth to advocate for themselves.

For the opposition, relationships with urban migrant workers are used to claim 'the youth vote', and an account of how the weakened CNRP might achieve a political renaissance. However, urban wage-earners are a minority of Cambodian youth and their attitudes and concerns cannot be generalised to rural family farm workers. In the stifling political context of post-conflict Cambodia an effective civil society that might build bridges between different sections of youth has not emerged and different youth groups frequently appear at odds with one another. Furthermore the survey cited shows no evidence of different political attitudes between younger and older people to justify attributing recent electoral upsets to the 'youth vote'. The data suggest instead more generalised discontent with government development policies. Continued preoccupation with imagined delinquent youth and 'colour revolution' obscures and depoliticises socio-economic fissures emerging more broadly from neoliberal development.

Conclusion

Since the war, observers of Cambodia have worried about youth as a problem for peace, as headlines were repeatedly captured by striking workers, teenage gangs and violent protestors. However, as Okoi observes in Chapter 2, in his account of peacebuilding in the Niger Delta, the government has shown little interest in providing different groups of young people with a political voice. In fact the government has been slow to address issues specific to youth. Although the opposition CNRP organised among urban factory workers, rural youth in particular have been generally absent from policy discussions and political speeches for twenty years, except as a potential law-and-order problem.

The unexpectedly close election result in 2013, attributed to a discontented 'youth vote', changed the situation somewhat, as young people became central to political strategising. For the increasingly marginalised Cambodian opposition a 'people power' movement led by a young freedom-loving generation represents a major hope. For the government, talk of a 'colour revolution' calls youth to rally against such a prospect. Underlying both of these visions is a characterisation of youth as a potentially disruptive force. The Cambodian government's response, like that of the Nigerian government as documented by Okoi, has been 'anti-political', comprising better social benefits offered to the most dangerous youth constituency – young factory workers – and anodyne publicity stunts to evoke national pride among the poorest constituency – young agricultural workers – alongside tightening surveillance control of young bloggers and human rights activists.

The survey data presented here suggest that Cambodian youth themselves view the situation somewhat differently. They are generally conservative and family-oriented, neither an organised political threat nor a particularly destabilising social or economic factor. Their disapproval of government policies is rather less than that of older generations. Youth appear disconnected from one another, more preoccupied with family, work and religion than with either politics or leisure. The precarity of young people in the political economy suggests an intensification of reliance on immediate family. This is combined, in Cambodia as in Nigeria, with the insertion of the household in politicised rural patronage structures as the key to survival. At the same time Cambodian youth are a differentiated group, and, as Fett warns in Chapter 3, the presumption that they share a political objective is unfounded. Political campaigns to inspire youth to entrepreneurial and leadership activities have been highly publicised in Cambodia, but they are uniformly elite-led, and disguise powerful faultlines of political identity and economic status that persist in Cambodian society 25 years after the war formally ended.

A key issue for countries like Cambodia, emerging from conflict in the era of late neoliberal development, is how to address shortcomings in the postwar political settlement while at the same time coping with the pressures of neoliberal development. The postwar political settlement in Cambodia, like that of Nigeria described in Okoi's chapter, was based on the presumption that profits from 'development' can be captured and shared amongst elites. This leaves young people – whether urban or rural – bearing a heavy share of the burden of neoliberal 'competitiveness', but a small share of the reward. The response of political actors has been to deploy twin strategies of co-optation and repression, as a means to contain and disempower young people. These strategies have been largely successful, since few really existing 'youth movements' present a significant threat to the postwar order. The adverse incorporation of youth into the postwar economy but their continued alienation in the political sphere raises important questions for the quality of Cambodia's 'peace'.

References

Aun, Pheap, and Simon Henderson. 2013. 'Flying the CPP Flag, "Pagoda Boys" Have Mixed Allegiances.' *The Cambodia Daily*, 19 July 2013 https://english. cambodiadaily.com/news/flying-the-cpp-flag-pagoda-boys-have-mixed-alle giances-35718/. Accessed 30 November 2023.

Bellamy, Alex J., Paul D. Williams and Stuart Griffin. 2010. *Understanding Peacekeeping*. Cambridge: Polity Press.

Bynum, Eliot, and Franziska Pfadt. 2019. 'Increased Repression, Declining Demonstrations, an Analysis of Cambodian Demonstrations.' Armed Conflict Location and Event Data Project (ACLED) Country Analysis. https://www.acleddata. com/2019/02/22/increased-repression-declining-demonstrations-an-analysis-of-cambodian-demonstrations-2010–2018/. Accessed 30 November 2023.

Cambodia Development Resource Institute. 2019. *Cambodia's Older and Younger Generation: Views on Generational Relations and Key Social and Political Issues*. Phnom Penh: CDRI.

Cerny, Philip. 2010. 'The Competition State Today: from *Raison d'Etat* to *Raison du Monde*,' *Policy Studies* 31 (1): 5–21.

Cock, Andrew. 2016. *Governing Cambodia's Forests: The International Politics of Policy Reform*. Copenhagen: NIAS Press. Doorenspleet, Renske. 2005. *Democratic Transitions: Exploring the Structural Sources of the Fourth Wave*. Boulder: Lynn Rienner.

The Economist. 2013. 'Feeling Cheated: Cambodia's Election.' 29 July 2013.

Eng, Netra, and Caroline Hughes. 2017. 'Coming of Age in Peace, Prosperity, and Connectivity: Cambodia's Young Electorate and Its Impact on the Ruling Party's Political Strategies/.' *Critical Asian Studies* 49 (3): 396–410.

Everett, Silas. 2013. 'Cambodia's 2013 Elections: a Measure of Political Inclusion?' *In Asia Weekly Insights and Analysis.* Bangkok: Asia Foundation.https://khmerization.blogspot.com/2013/07/cambodias-2013-elections-measure-of.html. Accessed 14 December 2023.

FAO and Humboldt University of Berlin. 2019. *Preparing and Accessing Decent Work amongst Rural Youth in Cambodia.* Rome: FAO.

Fresh News Asia. 2018. 'PM Hun Sen Urges Youth to Prevent Color Revolution at All Cost.' 27 November 2018. http://m.en.freshnewsasia.com/index.php/en/12062-2018-11-27-15-04-01.html. Accessed 30 November 2023.

Gender and Development for Cambodia. 2003. *Paupers and Princelings: Youth Attitudes towards Gangs, Violence, Rape, Drugs and Theft.* Phnom Penh: Gender and Development for Cambodia. https://www.eldis.org/document/A13489. Accessed 30 November 2023.

Harvey, David. 2007. *A Brief History of Neoliberalism.* Oxford: Oxford University Press.

Hensengerth, Oliver. 2008. 'Social and Political Fractures after Wars: the Role of Youth Violence in Post-1993 Cambodia.' Project Working Paper No. 4, *Social and Political Fractures after Wars: Youth Violence in Cambodia and Guatemala.* Essen: Universitet Duisberg Essen Faculty of Social Sciences Institute for Development and Peace.

Hughes, Caroline. 2003. *The Political Economy of Cambodia's Transition 1991–2001.* London: Routledge.

Hughes, Caroline. 2008. 'Cambodia in 2007: Development and Dispossession,' *Asian Survey* 48 (1): 69–74.

Hughes, Caroline, and Netra Eng. 2019. 'Facebook, Contestation and Poor People's Politics: Spanning the Rural-urban Divide in Cambodia.' *Journal of Contemporary Asia* 49 (3): 365–88.

International Labor Organization. 2018. 'Living Conditions of Garment and Footwear Sector Workers in Cambodia.' *Cambodia Garment and Footwear Sector Bulletin* 8 (December): 1–11.

ILO and ADB. 2015. *Cambodia: Addressing the Skills Gap, Employment Diagnostic Study.* Metro-Manila: ADB.

Kawazu, Erin, and Hyun Kim. 2019. 'Mass Fainting in Cambodian Garment Factories.' *Global Epidemiology.* https://doi.org/10.1016/j.gloepi.2019.100008. Accessed 30 November 2023.

Kuch, Naren, and Simon Lewis. 2013. 'Subedi Protest Linked to CPP-aligned Youth Group.' *The Cambodia Daily*, 23 May 2013. https://english.cambodiadaily.com/news/subedi-protest-linked-to-cpp-aligned-youth-group-26156/. Accessed 30 November 2023.

LICADHO. 2001. *Rape and Indecent Assault: Crimes in the Community.* Special Report, February 2001, Phnom Penh: Cambodian League for the Promotion and Defence of Human Rights (LICADHO).

Marcher, Anette. 1999. 'Arranged Marriage Blamed for Failing Families,' *Phnom Penh Post,* 20 August. https://www.phnompenhpost.com/national/arranged-marriage-blamed-failing-families. Accessed 14 December 2023.

Ministry of Employment, Youth and Sport (MOEYS). 2011. *National Policy on Cambodia Youth and Development,* Endorsed by the Council of Ministers. Phnom Penh, 24 June 2011. Ministry of Planning. 2012. *Migration in Cambodia: Report of the Cambodian Rural Urban Migration Project (CRUMP).* Phnom Penh: Ministry of Planning.

Mu, Sochua, 2017. 'There is Still Hope for Cambodia's Democracy.' Opinion/ Democracy, Al Jazeera. 16 November 2018. https://www.aljazeera.com/ indepth/opinion/hope-cambodia-democracy-181113151712889.html. Accessed 30 November 2023.

Mun, Vong. 2022. 'State Mobilization in Authoritarian Regimes: Youth Politics and Regime Legitimation in Cambodia.' *Journal of East Asian Studies* 22 (3): 411–34.

The Nation. 2023. 'Rainsy Puts His Faith in Youth.' 13 December. https://www. nationthailand.com/international/30211323. Accessed 14 December 2023.

OECD Development Centre. 2017. *Youth Well-being Policy Review of Cambodia.* Paris: EU-OECD Youth Inclusion Project.

Ovensen, Jan, Ing-Britt Trankell and Joakim Ojendal. 1996. *Where Every Household Is an Island: Social Organization and Power Structures in Rural Cambodia.* Stockholm: SIDA.

Phok, Dorn, and Dene-hern Chen. 2012. 'Scouting Out the Next Generation of CPP Supporters.' *The Cambodia Daily.* 25 January 2012, https://english.cambo diadaily.com/news/scouting-out-the-next-generation-of-cpp-supporters-1550/. Accessed 30 November 2023.

Reuters. 2013. 'Opposition Vows Mass Protest over Election Deadlock.' 6 August, 1:19 AM EDT.

Seiff, Abby. 2013. 'Cambodia's Youth Begin Demanding Change.' Al Jazeera. 27 July 2013. Springer, Simon. 2010. *Cambodia's Neoliberal Order: Violence, Authoritarianism and the Contestation of Public Space.* London: Routledge.

Supreme National Economic Council of Cambodia (SNEC). 2007. *The Report of Land and Human Development in Cambodia.* Phnom Penh: RGC. https://www. un.org/esa/agenda21/natlinfo/countr/cambodia/land.pdf. Accessed 14 December 2023.

UNESCO, UNDP, IOM and UN Habitat. 2017. *Overview of Internal Migration in Cambodia,* Policy Briefs on Internal Migration in Southeast Asia Series. Bangkok: UNESCO. http://bangkok.unesco.org/content/policy-briefs-internal-migration-southeast-asia. Accessed 14 December 2023.

UNFPA. 2016. *Cambodia Youth Fact Sheet.* https://cambodia.unfpa.org/sites/default/ files/pub-pdf/Flyer_Cambodia_Youth_Factsheet_final_draft_%28approved%29. pdf. Accessed 30 November 2023.

UNICEF. 1996. *Towards a Better Future: An Analysis of the Situation of Children and Women in Cambodia.* Phnom Penh: UNICEF.

United Nations Country Team Cambodia. 2009. *Situation Analysis of Youth in Cambodia.* Phnom Penh: Office of the United Nations Resident Co-ordinator in Cambodia.

US State Department Bureau of East Asian Affairs. 2003. 'Report to Congress on the Anti-Thai Riots in Cambodia January 29 2003.' Bureau of East Asian Affairs, 14 May 2003. https://2001–2009.state.gov/p/eap/rls/rpt/20565.htm. Accessed 30 November 2023.

Voun, Dara. 2018. 'Cambodian Scouts to Be Trained in New Digital Technologies.' *Phnom Penh Post.* 5 December 2018. https://www.phnompenhpost.com/national/cambodian-scouts-be-trained-new-digital-technologies?__cf_chl_jschl_tk__=585917e365f33b5f7b91f8803ed25dcfc71044ca-1592487789–0-AdXoihO7zgJM-coOCQeGyT4HL-Zqs1GIe4V22Ire_S9l50QYE1pOyK3qfirF-. Accessed 30 November 2023.

Wallace, Julia. 2019. 'Cambodia Ruler's Recipe for Youth Appeal? An 8,900 Pound Sticky Rice Cake.' *New York Times.* 23 January 2019. https://www.nytimes.com/2019/01/23/world/asia/cambodia-hun-sen-world-records.html. Accessed 30 November 2023.

Yun, Samean. 2004. 'Pagoda Boys Accused of Interference at Strike.' *The Cambodia Daily*, 12 April 2004. https://english.cambodiadaily.com/news/pagoda-boys-accused-of-interference-at-strike-39993/. Accessed 30 November 2023.

2

The challenge and promise of transforming youth insurgency in Nigeria's oil region

Obasesam Okoi

Nigeria's oil economy has the potential to transform significantly the living conditions of minority groups in the Niger Delta region. Paradoxically, however, six decades of oil extraction in Nigeria has brought unprecedented prosperity to multinational corporations and a tiny indigenous elite while millions of citizens in communities with an abundance of oil wealth lack good roads, electricity, clean water, health facilities, high-quality schools and economic opportunities. The cumulative effects of oil extraction on the environment and poverty have been a source of long-standing discontent among ethnic minorities, whose agitation for resource control and environmental justice was initially expressed through non-violent protests championed by environmental rights activists. The polarising impact of the struggle gained scholarly attention in the 1990s when the Nigerian state began to exact reprisal on peaceful protesters including the prosecution and killing of environmental rights activists from the Ogoni ethnic nation (Okonta and Douglas 2003). As a result of these contradictions, community youths have been challenging the state and oil multinationals to pay attention to the suffering of ethnic minorities in the oil region. The importance of this challenge was powerfully demonstrated in the state's commitment to an unconditional amnesty for thousands of youth insurgents in 2009. Amnesty served as a precondition for the implementation of peacebuilding measures that laid the foundation for safeguarding the communities to which the insurgents would be returning while building capacity for peace, security and development in the oil region.

To date, analytical attention has focused on the marginalisation of minorities (Ikelegbe 2005; Obi 2009; Idemudia 2009; Arowosegbe 2009; Folami 2017); environmental injustices (Okonta 2005; Idemudia and Ite 2006; Elum, Mopipi and Henri-Ukoha 2016); and the monetisation of peace (Davidheiser and Nyiayaana 2011; Ajayi and Adesote 2013; Ushie 2013; Obi 2014; Okonofua 2016; Schultze-Kraft 2017). There has been less scholarly effort to understand the social dynamics of peacebuilding – the fact that disarmament, demobilisation and reintegration (DDR) practices became a politico-economic activity of breaking the leadership structure of the insurgent groups by paying off the leaders and their followers to be peaceful. These dynamics led to the exclusion of thousands of former insurgents from the economic incentives of peacemaking, mostly orchestrated by their leaders, in connivance with the peacebuilders. This chapter examines the challenge and promise of transforming youth insurgency in Nigeria's oil region. This chapter argues that Nigeria's peacebuilding infrastructure, initially designed to transform the insurgency that debilitated the nation's oil economy, constituted itself into an anti-peace machine by transforming the DDR programme into an industry racket that enables former youth insurgents to exploit violence for material gains. Underlying the anti-peace machine is the framing of peace as an economic problem requiring the state to buy peace from the ex-insurgents by paying them a monthly stipend. This enables the peacebuilders to direct their interventions mainly on sustaining the peace economy with monetary incentives while ignoring the social inequities in the local communities from where insurgency grows. The evidence draws on qualitative and quantitative data obtained from field research in Rivers, Bayelsa and Akwa Ibom states between 2017 and 2018. Rivers and Bayelsa states are the hotspots of insurgent activities due to the presence of notorious armed groups. In contrast, insurgent activities in Akwa Ibom state are relatively low. The participants in this study are former youth insurgents who participated in the Presidential Amnesty Program (PAP) established by President Musa Yar'Adua in 2009 to co-ordinate the implementation of DDR activities as an instrument for post-conflict peacebuilding.

The amnesty database comprises thirty thousand registered participants from the nine states of the oil region. The population is composed of individuals between thirty and forty-five years of age who identified as youth, and 84 per cent of the respondents were male, while 16 per cent were female. Thousands of youths have experienced a positive change in their economic status through participation in the peacebuilding programme, while 90 per cent of the ex-insurgents I surveyed expressed an intense feeling of exclusion from the peace economy and are more apt to rearm and disrupt the peace process in the future (Okoi 2019a). I used snowballing sampling to recruit the participants and administered 396 questionnaires representing 2 per cent of the population captured in the amnesty database from Rivers, Bayelsa and Akwa Ibom. I performed simple descriptive statistics that provided summaries about the survey responses, displayed in frequency tables. In addition to this I obtained qualitative data through interviews with forty-five purposefully selected informants recruited on the basis of their experience in the peacebuilding programme.

For analytical convenience this chapter is organised in five sections. Section one introduces the context, argument and methods. Section two provides a brief overview of the nature of the insurgency. Section three examines the promise of transforming the insurgency while section four examines the challenges emerging from the peacebuilding efforts. The concluding section appraises the key argument. Two key challenges are worth emphasising in this chapter. The first is mobilisation of youth as a source of identity within the broader struggle for social justice in the oil region. This conception of youth serves as a catalyst for peace and justice. The second, and more problematic, is the political construction of youth as a source of agency easily mobilised by armed groups to negotiate their access to the peace economy. The contextualisation of youth is important in developing a critical analysis of the anti-peace machine, and makes a unique contribution to this volume. The broader contribution of this chapter to the volume is that it provides an analysis of the consequences of the government's attempt to co-opt the 'leadership' of the insurgent groups by patronising it to prevent a relapse into insurgency. This development alienated thousands of former youth insurgents, which leaves the Nigerian government in a bind of perpetually paying for peace.

The challenge of transforming youth insurgency in Nigeria

DDR is generally assumed to be a necessary intervention for ensuring the stability of post-conflict societies. In Nigeria the goal of post-conflict stability is achieved against the backdrop of the federal government's intent to transform the youth insurgents into responsible and law-abiding citizens. But when DDR interventions are politicised, as they are in the context of the Niger Delta, they none the less produce a host of unintended consequences, such as the translation of the political realities of poverty, environmental pollution and marginalisation into technical problems that marginalised many ex-insurgents. The youth who feel alienated from the emerging peace economy now constitute a threat to sustainable peace in the oil region. They threaten to rearm and disrupt the peace process if their needs are not met. I describe this development as the *anti-peace machine*. The concept of the anti-peace machine was inspired by James Fergusson's *Anti-Politics Machine*, written as a critique of 'development'. It makes specific reference to the consistent failure of development agencies to bring about economic stability in Lesotho due to the depoliticisation of development (Ferguson 1990). The overarching argument of this chapter is that the Niger Delta peacebuilding framework represents such a machine that seeks to depoliticise peace in pursuit of stability by framing peacebuilding primarily as an economic problem requiring monetary solutions. Moreover, the peacebuilding machinery depoliticises peace by focusing conflict resolution interventions mainly on sustaining the peace economy with monetary solutions while ignoring the underlying social inequities in the oil region.

It is important to note that Nigeria's DDR programme was designed as a process of decapitating the organisational structures of the insurgent groups and separating the leaders from young insurgents. The federal government successfully lured the leaders of the various insurgent groups to the negotiation table with the promise of security and peacebuilding contracts and technical training. Thousands of youth who disarmed to accept amnesty under the influence of their leaders became pawns to their own leaders' selfish desires. Most of them were denied the financial and training incentives. Thousands of youths who were alienated from these incentives became the anti-peace machine. The peacebuilding programme thus constitutes an anti-peace machine because the peacebuilders chose to limit their interventions to technical solutions that have been successful in elevating the status of some ex-insurgents and a few privileged non-insurgents, while ignoring the insecurities that threaten the wellbeing of marginalised youths in the rural communities who are equally capable of picking up arms to resume insurgency at the slightest discontent. In this context the anti-peace machine constitutes what Johan Galtung describes as a state of negative peace (the absence of violence). For Galtung the absence of violence does not imply the achievement of peace. Thus he sees peacebuilding as the elimination of contradictions at the root of conflict formation (Galtung 1996, 103). Peacebuilding aims to address conflicting relationships that lie at the root of injustice while enhancing prospects towards positive peace based on social justice and equity (Galtung 1975, 297–304; Gawerc 2006, 439). This involves a deep-level transformation of violent actors and structures, enabling the achievement of positive peace.

This line of thinking is significant given that the oil communities contribute more than 90 per cent of Nigeria's export revenue (Adeola 2009; Etekpe 2009; Chukwuemeka, Anazodo and Nzewi 2011; Okorobia and Olali 2013; Nwankwo 2015) and therefore deserve interventions that move beyond palliative measures focused on stabilising the security situation without necessarily addressing the underlying inequities in the oil region. The UNDP Human Development Report has further confirmed the appalling contradiction between opulence and poverty in the Niger Delta (UNDP 2006). Nowhere is inequality more visible than in Bayelsa state where the ratio of physicians to the population is 1:150,000 (Watts 2007, 1). Social inequality also manifests itself in the level of illiteracy in rural communities where many young people cannot read, write or communicate in English. The level of illiteracy in the rural communities poses a security threat to the oil region because it limits employment prospects for youths. The high level of illiteracy is a critical factor in understanding some technical challenges emerging from the peacebuilding programme. Many participants I met during an entrepreneurship training in Calabar – the headquarters of Cross River state and one of the cities in the Niger Delta region – expressed a lack of familiarity with the technical concepts the trainers were teaching and could barely benefit from the knowledge. I discovered that most ex-insurgents who had difficulty with written or verbal communication attended the entrepreneurship training only to benefit from the financial incentives. In addition to their being paid a monthly stipend that is twice the federal government minimum wage to ensure they are peaceful, they also receive allowances for participating in the entrepreneurship training. But the insurgents I met in Calabar in January 2018 were uninterested in the training that brought them from Rivers and Bayelsa states to Calabar. Of the two hundred participants who attended the entrepreneurship training, only 2 per cent were attentive. The rest expressed greater interest in their training allowance than the training itself. I discovered, however, that the general lack of interest in the training was because they do not have land for the type of agroenterprise they were trained to pursue. Their lands have been devastated by oil pollution and cannot support agriculture.

The fact remains that, while the peacebuilding programme has been successful in incentivising violence for material rewards by building the technical capacity of many ex-insurgents through a range of training programmes, it none the less ignores fundamental insecurities in the rural communities. The programme ignores thousands of illiterate youths in the rural communities who depend on the environment for their daily survival, yet do not benefit from the peace programme because they did not participate in the insurgency or have no connection to the peacebuilders. While the federal government did extend the programme to include community youths who did not participate in the insurgency, the nepotistic tendencies of the peacebuilders ensured that they mobilised the beneficiaries on the basis of family and ethnic ties while marginalising other youths with no such connections. The youth who are left out now constitute a threat to sustainable peace in the oil region. They constitute the anti-peace machine.

The promise of transforming youth insurgency

Youth insurgency in the Niger Delta had enormous effects on the nation's economy. The federal government lost approximately US$92 billion in export revenue from crude oil theft and production shutdowns between 2003 and 2008 (Davis 2009, 6). Renewed insurgency in 2016 cut Nigeria's oil production from 2.2 million barrels per day to approximately 1.5 million barrels per day (Gaffey 2016). The economic impact of the youth insurgency prompted President Musa Yar'Adua to commission a technical committee in 2008 to review the various reports on the Niger Delta and recommend a sustainable solution to the problem. The technical committee recommended the implementation of amnesty within a comprehensive disarmament, demobilisation and reintegration programme. The terms of amnesty include the willingness of the insurgents to 'disarm and unconditionally renounce' insurgency (Kuku 2015, 22–3). The presidential proclamation of amnesty included a sixty-day moratorium between 6 August and 4 October 2009. The moratorium created a safe and secure environment for disarming the initial 20,192 youth insurgents as well as developing management programmes for the storage and destruction of arms and ammunition. The purpose of disarming the insurgents is to create a secure environment for 'nurturing the peace process' (Knight 2008, 28) by 'eliminating the means by which wars are executed, while building confidence among conflict parties and the civilian population' (Alden, Thakur and Arnold 2011, 14).

Following the declaration of amnesty, the leaders of various insurgent groups who have been responsible for the violence and criminality in the oil region for which an amnesty was warranted, such as the Movement for the Emancipation of the Niger Delta (MEND), Niger Delta Volunteers, The Outlaw Group and Niger Delta Strike Force mobilised their members to disarm and accept amnesty. The federal government recovered 520 arms, 16 gunboats and 95,970 rounds of ammunition in Bayelsa state (Gilbert 2010, 63). In 2012 the federal government awarded the Oil Pipeline Surveillance and Protection (OPSP) contract to these leaders and mobilised the national interest rhetoric to justify its action against public outrage. The first beneficiary of a US$103 million OPSP contract was 'General' Government Ekpemupolo (Tompolo) through his company Global West Vessel Specialist Limited (Adibe 2016, 343). This was in addition to a US$22 million contract awarded to him through another company, Egbe Security River One. Asari Dokubo also benefited from a US$9 million contract through his company Security Gallery, while Ateke benefited from a US$3.8 million contract through his company Close Body Protection. General Boyloaf received a total of US$3.8 million in security contracts through his companies Adex Energy Security, Donyx Global Concept, Oil Facilities Surveillance and New Age Global Security (Adibe 2016). While these leaders did transform the peace process into an opportunity to emerge as security contractors that gave them access to material wealth, they did not carry most of their followers along. Regular ex-insurgents who are no longer loyal to these leaders have been excluded from the monthly stipend because these payments have been contracted to the leaders. I realised, however, that thousands of youth insurgents had initially expressed their unwillingness to comply with the terms of the amnesty due to lack of trust in the federal government's true intent. These participants were mostly ex-insurgents who initially had disarmed but were unwilling to accept amnesty due to its consequences. They perceived the amnesty not as a genuine reconciliation process but as a tactical ploy to disarm and prosecute them for violence and alleged criminal transgressions targeting the nation's oil and gas infrastructure. They later changed their minds upon realising the incentives of participating in the peacebuilding programme.

An opportunity presented itself for insurgent youths who did not comply with the initial 4 October 2009 grace period to accept amnesty. Between 2010 and 2012 the federal government enlisted 9,808 insurgent youths in the amnesty programme, comprising 6,166 delegates in 2010 and 3,642 in 2012 (Ikelegbe and Umukoro 2016: 39). In general thirty thousand insurgents enrolled in the DDR programme (Kuku 2012). However, not everyone in the list of thirty thousand delegates participated in the insurgency. I have met thousands of community youths in Cross River, Akwa Ibom, Rivers and Bayelsa who did not participate in the insurgency but were integrated into the peacebuilding programme. It is important to note that, in the context of the Presidential Amnesty Program, there is no clear distinction between DDR and peacebuilding. DDR is understood more broadly as the set of activities designed to achieve post-conflict peacebuilding. The practical limitation of circumscribing DDR within a peacebuilding programme is that it narrows the peace process to DDR activities that allow the federal government to temporarily stabilise the oil region by incentivising youths who somehow identified themselves as insurgents to benefit from the peace economy, even though they did not fight the insurgency. Many ex-insurgents eventually found themselves on the fringes when powerful political elites conspired with the peacebuilders to influence the incentives to benefit members of their ethnic groups, most of whom did not fight. It was the grievances generated by the perceived alienation of legitimate ex-insurgents that subsequently gave impetus to the anti-peace machine. Besides, there were concerns that restricting the peacebuilding incentives to ex-insurgents only might provoke the non-insurgents to disrupt the peace process by violent means. Thus the commitment by the federal government to the peacebuilding process led to the inclusion of more participants between October 2009 and October 2012 (Ikelegbe and Umukoro 2016, 39).

The demobilisation phase of the Niger Delta DDR programme commenced on 28 June 2010. Demobilisation activities at the Obubra camp include non-violent transformational training. Thousands of ex-insurgents from the nine states of the Niger Delta undertook their training at Obubra community in Cross River state, which the first participants completed on 10 July 2010. This strategy emphasised the psychological transformation of the ex-insurgents with the aim of reprogramming their minds to think as nonviolent actors (Ikelegbe and Umukoro 2016, 40; Okoi 2019a, 5). The inspiration behind this strategy was Martin Luther King Jr's nonviolence philosophy. This study finds that, as a result of the impact of DDR in elevating the status of some Niger Delta youths, there is a growing desire among former youth insurgents to seek *inward* and *outward* transformation as the basis of peace. Inward transformation refers to the impact of education in changing the mindset of the youth and their attitude to violent behaviour. For example thousands of youths who chose education as the path to peace and have been awarded the Presidential Amnesty Scholarship to pursue their dreams in foreign and local universities eventually return to the oil region as educated and refined citizens. Those who have experienced a change of economic and social status (outward transformation) through their exposure to Western education that gave them job opportunities are unwilling to participate in violence upon returning to the oil region. The economic incentives have subsequently become the motivation of youths seeking *inward* and *outward* transformation as the basis of peace. I coin the terms *inward transformation* and *outward transformation* to give expression to my experience interacting with the ex-insurgents.

I conducted a simple statistical analysis to test the impact of demobilisation training on the intrapersonal transformation of ex-insurgents. More than half (57.1 per cent) of the respondents strongly agree that transformational training has been successful in transforming the ex-insurgents into non-violent citizens while 35.1 per cent somewhat agree. In general more respondents (92.2 per cent) agree that the transformational training – a powerful DDR activity designed to achieve the goal of demobilisation – has been effective in transforming the ex-insurgents into peaceful, non-violent citizens (see Figure 2.1). It was important, as part of this study, to measure the extent to which demobilisation interventions have weakened the capacity of insurgent groups, making it almost impossible for the oil region to relapse into repeated cycles of insurgency. Successful demobilisation programmes across Africa have shown that the process of breaking up insurgent groups socially can be eminently rewarding. For example, the majority (87.2 per cent) of the respondents agree that the demobilisation programme has successfully weakened the capacity of the insurgent groups (see Figure 2.2). In general, 77.7 per cent of the respondents agree that the peacebuilding programme has broken the structure of the insurgent groups (see Figure 2.3). By implication those who hold an optimistic view of the impact of the peacebuilding programme in reprogramming the minds of ex-insurgents against violent behaviour, as well as its capacity to break the organisational structure of the armed groups, are more compared to those who think otherwise.

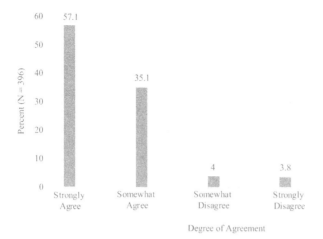

Figure 2.1 Effectiveness of demobilisation training

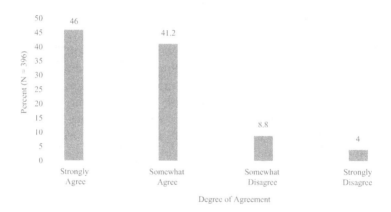

Figure 2.2 Effectiveness of amnesty in weakening the capacity of armed groups

The statistical data give credence to the qualitative evidence which shows that the transformational training activities undertaken as part of DDR have 'inspired many ex-insurgents to resist criminal behaviours that promise immediate financial returns' (Okoi 2019b, 5). It brought about the awareness that the pursuit of peace is the strongest weapon that could be deployed by courageous individuals in search of justice. Many ex-insurgents have been inspired by this philosophy to become peace ambassadors in their communities.

Following the end of the demobilisation programme on 29 September 2011 the federal government began the process of reintegrating the

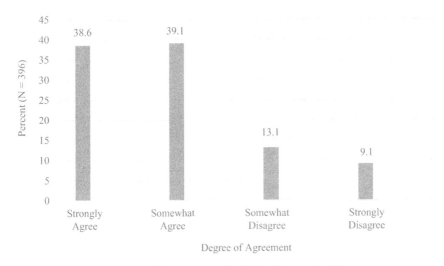

Figure 2.3 Impact of amnesty in the disbandment of militant groups

ex-insurgents into civilian society. Reintegration activities were designed to help the ex-insurgents transition into civilian society and participate in the economic life of their communities, and included financial empowerment, skill training, education and entrepreneurship implemented in partnership with the private sector and non-governmental organisations. They involved providing education and skill training to ex-insurgents in technical vocations that the federal government considers as critical to national development. These included pilot training and aircraft maintenance, marine technology, electrical installation, welding and fabrication technology, oil and gas exploration, production and process engineering, and hospitality management. These occupations were chosen by the peacebuilders on the basis of the federal government's priorities and dangled in front of the insurgents to commit them to the peace process. While a handful of them were fortunate to find employment in their choice of vocations, thousands of them who have received training in preparation for job placements in these vocations are redundant. It is obvious that the technical interventions benefited the male fighters while marginalising the female ex-insurgents who were mostly absent in these training opportunities. Gender disparity was one of the concerns I raised during my interview with the peacebuilders. They acknowledge the disparity but argue that women did not bear arms but were conscripted into the insurgency as 'sex workers' and intelligence agents. Their perception of women's agency reveals the patriarchal culture driving the implementation of post-conflict peacebuilding practices. None the less the programme has transformed the lives of thousands of youths from the oil region through scholarships in local and foreign universities. It also has produced an explosion of local entrepreneurs, in addition to a skilled labour force in highly demanding trades and professions. To date the federal government has invested billions of dollars in peacebuilding.

Following the inauguration of the amnesty programme in June 2009 the federal government allocated an initial 50 billion naira US$50 million) for peacebuilding and later increased the budget to 68 billion naira (US$68 million) (Nigeria Stability and Reconciliation Program 2014: 3). The budget was intended to address the needs of the initial 20,192 registered insurgents in 2009, and subsequently 26,000 in 2010 and 30,000 in 2012. Between 2009 and 2012 the federal government had invested over US$1 billion to cover the allowances and training costs for amnesty delegates deployed both locally and internationally for training and education (Nigeria Stability and Reconciliation Program 2014: 4).

Despite the promise of the peace process, its biggest challenge had been the management of peacebuilding activities, particularly the payment of monthly stipends to ex-insurgents that were initially designed as reinsertion but have continued indefinitely. Expert opinion suggests that 'the strategy of buying off militant leaders and clamping down militarily and with the force of the law on those who continued to operate, has been largely successful' (Nigeria Stability and Reconciliation Program 2014: 3). Some analysts contend that 'the amnesty program has served a strategic purpose of increasing stability in the Niger Delta, which has enabled the state to pursue its economic interests' (Ushie 2013: 32). Others argue, however, that amnesty poses a major challenge to lasting peace in the region because the state ignores the 'widely shared grievances' of local populations, and the structural violence in which militancy grows (Davidheiser and Nyiayaana 2011: 45). The context of structural violence refers to the systematic ways in which minority groups in the oil region are hindered from equal access to political and economic opportunities. Sustainable peace remains elusive due to the materialistic nature of DDR.

Contextualising the nature of youth insurgency

A fundamental concern that this chapter raises is what 'youth' really means in the context of the Niger Delta insurgency. While most insurgents are below the age of thirty-six, which is the official age for youth in Nigeria, I discovered through my research that many insurgents mobilise as youth because of their shared identity. Therefore, in this study, the term 'youth' is used not as a demographic variable but as a social construction

(Kehily 2013). Young people with a shared ethnic identity often mobilise as youth to achieve a political objective. In this context, youth is not something that is given but is a political construct that enables people of shared identity to give legitimacy to their struggle. Youth identity has become the driving force behind the emergence of Ijaw youth activists who asserted themselves as a powerful political force in the struggle for self-determination from the late 1990s to the early 2000s. What deserves attention is the political construction of youth in the broader context of the struggle against ethnic domination. Youth, I argue, is a concept that gives legitimacy to the actions of identity groups in their struggle to achieve a political objective. But this struggle did not emerge in a historical vacuum. It is embedded in Nigeria's colonial history.

Youth insurgency in the oil region is one of the legacies of colonialism in Nigeria. The British colonial government divided Nigeria into administrative regions corresponding to the dominant ethnic groups, such as Ibo in the south-east, Hausa in the north and Yoruba in the south-west. Other ethnic groups who did not fit in these three categories but were forced to live together under the colonial administrative structure became minorities in the various regions. Ethnic sentiments grew among minority groups of the south, who began to express legitimate concerns about their status within the postcolonial political configuration whereby power was monopolised by the dominant ethnic groups to award privileges in their favour while alienating the minorities (Anugwom 2011; Joab-Peterside, Porter and Watts 2012; Jack-Akhigbe 2013). Since the 1960s the postcolonial state in Nigeria has grappled unsuccessfully with the complex challenge of nation-building in ways that transcend primordial ethnic loyalties.

Eghosa Osaghae and his colleagues have also traced the insurgency in the oil region to the failure of Indigenous elites to develop their local communities (Osaghae et al. 2007). Their study shows how these challenges provided the political context for Ijaw activists to mobilise a youth insurgency. There have been several efforts to address the development challenges in the oil region which none the less became an opportunity for predatory elites to reward ethnic loyalty. In this context youth insurgency epitomises the structural inequalities that arose from the postcolonial nation-building project, which downplayed the underdevelopment of the oil region. At the heart of this paradox is Nigeria's inability to translate its natural resource wealth into rising living standards for its growing population (Okoi 2019b). Terry Karl has argued that developing countries with an abundance of natural resource wealth are at a greater risk of experiencing violent conflict due to bad governance compared to those without natural resources (Karl 1997). Underlying the youth insurgency, therefore, is the spatial expression of power and agency between the state and insurgent youths over the control of oil resources. These contestations underline a 2006 study by Sylvia Washington, Paul Rosier and Heather Goodall who observed that how communities construct their struggle for justice is an essential way in which 'place' conveys its meaning for the people who inhabit that community (Washington, Rosier and Goodall 2006). Their observation offers a critical lens into the dynamics of identity politics in the oil region and the role that identity plays in the spatial politics of youth insurgency. While youth identity can be tied to 'place', in the Niger Delta context, people mobilise as youth to gain access to oil rents in relation to the spatial politics of peacebuilding.

Conclusion

This chapter examined the promise and challenge of transforming youth insurgency in Nigeria's oil region. Currently the peacebuilding programme provides palliative measures that have been successful in preventing a relapse into insurgency using a range of strategies including economic incentives, rather than a strategic institutional response to the complex development challenges prevailing in the oil region and the suffering of Niger Delta youths. The peacebuilding infrastructure thus constituted itself into an anti-peace machine that encourages youths who feel marginalised to exploit violence as a means to an end. The implications of this machine are evident in the achievement of temporary successes while ignoring the fundamental realities of marginalisation, hopelessness and suffering from where insurgency grows. In this context the peacebuilding programme is embroiled in a vast array of political challenges that make progress towards sustainable peace increasingly difficult to achieve. Such challenges give considerable attention to the danger of marginalising a fraction of former insurgent youths from the oil region who feel that their decision to disarm did not lead to any meaningful change in their lives and are more apt to rearm.

At the core of this chapter is the economic expediency of peacebuilding, which encourages youths in search of hope to mobilise insurgency as a strategy for negotiating material benefits from the state. Other considerations give primacy to the total disregard for environmental justice in a region where the very basis of survival in the rural communities depends heavily on the immediate ecosystem. It is through these dynamic processes that the anti-peace machinery operates. The key lesson is that peacebuilding design and implementation can have a significant impact on whether ex-insurgent youths who have been successfully disarmed and demobilised will change their behaviour when there are considerable disparities in their living conditions.

This chapter concludes that the prospects for sustainable peace in Nigeria's oil region are mixed. On one hand the Nigerian government has implemented sweeping measures to address the long-standing grievances of ethnic minorities in the region, such as launching the Presidential Amnesty Program to reintegrate former insurgents into society. On the other hand the underlying drivers of the Niger Delta insurgency, which include environmental degradation, social inequality and a lack of economic opportunities, remain deeply entrenched. To attain sustainable peace in the oil region a long-term commitment from both the Nigerian government and oil multinationals operating in the region is necessary. These stakeholders must prioritise efforts to address environmental, social and economic vulnerabilities. Furthermore, the Nigerian government must tackle issues of governance and corruption in the peacebuilding programme that perpetuate insurgency. In this regard the prospects for sustainable peace must emphasise the importance of involving marginalised youth in peacebuilding efforts. This approach ensures that the needs and concerns of both former insurgents, who feel marginalised in the peace process due to corruption, and community youth, who were not involved in the insurgency but are affected by the environmental and economic conditions in the oil region, are adequately addressed as part of the peace process.

In order to achieve sustainable peace in the Niger Delta it is crucial to involve community youth in peacebuilding efforts, as they are often impacted by the region's environmental and economic conditions, which can contribute to their grievances and potential involvement in armed insurgency. Addressing the needs and concerns of community youth as part of the peace process can increase the likelihood of achieving lasting peace in the region. Furthermore, engaging youth in peacebuilding efforts can empower them to become agents of positive change and contribute to the development of their communities. Therefore it is essential to prioritise the participation of youth in peacebuilding efforts and recognise their perspectives and contributions in building sustainable peace in the Niger Delta.

References

Adeola, Francis O. 2009. 'From Colonialism to Internal Colonialism and Crude Socioenvironmental Injustice: Anatomy of Violent Conflicts in the Niger Delta of Nigeria.' In *Environmental Justice in the New Millennium: Global Perspectives on Race, Ethnicity, and Human Rights*, edited by Filomina Steady, pp. 135–63. New York: Palgrave Macmillan.

Ajayi, Adegboyega I., and Adesola S. Adesote. 2013. 'The Gains and Pains of the Amnesty Programme in the Niger Delta Region of Nigeria, 2007–2012: a Preliminary Assessment.' *Journal of Asian and African Studies* 48 (4): 506–20.

Alden, Chris, Monika Thakur and Mathew Arnold. 2011. *Militias and the Challenges of Post-Conflict Peace: Silencing the Gun.* London: Zed Books.

Anugwom, Edlyne. 2011. 'Something Mightier: Marginalization, Occult Imaginations and the Youth Conflict in the Oil-Rich Niger Delta.' *Africa Spectrum* 46 (3): 3–26.

Arowosegbe, Jeremiah O. 2009. 'Violence and National Development in Nigeria: the Political Economy of Youth Restiveness in the Niger Delta.' *Review of African Political Economy* 36 (122): 575–94.

Chukwuemeka, Emma E. O., Rosemary Anazodo and Hope Nzewi. 2011. 'Social Conflict in the South-South Nigeria: Implications for Foreign Investment. *African Journal of Political Science and International Relations* 5 (6): 335–40.

Davidheiser, Mark, and Kialee Nyiayaana. 2011. 'Demobilization or Remobilization? The Amnesty Program and the Search for Peace in the Niger Delta.' *African Security* 4 (1): 44–64.

Davis, Stephen. 2009. *The Opportunity for Peace in the Niger Delta.* Global Energy and Environment Initiative. Washington, DC: The Paul H. Nitze School of Advanced International Studies.

Elum, Z. A, K. Mopipi and A. Henri-Ukoha. 2016. 'Oil Exploitation and Its Socioeconomic Effects on the Niger Delta Region of Nigeria.' *Environmental Science and Pollution Research* 23 (13): 12880–9.

Etekpe, Ambily. 2009. *Policy Options and Adaptation: A Comprehensive Study of the Niger Delta and Other Deltas of the World.* Monograph Series, No. 003. Department of Political Science, Niger Delta University, Bayelsa State.

Ferguson, James. 1990. *The Anti-politics Machine: 'Development,' Depoliticization and Bureaucratic Power in Lesotho.* Cambridge: Cambridge University Press.

Folami, Olakunle Michael. 2017. 'Ethnic-conflict and Its Manifestations in the Politics of Recognition in a Multi-ethnic Niger Delta Region.' *Cogent Social Sciences* 3 (1). https://www.tandfonline.com/doi/full/10.1080/23311886.2017.1 358526?scroll=top&needAccess=true. Accessed 20 July 2018.

Gaffey, Conor. 2016. 'Niger Delta Avengers Threaten Further Violence in Oil-Producing Region.' *Newsweek.* 14 June. www.newsweek.com/nigeria-niger-de lta-avengers-threaten-further-violence-oil-producing-region-470073\. Accessed 20 June 2018.

Galtung, Johan. 1975. 'Entropy and the General Theory of Peace.' In *Peace: Research Education Action*, pp. 186–220 Essays in Peace Research Series, Volume 1. Copenhagen: Ejlers.

Galtung, Johan. 1996. *Peace by Peaceful Means: Peace and Conflict Development and Civilization.* London: SAGE Publications.

Gawerc, Michelle I. 2006. 'Peace-building: Theoretical and Concrete Perspectives.' *Peace and Change: A Journal of Peace Research* 31 (4): 435–78.

Gilbert, Lysias D. 2010. 'Youth Militancy, Amnesty and Security in the Niger Delta Region of Nigeria.' In *Checkmating the Resurgence of Oil Violence in the Niger Delta of Nigeria*, edited by Victor Ojakorotu and Lysias Dodd Gilbert, pp. 51–88. Potomac, MD: Institute for the Analysis of Global Security. http://www.iags.org/Niger_Delta_book.pdf. Accessed 21 December 2023.

Idemudia, Uwafiokun. 2009. 'The Changing Phases of the Niger Delta Conflict: Implications for Conflict Escalation and the Return to Peace.' *Conflict, Security and Development* 9 (3): 307–31.

Idemudia, Uwafiokun, and Uwem W. Ite. 2006. 'Demystifying the Niger Delta Conflict: Towards an Integrated Explanation.' *Review of African Political Economy* 33 (109): 391–406.

Ikelegbe, Augustine. 2005. 'Encounters of Insurgent Youth Association with the State in the Oil Rich Niger Delta Region of Nigeria.' *Journal of Third World Studies* 27 (3): 87–122.

Ikelegbe, Augustine, and Nathaniel Umukoro. 2016. *The Amnesty Programme and the Resolution of the Niger Delta Crisis: Progress, Challenges and Prognosis.* Monograph Series No. 14. Benin City: Centre for Population and Environmental Development.

Jack-Akhigbe and Okouwa Peace. 2013. 'The State and Development Intervention in the Niger Delta Region of Nigeria.' *International Journal of Humanities and Social Science* 3 (10): 255–63.

Joab-Peterside, Sofori, Dough Porter, and Michael Watts. 2012. *Rethinking Conflict in the Niger Delta: Understanding Conflict Dynamics, Justice and Security.* Niger Delta Economies of Violence Working Paper No. 25. Berkeley: University of California. https://geography.berkeley.edu/sites/default/files/watts_26.pdf. Accessed 30 November 2023.

Karl, Terry Lynn. 1997. *The Paradox of Plenty.* Berkeley, CA: University of California Press.

Kehily, Mary Jane. 2013. 'Youth as a Social Construction.' In *Working with Young People*, edited by Sheila Curran, Roger Harrison and Donald Mackinnon, pp. 13–23. London: Sage Publications, Inc. in Association with the Open University.

Knight, Andy W. 2008. 'Disarmament, Demobilization, and Reintegration and Post-conflict Peacebuilding in Africa: An Overview.' *African Security* 1 (1): 24–52.

Kuku, Kingsley. 2012., 'Nigeria Enlists 30000 Ex-militants in Presidential Amnesty Programme, Says Kuku.' *Premium Times*, 24 December 2012. www.premium timesng.com/news/112493-nigeria-enlists-30000-ex-militants-in-presidential-amnesty-programme-says-kuku.html. Accessed 14 December 2016.

Nwankwo, Beloveth Odochi. 2015. 'The Politics of Conflict over Oil in the Niger Delta Region of Nigeria: a Review of the Corporate Social Responsibility Strategies of the Oil Companies.' *American Journal of Educational Research* 3 (4): 383–92.

Obi, Cyril. I. 2009. 'Nigeria's Niger Delta: Understanding the Complex Drivers of Violent Oil-related Conflict." *Africa Development* 34 (2): 103–28.

Obi, Cyril. I. 2014. 'Oil and the Post-Amnesty Programme (PAP): What Prospects for Sustainable Development and Peace in the Niger Delta?. *Review of African Political Economy* 41 (140): 249–63.

Okoi, Obasesam. 2016. 'Why Nations Fight: The Causes of the Nigeria-Cameroon Bakassi Peninsula Conflict.' *African Security* 9 (1): 42–65.

Okoi, Obasesam. 2019a. 'Peacebuilding and Transformational Change in Nigeria's Oil Region.' *Conflict Resolution Quarterly* 19 (1): 1–16.

Okoi, Obasesam. 2019b. 'The Paradox of Oil Dependency in Nigeria.' *Africa Portal.* https://www.africaportal.org/features/paradox-nigerias-oil-dependency/. Accessed 30 November 2023.

Okonofua, Benjamin A. 2016. 'The Niger Delta Amnesty Program: The Challenges of Transitioning from Peace Settlements to Long-Term Peace.' *SAGE Open* 6 (2): 1–16.

Okonta, Ike. 2005. 'Nigeria: Chronicle of a Dying State.' *Current History* 104 (682): 203–8.

Okonta, Ike, and Oronto Douglas. 2003. *Where Vultures Feast: Shell, Human Rights, and Oil in the Niger Delta.* London: Verso.

Okorobia, Atei Mark, and Stepehn Temegha Olali. 2013. 'Ethno-Nationalism and Identity Conflicts in Nigerian History: The Niger Delta Situation to 2012.' *Mediterranean Journal of Social Sciences* 4 (4): 431–47.

Osaghae, Egosa E., Augustine Ikelegbe, Omobolaji O. Olarinmoye and Stephen I. Okhonmina. 2007. *Youth Militias, Self Determination and Resource Control Struggles in the Niger Delta Region of Nigeria.* Dakar: Council for the Development of Social Science Research in Africa (CODESRIA) and ASC Leiden Consortium for Development Partnership Research Report No. 5, Modules 5 and 6.

Schultze-Kraft, Markus. 2017. 'Understanding Organised Violence and Crime in Political Settlements: Oil Wars, Petro-criminality and Amnesty in the Niger Delta.' *Journal of International Development* 29 (5): 613–27.

United Nations Development Program (UNDP). 2006. *Niger Delta Human Development Report.* Abuja: UNDP Nigeria. http://hdr.undp.org/en/content/human-development-report. Accessed 30 November 2023.

Ushie, Vanessa. 2013. 'Nigeria's Amnesty Programme as a Peacebuilding Infrastructure: a Silver Bullet?' *Journal of Peacebuilding and Development* 8 (1): 30–44.

Washington, Sylvia Hood, Paul C. Rosier, and Heather Goodall. 2006. 'Introduction.' In *Echoes from the Poisoned Well: Global Memories of Injustice*, edited by Sylvia Hood Washington, Paul C. Rosier and Heather Goodall, pp. xiii–xxiii. Lanham, MD: Lexington.

Watts, Michael. 2007. 'Petro-insurgency or Criminal Syndicate? Conflict & Violence in the Niger Delta.' *Review of African Political Economy* 114: 637–60.

3

Why all the 'emphasis on youth'? A Cold War perspective on contemporary US youth bulge talk

Anna Fett

The Youth, Peace and Security (YPS) Act, a bipartisan bill first introduced into the US House of Representatives in March of 2020, opens with a series of ten 'findings': '(1) There are currently 1.8 billion youth in the world, the largest number ever to have existed' (USYPS 2020).[1] This first finding, which suggests that a category of persons called youth should matter to Congress because of their unprecedentedly large number, employs the logic of *youth bulge* talk. Marc Sommers explains that the 'demographic phenomenon known as the "youth bulge" signifies an unusually high proportion of youth in an adult population' yet what constitutes unusually high is rarely made clear by those who employ this rhetoric (Sommers 2019, 10).

For example, the '1.8 billion' number in the 2020 US YPS Act is said to come from the approximate number of the global population between the ages of fifteen and twenty-nine years old (SCFG 2023). Yet the bill later defines 'youth' as those 'who have attained the age of 16 but have not attained the age of 30' – a definition that also diverges from the 2015 United Nations (UN) Security Council Resolution 2250 which defines youth as 'persons of the age of 18–29 years old' (UNSCR 2250 2015). The second finding of the 2020 Act goes on to state: 'Youth represent the majority of the population in many conflict-affected countries, where on average 50 percent of the population is below the age of 20, and in some countries more than 70 percent of the population is below the age of 30' – statistics which not only confuse the cut-off for when youthhood ends but also include those younger than fifteen, even infants. Despite the haphazard slippage concerning age cohorts given in these findings, which may not correlate in any meaningful way to a purportedly universal, aged cohort known as youth, these kinds of statistics lend youth bulge talk the veneer of scientific credibility. The notion that 'youth' should matter to US policy-makers, as well as the international peacebuilding community, because there are so many (read: *too* many) of them is made to feel axiomatic.

More importantly, youth bulge discourse inevitably constructs the allegedly high demographic of youth as a problem-to-be-solved. As Sommers explains, 'the concept implies the presence of an abnormal situation that could get worse: a "bulging" youth population just might explode' (Sommers 2019, 10). Some youth advocates and development experts have tried to reconceptualise youth bulges in a positive light by framing the too high global proportion of youth as a potential 'resource' or 'asset' that remains underutilised and can be harnessed in support of, often neoliberal, development projects, yet, as Siobhán McEvoy-Levy has argued, this framing still reinforces the underlying presumption that youth bulge populations are a potential problem in need of fixing (McEvoy-Levy 2013, 300–3). For instance the 2020 Act states that '(4) Violence impacts over 1 billion people globally each year.' This fourth finding does not explicitly name 'youth' as the driver of global 'violence', but the earlier claims to the high demographic of youth – the 'largest number ever to have existed' – at the very least implicitly offers a plausible culprit. This assumption that youth are potential, if not already actual, drivers of physical forms of violence is reinforced by findings 7–9 which all mention youth-related (7) 'approaches', (8) 'programs' and (9) 'strategies', for 'reducing' or otherwise discouraging 'violence', 'political violence', and 'violence and extremism'. Therefore, even when the fifth and sixth findings positively highlight youth for playing 'critical' roles in both 'strengthening a culture of peace and security' and 'in grassroots community development', respectively, the logic of this legislation implies that this will happen again only if Congress intervenes quickly in order to harness youth's collective critical 'capacity'.

According to the international non-governmental peacebuilding organisation Search for Common Ground which actively supports the adoption of this proposed legislation, the 2020 Act 'would adapt US foreign policy to an age of emergent youth power' – a 'power' apparently derived from the unusually large global proportion of youth (USCG 2023). To do this the bill calls for developing an inter-agency 'strategy' across multiple governmental departments, mandating 'training for Foreign Service Officers', and naming a new 'Youth Coordinator' within the US Agency for International Development (USAID) as well as designating 'a Youth Point of Contact (YPOC) in diplomatic overseas missions'. Given that the US YPS Act is the first piece of legislation to attempt to translate the international UN YPS Agenda into a country-specific strategy that may provide a model for other states in the future if it ever passes – it is worth pausing to evaluate an earlier moment in US history when youth bulge talk inspired the US government to craft another inter-agency strategy targeting 'youth'.

In the early 1960s 'youth' became something of a buzzword throughout US governmental agencies thanks in no small part to the work of President John F. Kennedy. Soon after his passing, President Kennedy's brother

Robert F. Kennedy reflected, 'the current world-wide contest for the hearts and minds of youth, particularly the youth of underdeveloped nations ... was of intense personal interest to President Kennedy who became identified with young people throughout the world to an extent many did not realize during his life' (R. Kennedy 1964). Often remembered as the youngest American president, entering the White House at the age of 43, what is less well-known about Kennedy is his administration's effort to launch the Inter-Agency Youth Committee (IAYC) in 1962 to carry out a covert 'Emphasis on Youth' foreign policy directive on a global scale. The IAYC co-ordinated its efforts across an impressive number of governmental bodies including the Central Intelligence Agency, the Department of Defense, the Department of State, USAID and US diplomatic posts around the world.

Combining approaches from US foreign relations history along with Critical Youth Studies and Peace Studies, this chapter analyses the discursive logic of the 'Emphasis on Youth' directive and how it validated the agenda of the IAYC. Ostensibly building on the fear of the (too quickly) growing demographic of young people globally in the early 1960s, the Kennedy administration used this youth bulge talk to justify its establishment of a new government-wide apparatus to surveil, contact and, ultimately, try to influence strategic foreign youth with leadership potential, generally by increasing youth participation in a number of US governmental programmes. Confidential correspondence between the central committee in Washington, DC, and US overseas missions reveals that the IAYC constructed a category of persons called youth that was seen as both a risk *and* an untapped asset with the capacity to either thwart or support US foreign policy objectives in the midst of the Cold War. Building on Christina Klein's insight that early Cold War Americans developed not only a 'global imaginary of containment' but also a 'global imaginary of integration' (Klein 2003, 19–49), I argue that the IAYC's attempts to cultivate intimate, friendly contact with promising young foreign leaders complemented simultaneous approaches by the Kennedy and later the Lyndon B. Johnson administrations to repress other transnational alliances amongst young persons deemed too radical. Rather than cast these negative and positive tactics in opposition to each other, I argue that these approaches were intended to work together to expand US state power during the Cold War.

Cold War youth bulge talk

While Robert Kennedy never referred to a 'youth bulge', his 1964 speech to the Canadian press in Toronto had all the hallmark traits of this rhetoric:

In the unsettled atmosphere of the world today, there is a premium on the qualities of young people. They are more important to themselves, to their nations and to the ideas that they espouse then [*sic*] ever before. Quite apart from that, however, *the young have a special importance today simply because there are so many of them*. In numbers alone, they are a substantial majority in the developing nations of Africa, Asia and Latin America. In Pakistan, for example, 60% of the population is under the age of twenty-five. In the Congo, the figure is 54% ... There are comparable figures for most other developing nations, higher figures for several [*emphasis added*]. (R. Kennedy 1964)

In the early 1960s it was easy for Kennedy's Canadian and American listeners to feel like there were more young people than ever before. In the United States, following the postwar baby boom, the population of young Americans did rise rapidly. By 1970 those aged 14 to 24 would reach 40 million – an increase of 52 per cent from the number in 1960 (cited in Klatch 1999, 4). During the 1950s public anxiety about younger generations intensified, fuelling greatly exaggerated fears over rising rates of so-called juvenile delinquency (Gilbert 1986). In the early 1960s Kennedy's speech helped his audience imagine 'the young' as one homogeneous age demographic quickly becoming the majority of the world's population at home and now abroad as well. Although he later admitted in his speech that the demographic figures he mentioned 'include children, [and] the very young', Kennedy had no problem invoking these figures to support his claim that his listeners should turn their attention on youth 'because there are so many of them'. Fears of overpopulation, especially in the Global South, eventually shaped USAID's 'family planning' efforts during the end of the Kennedy administration and even more so during the Johnson administration (Connelly 2010, 195–252).

And yet, in emphasising these numbers, Kennedy did not, in reality, intend for his audience, or the US government, to actually deal with all those he so fuzzily lumped into that category. He may have opened with youth bulge talk, but the rest of his speech exposed the fact that Kennedy really cared about a particular subset of young persons: those who were 'leading their nations' and 'in positions of significant political power' (R. Kennedy 1964). Here Kennedy paused to list one-by-one popular nationalist leaders in countries such as Angola, Cuba, Congo, Guinea, Kenya and the Philippines who were in their early to mid-thirties. Even as he acknowledged that his brother had 'of course, appointed many young men to high positions in our government' – himself included, elected the youngest US Attorney General ever at the age of 35 – Kennedy argued that the age of *these* leaders was a matter of 'special importance' that necessitated further examination.

From the end of the Second World War to 1960 approximately forty states gained independence from their former colonial powers (cited in Latham 2000, 2). The Kennedy brothers had themselves grown up witnessing new leaders around the world topple established power regimes. When President Kennedy took office in 1961, his administration was consumed with the desire to win the political and economic allegiance of newly independent nations before the Soviet Union did by helping these countries 'modernise' through foreign aid (Latham 2000, 28–30 and 69–108). But the Kennedy brothers worried that aid in itself would not be enough. Robert Kennedy personally came to this conclusion in February of 1962 on a visit to various East Asian countries where he witnessed firsthand the widespread antagonism many educated young people felt towards the United States (Battle 1963).

In his 1964 speech Kennedy drew a direct link between the emerging leaders in what he called developing countries and a recent wave of student protests around the world. From the Hungarian and Polish student protests of 1956 to other 'student riots' first in Peru and Venezuela and then in Japan, Korea, Turkey and Vietnam, Kennedy traced a monolithic line connecting them all:

> We must recognize that the young in many areas of the world today are in the midst of a revolution against the status quo … If they have to pull governments tumbling down over their heads, they will do it. But they are going to win a share of a better, cleaner world. (R. Kennedy 1964)

Thus the real threat Kennedy worried about was not the quickly growing proportion of youth globally but the up-and-comers who were replacing the current political leadership in many strategic countries – those 'young people' who were 'only a few short years away from the presidential palace'. Worried that Western countries were not taking these emerging political leaders seriously enough, Kennedy argued that the United States and Canada must make 'a conscious effort' in 'seeking out the young'. Within the ideological competition of the Cold War, Kennedy argued that Westerners needed to act fast before the Soviets beat them to it (for example, Hornsby 2016).

Kennedy's listeners may not have been familiar with all of the student protests that he referenced, but many could envisage recent student protests closer to home. By the end of 1960 sit-in lunch-counter demonstrations occurred in 104 US cities. While roughly fifty thousand people took part in them, most Americans associated this particular desegregation tactic with the Black college students who employed it in Greensboro, North Carolina, some of whom then went on to help organise the Student Nonviolent Coordinating Committee. That same year, other predominantly White students from the University of California at Berkeley gained notoriety when police used fire hoses to break up their demonstrations against the House Un-American Activities Committee hearings held in San Francisco (cited in Scott 2016, 18 and 33). Although Kennedy never explicitly named these US student protests in his speech, he did not need to. His audience could conjure a picture of these students from what they saw on their television screens (Scott 2016, 33–54). Regardless of their age and socio-economic status – let alone whether these various groups of students self-consciously identified as 'youth' or not (Scott 2016, 118–36) – Kennedy cast them all as a potential threat. That he cared much more about students with rising political power rather than the large demographic of global youth was tellingly evidenced when he conceded in his 1964 speech that 'students in the world today are a dynamic force with an importance *all out of proportion to their numbers* [*emphasis added*]'. It was really only rising foreign leaders that he meant when he said: 'We must be concerned with these young people, with who they are and where they live, with what they are thinking and saying, and with what we are saying to them.'

In order to win over young emerging leaders in newly independent countries, the Kennedy administration crafted the 'Emphasis on Youth' directive to be carried out covertly by a new inter-agency youth task force – the IAYC. In its early years the central committee in Washington, DC, developed training seminars at the Foreign Service Institute and then for other agencies and departments including USAID and the Department of Defense. The IAYC expected all overseas missions to set up their own Country Team Youth Committees led by new Youth Coordinators. To make clear that the directive viewed youth as *politically* significant actors, the IAYC central committee encouraged Political or Economic Affairs Officers, if not Deputy Chiefs of Missions, to take the lead in carrying out the new directive. Fittingly, the US Secretary of State Dean Rusk also had copies of Robert Kennedy's 1964 speech sent to all State Department, USAID and military officers, claiming that it aptly 'expressed the concern felt by this Government' regarding the 'Emphasis on Youth' directive (Rusk 1964). In 1965 the Department of State published a confidential training booklet *Emphasis on Youth: Reaching and Influencing Rising Young Leaders*, copies of which were sent to US missions abroad. The booklet began by explaining that the 'goal' of the 'youth policy' was to 'gain decisive influence with the rising young leaders of the developing countries and to assist them to solve their problems by democratic means'. Indeed the booklet claimed that the newly 'coordinated approach by the US government' signalled 'another dimension in diplomacy' altogether (*Emphasis* 1965, 1).

The booklet also confirmed that neither the age of youth nor their numbers actually mattered to the IAYC: 'The simple fact that various government programs reach people of a certain age will not spell success in carrying out the youth policy. Nor are we focusing on the masses' (*Emphasis* 1965, 2). The quickly growing number of the young 'masses' may have provided a convenient justification for the work of the IAYC, but they would not be the main focus of the intervention. Instead 'The youth policy is aimed at potential leaders selected out of those sectors of a society that can be expected to produce the future national leaders' (2). If there was one overarching qualification to be considered a youth according to the IAYC, it was being a person (*read* man) poised on the brink of holding significant political, economic or military power in his society: the 'selected persons beneath the leadership layer whom we may not now be reaching through mission programs' (2). Thus, according to the logic of the 'Emphasis on Youth' directive, the status of youthhood ended when a person formally assumed a position of leadership (in comparison, see Catherine E. Bolten, Chapter 5). It would be the IAYC's job to influence strategic young people *before* they grew up, i.e. when they were still outside the official 'leadership layer'.

Overconfidence in(fluencing) youth

The *Emphasis on Youth* booklet broke down the directive into three core steps: (1) 'spotting' youth with leadership potential, (2) 'contacting' them and 'cultivating' relationships with them and (3) 'influencing' them (*Emphasis* 1965, 35). The IAYC's confidence in its capacity to influence the hearts and minds of strategic foreign youth reflected the committee's prevailing faith in leading American theories in the field of child development which constructed youthhood as a universal (meaning, international and cross-cultural) transitory phase between childhood and adulthood – one marked by acute malleability and, consequently, influenceability (Fett 2023). The plan also reflected faith in leading American theories of *economic* development which suggested that 'contact with the West' – particularly via USAID's 'modernisation' projects – would inevitably 'produce a beneficial, catalytic effect on "backward" societies' as 'developed' nations 'push[ed] more "primitive" ones toward the endpoint of modernity' (quoted in Latham, 59). The training booklet claimed that 'The most effective of all US Government assets in reaching potential leaders is personal, face-to-face contact ... where ideas are exchanged and friendships established' (*Emphasis* 1965, 36) – a logic that took for granted that the American points of contact would be able to 'exchange' ideas with foreigners without risk of being influenced *themselves*.

The IAYC expected a truly government-wide effort toward cultivating intimate relationships with targets: 'This contact is the obvious responsibility of everyone associated with the mission, from the Ambassador down to contract personnel', and, of course, 'in all these contacts we are trying to *develop a relationship* that will make it possible to *implant ideas* [*emphasis added*]' (*Emphasis* 1965, 36–7). To do this, military personnel should be on the lookout for promising leaders during its 'counterinsurgency' trainings; USAID personnel should do the same each time it sponsored 'community development and land reform projects' (*Emphasis* 1965, 37). Names of promising youth should be passed on to the State Department's Bureau of Cultural and Educational Affairs to be recommended for 'foreign leadership' grants and other student exchange programs (37). The Bureau, already confident in the power of intercultural exchanges as an effective tool of US cultural diplomacy (Bu 2003, 145–246), began putting extra care into the selection of foreign youth for its exchange programmes (*Emphasis* 1965, 37). Overall, the IAYC's purportedly novel plan of action basically came down to increasing participation of strategic youth in pre-existing governmental programmes.

Already by the spring of 1963 the IAYC reported that 99 US embassies around the world had established their own Youth Committees led by newly named Youth Coordinators (cited in Klimke 2010, 148; see also 144–50). Embassies in Guatemala and Mexico were praised for developing sophisticated systems of identification and surveillance. Others in Afghanistan, India, Pakistan, Syria and Turkey also made serious strides towards preparing lists of potential leaders and developing creative ways of increasing contact with them. Meanwhile embassy officials in East Asia were scolded for failing to grasp the political aims of the programme and told to do more to '[find] and [move] in on present and potential leaders of real following and creative vitality (such as we lack now at the top in Viet Nam [*sic*], Korea, and Taiwan, for example)' ('Youth' Reports 1963–1965). Of course the internal record-keeping of the IAYC tells us little about how foreign targets reacted to the IAYC's overtures. What is at least clear is that the task of identifying young people with leadership potential across various sectors of society in 'developing' countries, contacting them and even providing them greater access to US development and exchange programmes in the *short term* proved far easier than the *long-term* goal of maintaining influence over these foreigners once they reached positions of real political power.

In reality the committee's attempts to reach and influence strategic foreign youth in the 1960s occurred amidst a backdrop of a rising number of, what the IAYC considered to be, unsanctioned transnational exchanges and alliances amongst young radical activists (Klimke 2010, 10–142; and Young 2006, 18–53 and 184–208). In one of the last documents President Kennedy signed in November of 1963 prior to his death, he underscored the nature of this threat:

> In this effort we should be very precise about what we mean by 'youth.' It is neither feasible nor necessary to reach all people under a certain age. Rather, we are interested in young leaders and potential leaders ... We are also interested in reaching, directly or through potential leaders, those young people who are not really leaders, but who have a capacity, in the classroom or in the streets, to frustrate the achievement of our objectives. (J. Kennedy 1963)

According to the IAYC it was the job of everyone who worked for the US government 'to reach these people' since 'they are not going to come to us' (*Emphasis* 1965, 3). US missions abroad, alongside all US governmental agencies, shared the responsibility to 'break through the various rings of English speakers, friendly nationals, and official contacts who surround us and take up much of our time to reach these nationalistic, antagonistic, non-English-speaking individuals *who would prefer that the United States leave them alone [emphasis added]*' (3). When President Johnson took office at the close of 1963, his administration continued to support the work of the IAYC just as it continued to enable various governmental agencies and departments to suppress radical activists both at home and abroad through travel restrictions, by propaganda campaigns and by breaking up demonstrations (Gaines 2006). From the 1960s to the early 1970s the Federal Bureau of Investigation conducted its own covert surveillance and 'counterinsurgency' measures including secretly funding efforts to break up organisations that sought to foster transnational alliances and even inciting police violence against Black activists in the United States (O'Reilly 1991). The Johnson administration also crafted new methods of surveillance in the guise of social programmes, incorporating anti-delinquency measures including increased police patrolling, surveillance and detention into 'equal opportunity' initiatives for use in racially segregated communities (Hinton 2015, 101). In fact Martin Klimke has demonstrated that the IAYC shifted much of its focus in the latter half of the 1960s from relationship-building with youth in so-called developing countries to defusing radical youth organisations with anti-US sentiments in Europe (Klimke 2010, 151–93). I argue that the IAYC's original strategy of courting select foreign youth was not a *challenge* to other containment-oriented youth programmes established under these two administrations but rather a *complement* to them.

In the face of new waves of student protests around the world in the late 1960s (Suri 2003, 164–212; and Scott 2016, 93–154), the IAYC redoubled its efforts, making contributions to the Johnson administration's newly formed inter-agency 'Student Unrest Study Group' (Klimke 2010, 194–213). The Central Intelligence Agency's 1968 'Student Unrest' report described the 'world-wide phenomenon' of 'youthful dissidence, involving students and non-students alike' as a homogeneous group of 'adolescents' and 'post-adolescents' that shared a common propensity towards 'emotional crises attendant on both stages of development' (quoted in Suri 2007, 217 and 219; see also 216–38). By the early 1970s, however, hopes for a government-wide co-ordinated approach to engaging and influencing promising young leaders fizzled out. The IAYC disbanded its work altogether in 1973 (Klimke 2010, 228–34). President Richard M. Nixon lost much of his predecessors' faith in the influenceability of youth – as well as their faith *in* youth as assets to US foreign policy – and responded with even more repressive measures against radical activists (Suri 2003, 213–59; and Young 2006, 209–44) as well as harsher 'population control' methods (Connelly 2010, 254–60).

Throughout the IAYC's decade of work from 1962 to 1972 many field officers had remained sceptical of the claimed novelty of the 'Emphasis on Youth' directive. Accusations that the directive was all 'lip service' without providing adequate personnel and financial investment to see it through were common complaints ('Youth' Reports 1963–1965). The Youth Coordinator in Cambodia admitted that he 'thought it was a kind of fad and that most of the things they are doing now they were doing or would have done anyway' (McLaughlin 1963). More tellingly field officers struggled to apply the IAYC's supposedly cross-cultural conception of youthhood to their local contexts. Embassy officials in Tokyo, Japan, were encouraged by the expansion of American-style Junior Chamber of Commerce branches throughout the country as well as the growth of American–Japanese secondary school student exchanges; however, they stressed that, if the IAYC was 'concerned with the leadership 15 years from now, you must look to people who are now in their 30's and 40's' who, they assured the Washington office, were very much 'still influenceable' (Sheehan 1965).

In raising all the hullabaloo about the quickly expanding demographic of youth around the world, the Kennedy brothers had hoped to impress upon the US government and its allies that youth mattered in the fight to win the Cold War. But what they really meant was that a generation of rising leaders mattered – rather than *all* the youth. They established the IAYC to identify strategic foreigners presumed to still be influenceable – in advance of them reaching official leadership positions – and to cultivate relationships with them before the Soviets beat them to it. For anyone who resisted US Cold War objectives, whether at home or abroad, the Kennedy and Johnson administrations were prepared to apply methods of 'integration' alongside methods of 'containment'.

Conclusion

Even after the work of the IAYC came to an end, the utility of youth bulge talk for US government officials did not. In the 1990s quantitative studies of youth bulges circulated more widely, linking higher rates of young people in a society to social disturbance, political unrest or even physical violence (for example Fuller and Pitts 1990). Studies on youth bulges continued to proliferate with the rise of post-9/11 counter-terrorism agendas in the United States and other countries of the Global North (for example Urdal 2004). To date fear of youth bulges remains empirically unfounded. The vast majority of young people never engage in acts of physical violence nor do they join violent extremist organisations; moreover, as Sommers has reported, 'most countries with youth bulge populations have not had major conflicts' (Sommers 2019, 11). Yet the US government (for example USAID 2010) continues to employ this discourse under the guise of different security threats, often in ways that disproportionately negatively attempt to target, surveil and suppress young people of colour both at home in the United States and abroad in the Global South (Hartmann and Hendrixson 2005; and Sukarieh and Tannock 2018, 857–63). As the War on Terror enters its third decade, the US government has undertaken a range of self-described 'counter-terrorism' operations in at least 85 countries – many of which *have* very large young populations who must suffer the consequences of these interventions (Savell 2021).

The proposed 2020 US YPS Act uses youth bulge talk to justify a realignment of US foreign policy, yet it does not actually expect the US government to intervene in the lives of all '1.8 billion youth'. Rather the bill would offer 'assistance to expand training, technical assistance, and grant management managed and controlled by youth leaders' by setting up a Youth, Peace and Security Fund – although *who* will constitute an 'eligible' youth leader is less clear. The 2020 version of this legislation does specify that only youth in 'conflict-affected' and 'post-conflict' locations can be considered. This framing not only excludes American young people from being able to access this funding source but also reinforces the notion that the United States is not a 'conflict-affected' country[2] – despite American young people's experiences to the contrary (for example, Chapters 14 and 10 by de Leon and Bighorn and Lewis et al.; and Maira 2015). As peacebuilding advocates continue to revise their strategies for converting the UN YPS agenda's goals to increase 'youth participation' into sustainable peacebuilding practices that respond to young people's lived realities without further 'securitising' them (see Chapters 6 and 7 by Altiok and Berents), it is worth reconsidering the proposed framework of the US YPS Act. There is at least one pressing lesson that can be gleaned from the covert schemes of the Cold War-era IAYC: how might a revised, much more public 'inter-agency strategy' co-ordinated by the US government respond to those foreign young people who are desperate *not to participate* in US foreign policy but rather, as the IAYC once put it, 'prefer that the United States *leave them alone*'?

Coda

While this chapter primarily examines the original 2020 version of the US YPS Act, the proposed bill has continued to gain supporters each time it has been reintroduced in the US House of Representatives. When this legislation was reintroduced in July of 2023 (H.R. 5024), the revised Act opened with a significantly altered first 'finding' which states: 'As of 2023, there are an estimated 2.4 billion people in the world between the ages of 10–29 years of age, which represents the largest number of young people to have existed in human history, with 90 percent of youth (ages 15–24) in developing countries, and 1 out of every 4 young people directly affected by conflict, violence, and crisis' (USYPS 2023). The July 2023 version goes on to define youth as 'individuals who have attained 10 years of age and have not attained 30 years of age'. These greater fluctuations in age ranges associated with youthhood are striking if unsurprising, as the logic driving this youth bulge talk continues to be taken for granted and unquestioned. It is encouraging that the July 2023 version makes an effort to define 'conflict', acknowledging that it is an 'inevitable aspect of human interaction' on 'a continuum' that 'can be beneficial' or 'can be waged violently, as in war'. However, other parts of the text still refer to 'conflict-affected' countries, leaving intact the assumption that the United States is itself not a 'conflict-affected' country just as American young people remain excluded from this proposed legislation, at least for now. Finally, even though the July 2023 version highlights children and youth as particularly 'vulnerable' populations acutely affected by violence, the fifth 'finding' of the revised text continues to endorse the claim that: 'When we fail to effectively engage youth, it can lead to violence, instability, unrest, and irregular and forced migration.' This logic reinforces the notion that youth are potential instigators of 'violence' and that 'we' should, of course, identify them, contact them, and 'engage' them.

Notes

1 I am extremely grateful to the editors for their detailed feedback and guidance on this chapter.
2 My critique stems from peace studies theories of conflict transformation which make important distinctions between the 'epicentre' of deeper conflicts, including but not limited to longer-term societal structures and cultural patterns of inequality and oppression, and more visible 'episodic', shorter-term cycles of physical violence (Lederach 2014).

References

Battle, Lucius D. 1963. Memorandum to CU Area Directors, 'Inter-Agency Youth Committee', 3 May 1963 (37), box 161, Bureau of Educational and Cultural Affairs Historical Collection, Manuscript Collection 468, Special Collections of University of Arkansas Libraries, Fayetteville, AR (hereafter CU).

Bu, Liping. 2003. *Making the World Like Us: Education, Cultural Expansion, and the American Century*. Westport, CT: Praeger Publishers.

Connelly, Matthew. 2010. *Fatal Misconception: The Struggle to Control World Population*. Cambridge, MA: Harvard University Press.

Emphasis on Youth: Reaching and Influencing Rising Young Leaders, published by the Department of State, 1965 (15), box 162, CU.

Fett, Anna. 2023. 'The Teen-Age Program: the Expansion of a US Government Experiment in International Education from Postwar Germany and Austria to the Early Cold War World.' *Peace & Change* 48 1 (March): 132–51.

Fuller, Gary A., and Forrest R. Pitts. 1990. 'Youth Cohorts and Political Unrest in South Korea. *Political Geography Quarterly* 9: 9–22.

Gaines, Kevin K. 2006. *American Africans in Ghana: Black Expatriates and the Civil Rights Era*. Chapel Hill: The University of North Carolina Press.

Gilbert, James. 1986. *A Cycle of Outrage: America's Reaction to the Juvenile Delinquent in the 1950s*. New York: Oxford University Press.

Hartmann, Betsy, and Anne Hendrixson. 2005. 'Pernicious Peasants and Angry Young Men: the Strategic Demography of Threats.' In *Making Threats: Biofears and Environmental Anxieties*, edited by Betsy Hartmann, Banu Subramaniam and Charles Zerner, pp. 217–36. Lanham, MD: Rowman & Littlefield Publishers, Inc.

Hinton, Elizabeth. 2015. '"A War within Our Own Boundaries": Lyndon Johnson's Great Society and the Rise of the Carceral State.' *The Journal of American History* (June): 100–12.

Hornsby, Robert. 2016. 'The Post-Stalin Komsomol and the Soviet Fight for Third World Youth.' *Cold War History* 16 (1): 83–100.

Kennedy, John F. 1963 cited in Department of State memorandum to all American diplomatic posts, 'Joint State-USIA-AID-DOD-Peace Corps Message', 11 December 1963 (37), box 161, CU.

Kennedy, Robert F. 1964. 'Address to Canadian Press', Toronto, Canada, 14 April 1964 (13), box 162, CU.

Klatch, Rebecca E. 1999. *A Generation Divided: The New Left, the New Right, and the 1960s*. Berkeley and Los Angeles: University of California Press.

Klein, Christina. 2003. *Cold War Orientalism: Asia in the Middlebrow Imagination, 1945–1961*. Berkeley and Los Angeles: University of California Press.

Klimke, Martin. 2010. *The Other Alliance: Student Protest in West Germany and the United States in the Global Sixties*. Princeton: Princeton University Press.

Latham, Michael E. 2000. *Modernization as Ideology: American Social Science and 'Nation Building' in the Kennedy Era*. Chapel Hill: University of North Carolina Press.

Lederach, John Paul. 2014. *The Little Book of Conflict Transformation*. New York: Good Books.

Maira, Sunaina. 2015. 'Fighting with Rights and Forging Alliances: Youth Politics in the War on Terror.' In *The War of My Generation: Youth Culture and the War on Terror*. edited by David Kieran, pp. 60–82. New Brunswick, NJ: Rutgers University Press.

McEvoy-Levy, Siobhán. 2013. 'Youth.' In *Routledge Handbook of Peacebuilding*, edited by Roger Mac Ginty, pp. 296–307. New York: Routledge.

McLaughlin, Martin M. 1963. Draft of 'Interview with Cambodia Youth Coordinator', 4 October 1963, box 1, Records Relating to the Emphasis on Youth Program 1963–67, RG 59, National Archives and Records Administration, College Park, MD (hereafter NARA).

O'Reilly, Kenneth. 1991. *Racial Matters: The FBI's Secret File on Black America, 1960–1972*. New York: The Free Press.

Rusk, Dean, 1964. 'Joint Message to State-USIA-AID-Defense', 1 May 1964 (13), box 162, CU.

Savell, Stephanie. 2021. 'United States Counterterrorism Operations, 2018–2020.' *Costs of War*. https://watson.brown.edu/costsofwar/files/cow/imce/papers/2021/US%20Counterterrorism%20Operations%202018–2020%2C%20Costs%20of%20War.pdf. Accessed 10 March 2023.

Scott, Holly V. 2016. *Younger Than That Now: The Politics of Age in the 1960s*. Amherst, MA: University of Massachusetts Press.

Search for Common Ground (SFCG). Youth, Peace, & Security Act website. https://www.sfcg.org/youth-peace-security-act/. Accessed 10 March 2023.

Sheehan, Geraldine. 1965. 'My Conversation Today with Howard T. Robinson and Dr. Charles B. Fahs, CU Files,' 4 May 1965, box 1, NARA.

Sommers, Marc. 2019. *Youth and the Field of Countering Violent Extremism*. Washington, DC, Promundo-US. https://promundoglobal.org/wp-content/uploads/2019/01/Youth_Violent_Extemism.pdf.

Sukarieh, Mayssoun, and Stuart Tannock. 2018. 'The Global Securitisation of Youth.' *Third World Quarterly* 39 (5): 854–70.

Suri, Jeremi. 2003. *Power and Protest: Global Revolution and the Rise of Détente*. Cambridge, MA: Harvard University Press.

Suri, Jeremi. 2007. *The Global Revolutions of 1968*. New York: W.W. Norton.

United Nations Security Council Resolution (UNSCR) 2250 (2015). https://documents-dds-ny.un.org/doc/UNDOC/GEN/N15/413/06/PDF/N1541306.pdf?OpenElement. Accessed 10 March 2023.

US Agency for International Development (USAID). 2010. *Technical Brief: Youth Bulges and Conflict*. https://pdf.usaid.gov/pdf_docs/pnadt635.pdf. Accessed 10 March 2023.

US Youth, Peace, and Security (YPS) Act of 2020. Text of House of Representatives 6174 Bill introduced 10 March 2020. https://www.congress.gov/bill/116th-congress/house-bill/6174/text. Accessed 10 March 2023.

US Youth, Peace, and Security (YPS) Act of 2023. Text of House of Representatives 5024 bill introduced 27 July 2023. www.govtrack.us/congress/bills/118/hr5024/text/ih. Accessed 30 November 2023.

Urdal, Henrik. 2004. 'The Devil in the Demographics: the Effect of Youth Bulges on Domestic Armed Conflict, 1950–2000.' In World Bank, *Social Development Papers: Conflict Prevention & Reconstruction* 14 (July): 1–23. http://documents1.worldbank.org/curated/en/794881468762939913/pdf/29740.pdf.

Young, Cynthia A. 2006. *Soul Power: Culture, Radicalism, and the Making of a US Third World Left*. Durham, NC: Duke University Press.

Youth Program Activities, Country by Country Reports, 1963–1965, box 1, NARA.

Part II

Beyond inclusion: institutions and the
challenges of (transformative) participation

Introduction to Part II

Helen Berents, Catherine E. Bolten and Siobhán McEvoy-Levy

The global Youth, Peace and Security (YPS) agenda has brought into sharp focus questions and challenges around youth inclusion and participation in institutions such as: what do 'meaningful participation' and inclusive representation entail and how can they be implemented? Audre Lorde's resonant claim that 'the master's tools will never dismantle the master's house' (1984, 110) offers a ringing challenge to young people's hopes for substantive and transformative roles (as opposed to tokenistic inclusion) in formal mechanisms of peace and security. The argument that crosses the chapters in this section is that a focus on 'meaningful participation' does not replace the problems inherent in earlier attempts to recognise and include young people into peacebuilding processes, it merely creates different challenges. Together, these chapters offer nuanced examinations of the challenges youth and institutions face.

As context for our thinking about youth participation in formal peace and security processes, we note, that under-thirties make up less than 17 per cent of parliamentary representatives worldwide (Inter-Parliamentary Union 2018) and low levels of youth electoral participation persist (International Institute 2017). Lack of formal political involvement is not necessarily an indicator of lack of political interest, however, as shown by the energy and commitment that youth activists provide to grassroots movements (Taft 2011). Social media campaigns, heavily driven by young people, have powered mass movements and catalysed changes in government actions and decision-making (e.g. Saud and Margono 2021; Suwana 2020; Mun and Hok 2018), though impact varies by context and regime type (e.g. Shahzad and Omar 2021). These modes of political organising may be preferred by youth who distrust politics and political parties, and they are also part of the reason states fear youth as potential destabilisers. The failure of parties to reach out to youth, and structural barriers, such as minimum age requirements for running for office, also inhibit young people's formal political participation (Sloam 2014; Laiq 2013; Simpson 2018). The barriers to participation are often more subtle and ideologically based than are apparent in explicit laws. Importantly, young people have also indicated that they do not want inclusion in 'corrupt, undemocratic and oppressive structures' (Simpson 2018: xi). Indeed many young people's antipathy to being instrumentalised and co-opted by elite processes provides enough reason for them to eschew new global efforts like YPS.

In the YPS agenda, 'meaningful participation' of youth in conflict prevention and peace processes involves a rhetorical commitment to both broadening and deepening inclusion framed as 'a demographic necessity' and a 'democratic imperative' (Altiok and Grizelj 2019: 7), and both of these loaded terms identify the agenda as part of a liberal governance framework. YPS promotes young people's participation in peace negotiations, constitution-shaping and transitional justice as a means of legitimising those processes. Still, the UN-commissioned *We Are Here* policy report argues for the mainstreaming of youth and their expertise across all of the peace process sectors including DDR and security reform, electoral reform, employment and education (Altiok and Grizelj 2019). This *We Are Here* policy paper makes twenty-two recommendations for governments, international organisations and youth organisations that include access for youth organisations to flexible funding, trainings and networking opportunities, quotas for youth in peace negotiations and youth advisory teams for mediations, thus 'endorsing the view of youth as credible experts in relevant thematic issues' (Altiok and Grizelj 2019, 39). As well-meaning as these initiatives are, they still assume a fundamental difference between youth and older peacebuilders, and, in separating youth into a 'special' category of credible experts, further reify this difference. Many of the existing examples of youth participation illustrate that youth are deliberately included in a way that, paradoxically, highlights their difference from their 'older' counterparts, who organise and participate from the centre of these initiatives. For example young people are consulted about peacebuilding through youth councils, youth parliaments and other dedicated youth forums. The effectiveness, influence and credibility of these institutions vary greatly, however (Simpson 2018; Oosterom 2018).

Youth quotas – an increasingly popular mechanism for promoting formal involvement – also are not a guarantee of influence. Youth quotas have recently been introduced for elected bodies in Uganda, Rwanda, Kyrgyzstan, Kenya and after the 2011 uprisings in Egypt, Gabon, Morocco, and Tunisia, and they tend to accompany or follow gender quotas. Youth quotas, like gender quotas, increase 'democratisation' but may not translate to actual influence of the ideas and policies of women or youth (Dobbs 2020). Weak youth inclusion clauses in constitutions can lead to confusion and rivalry about the importance of youth participation (Dobbs 2020) and quotas are not always effective in increasing minority representation. They can instead lead to redistribution of power within minority groups with, for example, young women replacing young men in elected bodies, leaving intact the overrepresentation of older men (Belschner and de Paredes 2021). Transformative participation of young people in institutions is therefore much more complicated that merely being brought into those spaces.

The chapters in this section grapple with the complexities of representation of young people in peacebuilding institutions and the opportunities and obstacles that ideas of 'inclusion' and 'participation' in the YPS agenda present. Together they ask the reader to consider the political and social embeddedness of norms of youth participation and the underpinning assumptions that (the right kind of) young people will be hand-picked and invited into adult-led institutions and processes to participate in expected and particular ways. This approach further reinforces the securitisation of youth that was introduced in Part I, where youth must be 'handled' properly by adults in order to ensure that the right kind of participation occurs.

In the first contribution to this section Patrícia Nabuco Martuscelli focuses on transitional justice mechanisms, revealing the political nature of these processes and young people's inclusion within them. In her chapter Martuscelli analyses how children and youth's role as peacebuilders are constructed in two complementary transitional mechanisms created by the Colombian Peace Agreement between the National Government and FARC-EP in December 2016: The Special Jurisdiction for Peace (Jurisdicción Especial para la Paz – JEP) and the Truth, Coexistence and Non-Repetition Commission (Comisión para el Esclarecimiento de la Verdad, la Convivencia y la No Repetición – CV). Martuscelli traces the ways in which categories of victim are politicised, excluding certain children and youth and reinforcing particular narratives of the conflict. While the Peace Agreement opened the possibility of recognising children and youth as peacebuilders, the mechanisms of transitional justice do not guarantee their substantive participation. Given that many armed groups did not negotiate a peace agreement with the Colombian government, it is unclear if there is sufficient recognition of most young people's role to really support sustainable peace.

Catherine Bolten examines how young people in Sierra Leone *reproduce* social norms that curtail youth political participation in order to ensure a continued presence 'at the table', even if that presence is silent and largely symbolic. Bolten draws on Cynthia Enloe to examine how it is not enough for social subalterns to take up public space and nominally participate in political activities; they must be treated as people of consequence – they must be taken seriously – for that participation to be meaningful and potentially transformative for them. However, while youth are nominal participants in public life partly through the recommendations of the Truth and Reconciliation Commission, which set quotas for youth participation in politics at every level of public life, they themselves often do not take their peers seriously, and thus reproduce patterns of participation that reinscribe hierarchical relations with adults and fail to be transformative themselves.

The idea of the conditional participation of youth is also evident in the most elite spaces of peacebuilding discourse concerning youth. The emergent Youth, Peace and Security agenda encapsulates a significant and enduring tension between the persuasive and problematic narrative of young people's potential for violence and delinquency, and the idealistic notion of 'meaningful participation' of youth. Ali Altiok unpacks the ways in which the YPS agenda was born within the contradictions of the promise of youth inclusive peace and the pressures of global attention to countering violent extremism. In this we see a reproduction of securitised discourses of youth that serve to limit the spaces in which young people can participate, and a concomitant romanticisation of the notion of youth participation. Rather, Altiok points to the need for a more nuanced understanding of youth political participation that addresses the narrowing of focus of the agenda as it continues to develop. He argues that it is deeply counter-productive to link youth inclusion and participation with counter-terrorism and recommends that the YPS agenda should resist being paired with and operating within international counter-terrorism policies and approaches.

Complementing Altiok's concern with the securitising implications of elements of the YPS agenda, Helen Berents's chapter considers the consequences of institutionalising an agenda that was conceived as a radical interruption to how young people are usually seen and dealt with in peace and security policy spaces. To say that youth, particularly those affected by conflict or insecurity, should be included in discussions and decisions about addressing and resolving those issues and (re)building society has the potential to challenge notions of expertise and knowledge, upset established power relations and unravel embedded ideas of who and what 'youth' are and how they should participate. Tracing the agenda's emergence through relevant documents and key stakeholder interviews, Berents traces the tensions and opportunities of the Youth, Peace and Security agenda that sits between an agential vision for youth inclusion and the sometimes-depoliticising effects of institutionalising an agenda, to argue that the political project of youth inclusion must be kept in focus as the agenda is institutionalised.

The final chapter in this section by Caitlin Mollica draws attention to the political and politicised nature of youth participation in transitional justice while exploring ways in which formal and informal mechanisms may be bridged. Empowering young people in the design and implementation of transitional justice mechanisms can enable more responsive approaches to accountability and impunity. However, such mechanisms often rein-scribe institutional processes that nurture a 'politicised' form of justice over transformative models that are more able to recognise young people's contributions. Through exploration of examples from South Africa, Timor-Leste and Kenya, Mollica considers the enabling and constraining factors of transitional justice mechanisms for young people's engagement, drawing attention to the importance of informal arts-based forms of participation in (ex)pressing claims for justice.

Starting from the question of how youth participation in peace and security can be taken seriously, the chapters in this section highlight the fraught nature of concepts of 'meaningful participation' and 'inclusion' within formal structures and processes. The YPS agenda is opening novel opportunities for youth inclusion but, returning to Audre Lorde's concern about the 'master's house', it is clear that youth participation in institutions is often conditional on their being inculcated with established norms and practices of those institutions. Reliant on the continued good will of older gatekeepers who are inviting them into the conversation, it may be that young people, being focused for so long on getting into the house, will then pick up only the existing tools offered and try to work with them, helping to maintain the narrow, often wrongheaded, interests of existing power structures. If youth 'participation' is, by definition, young people walking into and somehow being incorporated – in very unimaginative ways – into existing structures of power, then transformative change will remain elusive. This is not to say these processes are not valuable or potentially useful; in many ways they have created opportunities and new spaces for young people's perspectives and voices on the issues that most affect them. However, contributors to this section highlight the inescapable political contexts in which young people contest and sometimes reproduce dominant assumptions about their capacity, contributions and potential. Recognising the truth of Audre Lorde's claims through their lived experience, many youth may prefer to participate outside of elder-established processes and innovate political involvement (e.g. Cammaerts et al. 2014; Chou et al. 2017; McEvoy-Levy 2018; Pruitt 2021). They can simultaneously be politi-cally engaged and disengaged or 'radically unpolitical' (Farthing 2010), and participating in ways that are not readily seen or appreciated by main-stream political actors or conventional expectations, a theme expanded upon in Part III of this volume.

References

Altiok, Ali, and Irena Grizelj. 2019. *We Are Here: An Integrated Approach to Youth Inclusive Peace Processes.* New York: Office of the Secretary General's Envoy on Youth.

Belschner, Jana, and Marta Garcia de Paredes. 2021. 'Hierarchies of Representation: the Re-distributive Effects of Gender and Youth Quotas.' *Representation: Journal of Representative Democracy* 57 (1): 1–20.

Cammaerts, Bart, Michael Bruter, Shakuntala Banaji, Sarah Harrison and Nick Anstead. 2014. 'The Myth of Youth Apathy: Young Europeans' Critical Attitudes toward Democratic Life.' *American Behavioral Scientist* 58 (5): 645–64.

Chou, Mark, John-Paul Gagnon, Catherine Hartung and Lesley Pruitt. 2017. *Young People, Citizenship and Political Participation: Combating Civic Deficit?* New York: Rowman & Littlefield.

Dobbs, Kirstie Lynn. 2020. 'Youth Quotas and "Jurassic Park" Politicians: Age as a Heuristic for Vote Choice in Tunisia's New Democracy.' *Democratization* 27 (6): 990–1005.

Farthing, Rys. 2010. 'The Politics of Youthful Antipolitics: Representing the "Issue" of Youth Participation in Politics.' *Journal of Youth Studies* 13 (2): 181–95.

Institute for Democracy and Electoral Assistance. 2017. *The Global State of Democracy: Exploring Democracy's Resilience.* Stockholm: First Edition.

Inter-Parliamentary Union. 2018. *Youth Participation in National Parliaments: 2018.* Geneva: Inter-Parliamentary Union.

Laiq, Nur. 2013. *Talking to Arab Youth: Revolution and Counterrevolution in Egypt and Tunisia.* New York: International Peace Institute.

Lorde, Audre. 1984. 'The Master's Tools Will Never Dismantle the Master's House.' In *Sister Outsider: Essays and Speeches*, 110–14. Berkeley: Crossing Press.

McEvoy-Levy, Siobhán. 2018. *Peace and Resistance in Youth Cultures: Reading the Politics of Peacebuilding rom Harry Potter to The Hunger Games.* London: Palgrave Macmillan.

Mun, Vong, and Kimhean Hok. 2018. 'Facebooking: Youth's Everyday Politics in Cambodia.' *South East Asia Research* 26(3): 219–34. https://doi10.1177/0967828X17754113.

Oosterom, Marjoke. 2018. 'Youth Engagement in the Realm of Local Governance: Opportunities for Peace?' *IDS Working Paper* 508: 1–31. https://opendocs.ids.ac.uk/opendocs/bitstream/handle/123456789/13550/Wp508%20Online.pdf?sequence=1&isAllowed=y. Accessed 5 May 2021.

Pruitt, Lesley J. 2021. 'Participatory Video: a New Outlook for International Relations Research.' *Australian Journal of International Affairs* 75 (2): 142–60.

Saud, Muhammad, and Hendro Margono. 2021. 'Indonesia's Rise in Digital Democracy and Youth's Political Participation.' *Journal of Information Technology and Politics* 18 (2): 1–12.

Shahzad, Sobia, and Bahiyah Omar. 2021. 'Social Network Matters: The Influence of Online Social Capital on Youth Political Participation in Pakistan.' *Journal of Information Technology and Politics* 18 (2): 1–13.

Simpson, Graeme. 2018. *The Missing Peace: Independent Progress Study on Youth and Peace and Security.* United Nations. https://www.youth4peace.info/system/files/2018–10/youth-web-english.pdf. Accessed 5 May 2021.

Sloam, James. 2014. '"The Outraged Young": Young Europeans, Civic Engagement and the New Media in a Time of Crisis.' *Information, Communication & Society* 17 (2): 217–31.

Suwana, Fiona. 2020. 'What Motivates Digital Activism? The Case of the Save KPK Movement in Indonesia.' *Information, Communication and Society* 23 (9): 1295–310.

Taft, Jessica, K. 2011. *Rebel Girls: Youth Activism and Social Change across the Americas*. New York: New York University Press.

4

How do children and youth participate in transitional justice mechanisms in post-accord Colombia?

Patrícia Nabuco Martuscelli

Through Resolution 2250 (2015), the United Nations Security Council (UNSC) recognised youth's positive contribution to maintaining and promoting peace and security. In this line many studies have highlighted the importance of youth for peacebuilding (McEvoy-Levy 2001; Alias 2015; Mollica 2017; Berents 2018). However, naming categories as important does not mean they will have substantive participation[1] in peacebuilding, especially in transitional justice mechanisms. Bolten in Chapter 5 shows direct and indirect challenges for youth participation in Sierra Leone for example. Additionally children and youth are generally denied participation in essential areas of peacebuilding since many peace agreements and foundational documents of transitional justice organs do not mention them.

Transitional justice is crucial to peacebuilding since it 'refers to the set of policies and measures that are implemented in countries emerging from repression and conflict to deal with the legacy of massive human rights abuses. Key elements of transitional justice include criminal prosecution, truth-telling, memorialization, reparations, and institutional reform' (Ramírez-Barat 2012: 1). However, transitional justice is political, based on political negotiations and views of stakeholders involved in the decision-making and implementation of these mechanisms about the role of actors involved in armed conflicts and violence. In that sense transitional justice mechanisms can construct and reproduce specific views, allowing some groups' participation and excluding others. Through this movement transitional justice mechanisms may recognise some people as peacebuilders who can be part of the formal processes.

Colombia has been facing an armed conflict with different armed groups, including guerrillas, paramilitaries, and state armed forces for the past sixty years. Many attempts of peace have been discussed since 1960.[2] Hopes of a durable peace rose when the government and the Fuerzas Armadas Revolucionarias de Colombia – Ejército del Pueblo (FARC-EP, the main guerrilla group fighting in the country) signed the 'Agreement for the Termination of the Conflict and the Construction of a Stable and Lasting Peace' on 24 November 2016.[3] The document created the mechanisms of the Comprehensive System of Truth, Justice, Reparation and Non-Repetition (Sistema Integral de Verdad, Justicia, Reparación e no Repetición – SIVJRNR) whose primary transitional justice organs are the Colombian Truth Commission (Comisión para el Esclarecimiento de la Verdad, la Convivencia y la No Repetición – CV) and the Special Jurisdiction for Peace (Jurisdicción Especial para la Paz – JEP).

The Colombian case is particularly interesting to understand how children and youth are constructed as peacebuilders in the foundational documents of these two transitional justice mechanisms now that they have started their work. The Colombian Peace Agreement considered different types of children and youth as participants of transitional justice mechanisms, adopting a differential approach considering gender, class, ethnicity and different collective communities (Koopman 2018). However, it was not clear how youth and children would participate in practice in these stances (Martuscelli and Villa 2018). Moreover it is essential to understand how particular views of which children and youth can participate will affect the implementation and work of these transitional justice mechanisms. Therefore it is necessary to understand if the Colombian transitional justice mechanisms adopt a preconceived approach that considers only the role of some children and youth (like direct and indirect victims of the armed conflict) or if they consider many experiences of different children and youth.

Children and youth who collectively suffered damage due to events after 1 January 1985, due to violations of the International Humanitarian Law or human rights issues connected to the internal armed conflict, are defined as victims in Colombia (Ley 1448 de 2011). They can also be considered victims if they suffered harm because they helped a victim or tried to avoid victimisation. If they are partners (including same-sex) or relatives in the first degree of a disappeared or dead person (who could be considered a direct victim), they are indirect victims. Children and youth can be perpetrators when they conduct events that create victims (according to the above definition). However, there are children and youth who were neither victims (direct or indirect) of the conflict nor perpetrators. Many children and youth engage in activities asking for peace in Colombia that could be defined as peacebuilders without being necessarily victims. Besides that there are children and youth who are siblings (especially sons and daughters of *guerrilleros*) born in the armed conflict but neither victims nor perpetrators. Since the Colombian armed conflict affected many generations, the categories of victims and perpetrators are not enough to understand the different types of children and youth that should engage in transitional justice mechanisms.

Leaving no children or youth behind is particularly crucial in the Colombia case because the Peace Agreement and its structures do not mean the end of the conflict. Violence continues to spread throughout the country with other active armed groups such as Bandas Criminales (BACRIM) and dissidents from FARC-EP violating human rights and recruiting children (UNSC 2019). Given the ongoing insecurity, inclusive efforts to seek justice, considering different stakeholders like children and youth, are more critical than ever in Colombia for the construction of a sustainable peace in the country. Hence this chapter aims to understand how children and youth's roles as peacebuilders are considered in the concrete mechanisms of the SIVJRNR created by the Colombian Peace Agreement. This will shape the possibilities of participation for children and youth in the post-accord context in Colombia, and this has direct implications for future peace in the country.

This preliminary analysis intends to verify if and how the JEP and CV's foundational structures recognise children and youth as peacebuilders in the Colombian peace process. It aims to understand how these two transitional justice mechanisms recognise the substantive participation of children and youth (Berents and McEvoy-Levy 2015). That is if the JEP and CV acknowledge the participation of different children and youth outside preconceived discourses of which children and youth are peacebuilders and can participate.

I conducted a content analysis of the documents, videos and other materials in the JEP and CV webpages to understand the actions and possibilities for childrens and youth participation. I conclude that JEP grants children and youth participation as victims of the armed conflict. Hence, their recognition as victims (according to the Colombian definition of a victim) is fundamental to understanding their possibilities as peacebuilders in this transitional justice mechanism. It does not recognise children and youth who are not victims in the armed conflict. However, the CV has more potential to recognise different categories of children and youth who are not victims, especially considering its decentralised structure and the different methodologies it uses to acknowledge the truth, reparation and non-repetition.

Children, youth, and transitional justice mechanisms

The concepts of children and youth are socially constructed.[4] This chapter uses both these concepts because they appear in the Peace Agreement and the transitional mechanisms' documents as different categories. The Peace Agreement mentions the word youth (*joven*) 13 times, boy (*niño*) 38 times,

girl (*niña*) 40 times, and adolescent (*adolescente*) 21 times. Colombian legislation has different definitions of these categories. Children are boys or girls
between 0 and twelve years old, and adolescents are people between twelve
and eighteen years old (Ley 1098 de 2006). Many documents employ the
expression boys, girls and adolescents (*niños, niñas y adolescents* – NNA),
referring to people under eighteen years old. Youth is connected with
citizenship in the Colombian legislation. Statutory Law 1885/2018 understands youth as people between fourteen and twenty-eight years old who
are consolidating their intellectual, physical, moral, economic, social and
cultural autonomy, and that is part of a political community and, in that
sense, exercise their citizenship.

The concepts of adolescence and youth partially overlap, considering
age requirements. However, adolescence is a passive idea, while youth
involves participation, social rights and citizenship. I also consider children
and youth because, as previously discussed, the armed conflict is not over,
and it has affected millions of Colombians from different generations. As
Salazar (2019) argues, 'We have lost three generations in the grip of the
so-called armed conflict.' Justifying the participation of youth and children
in the peace procedures, she continues, 'Young people of the recent past
and those of today know what war is, they live it in their flesh. ... But we
must also open up the possibility that they help us prevent boys, girls, and
adolescents of today, be recruited, violated or seduced by the conflict in its
new forms' (translated from Spanish by the author).

Youth are commonly portrayed as victims when put inside the categories
of children or 'problems' to the peace process (as the chapters in the first
part of this volume discussed) when their agency is expressed; however,
their role as peacebuilders tends not to be recognised (McEvoy-Levy
2001; Alias 2015; Pruitt 2015; Berents 2018; Mollica 2017). Berents and
McEvoy-Levy (2015: 119) understand that 'Young people's contributions
are perennially overlooked or viewed with suspicion within the structures, actors, and processes of the liberal peace'. Truth and Reconciliation
Commissions in Peru, South Africa, Sierra Leone and East Timor have considered youth. However, Mollica (2017) reflects that they were considered
as victims (children) or perpetrators (child soldiers or independent agents),
leaving behind experiences outside this dichotomy.

Children, on the other hand, tend to be perceived as passive victims
of armed conflicts, including in the United Nations Children and Armed
Conflict Agenda (Lee-Koo 2018). They form a static category based on the
idea of vulnerability (Billingsley 2018). Their participation in transitional
justice is not always recognised to avoid re-traumatising experiences in
favour of 'protection' narratives. However, children should participate
in transitional justice mechanisms with due consideration to their rights,

interests, best interest, child-friendly procedures and protection needs (Ramírez-Barat 2012). Children who actively participated in armed conflicts have received more attention in these discussions since they are considered both victims and perpetrators of atrocities. Steinl (2017) concludes that positive agency (contribution to conflict resolution and peacebuilding) and negative agency (harm and wrongdoing) of child soldiers should be considered in transitional justice mechanisms.

McEvoy and McConnachie (2012) study victimology to understand victims' roles in transitional justice procedures. They explain the importance of innocence to the construction of 'the victim'. This creates 'A hierarchy of victimhood [organized on] the "good" victims and "bad" victims, [that are based on] subjective views on the "justifiability" of the suffering that was visited upon such victims and the strategies and tactics deployed by such victims in the transition and their attitudes to dealing with the past' (McEvoy and McConnachie 2012, 532). Some categories of children and youth that fit specific classifications of victims (political discourse) receive more attention than others. Sanchez Parra (2018) indicates victims' hierarchies, recognising that some children are more visible inside the categories of children affected by the war in Colombia than others, e.g., child soldiers and displaced children. Children born as a consequence of sexual violence and transgender children and youth (for example) are silenced categories that receive little attention. Lee-Koo and Pruitt (Chapter 12) also show how young women face challenges to participating in peacebuilding in South Asia and the Pacific.

Considering children as innocent, traumatised and lacking agency and youth as problems to peace procedures prevents people who do not fit these preconceived categories from participating in formal structures of transitional justice. In that sense this chapter agrees with Mollica (2017, 372), studying the case of the Solomon Islands Truth and Reconciliation Commission, that those categories of victims and perpetrators silence 'the multiple identities to which youth often ascribe; the complex and unique relationship between youth, justice and reconciliation; and the contributions made by youth to post-conflict justice processes'.

In the report *Engaging Children and Youth in Transitional Justice Processes: Guidance for Outreach Programs* of the International Center for Transitional Justice (ICTJ) Ramírez-Barat (2012) recognises the importance of creativity and innovation to engage children and youth in transitional justice processes, including outreach programmes specifically designed for these groups considering their different rights, needs and experiences, and designing child-friendly procedures, materials, participatory activities and spaces for youth and children to express themselves (Ramírez-Barat, 2012: 2).

The foundation of transitional justice mechanisms must consider children and youth participation:

> Experience shows that if children and youth are not included from the outset, they are likely to be left behind or only partially included in the process and, therefore, inadequately served. To prevent this, recognition of their roles as stakeholders and rights bearers should be reflected in the founding documents of the TJ measure, and their participation should be specifically incorporated in the drafting of the general outreach program's strategic plan. (Ramírez-Barat 2012: 4)

Transitional justice should also contemplate different experiences of children and youth, avoiding generalising the categories of children and youth. Berents and McEvoy-Levy (2015, 123) recall that 'Age, class, race, and gender affect the experiences of youth in conflict and thus their engagements in peace'. Different children and different young people experience armed conflicts diversely according to their realities (Billingsley 2018). Transitional mechanisms should consider this diversity of experiences. Homogenising these categories of children and youth inside the idea of victim silences many experiences that should be acknowledged in peacebuilding procedures. Moreover, conditioning participation of people in transitional justice to their role as victims is complicated since people occupy many and multifaceted roles during armed conflicts and have complex identities. Therefore, this chapter aims to understand if or how these preconceived categories of children and youth are present in the foundational documents and activities of JEP and the CV in Colombia. I give particular attention to the hierarchy of victimhood discussed in the literature and its implications for the construction of a sustainable peace in Colombia.

Children and youth in the JEP

JEP and CV are complementary political components of the Colombian SIVJRNR. Their structure and foundational documents allow us to understand which children and youth should participate and how. The Special Jurisdiction for Peace (Jurisdicción Especial para la Paz – JEP) has the objective of guaranteeing the victims' right to justice, granting them the truth and contributing to reparation to build sustainable and lasting peace. The JEP analyses the gravest and most representative crimes of the armed conflict committed before 1 December 2016. It considers crimes committed by ex-members of FARC-EP, members of the Public Force and Agents of State and other civilians. The JEP started in 2018. It has a mandate of initially 15 years that can be extended for five years more (totalling 20 years of duration). As of June 2023 it had seven macro cases open (JEP 2020, 11).

A limitation of JEP is that it does not consider the experiences of children and youth involved in other armed groups (besides the FARC-EP) or affected by them. However, it adopts a holistic approach to consider the different experiences of children and youth involved in the armed conflict, as recommended by the literature. Gender, ethnicity and age are among the differential priorities stated in the legislation and JEP internal documents. This differential approach, in theory, means that JEP adopts a restorative justice lens considering the need and dignity of the victims, especially women and/or vulnerable groups (Indigenous, Afro-Colombians, other ethnic minorities, displaced people, refugees, religious, rural and disadvantaged communities, boys, girls and youth, LGBTI and older adults) (Ley 1957 de 2019). The legislation recognises the right of effective and equalitarian participation to all the victims, including the right to be designated as victims and presenting documents that can be used in the cases. However, this differential approach applies only to the categories of victims. Hence children and youth who are not direct or indirect victims of the armed conflict (more specifically of actions connected to the FARC-EP) cannot participate in JEP.

Being a child or adolescent (among other categories) is also a criterion for prioritisation of the JEP cases under the framework of the vulnerability of the victims. Youth is also considered a category for prioritisation when there is the intersectionality of the collective subjects (for example, rural youth victims of recruitment) (JEP 2018, 16). That is, when deciding about opening the cases and analysing materials, some categories of children and youth (connected to vulnerability) receive more attention than others, showing a hierarchy of victims in JEP's way of working. Besides these explicit prioritisation criteria in JEP, political struggles also may influence the issues that will receive more attention in JEP.

On the one hand JEP states the importance of guaranteeing the principle of the children's best interests during the documentation process and providing comprehensive protection, avoiding putting the child at risk (JEP 2018b: 21) and the holistic[5] impact of the armed conflict. On the other it has preconceived perceptions that exclude the substantive participation of children and youth who do not fit the definition of victims of the armed conflict. People involved in the armed conflict as children (child soldiers) are considered victims of the armed conflict. JEP's judges defend this approach, recognising the double condition as victims and perpetrators of children and youth above 18 years old (JEP 2020). This perception is illustrated in the video *En la JEP las víctimas Somos creíbles* (In JEP, we victims are credible) that tells the story of two young people (a man and a woman) who were recruited as children and say they were victims of the conflict for the past 20 years (since they started being victims as children and are now youth). Therefore, children involved in the armed conflict (even if they are adults now) can participate since they continue to be victims of the armed conflict.

The possibility of children and youth to participate in JEP is to be recognised as victims. Among the seven cases opened by JEP so far, two are mainly connected with children and youth's situations. Case 03[6] opened on 17 July 2018, about the illegitimate deaths (*falsos positivos*) presented as combat deaths by agents of the Colombian State, and case 07 opened on March 2019, about the recruitment and use of boys and girls in the Colombian armed conflict. JEP opened Case 03 because between 1988 and 2014 the Colombian General prosecutor identified 2,248 victims of these extrajudicial executions, especially between 2006 and 2008, and 48 per cent of them were young men between 18 and 30 when this crime happened in the country.[7] JEP opened Case 07[8] due to the high level of impunity in the crime of the recruitment and the use of boys and girls in the armed conflict. The JEP is currently accrediting the victims of illegal recruitment, sexual violence during the recruitment, and employment in other activities connected to the armed conflict between 1 January 1971 and 1 December 2016.

In March 2024, there were 9,446,572 people registered as victims in the Colombian system, 9.8 per cent children (0 and eleven years), 11.1 per cent adolescents (twelve to seventeen years) and 22.6 per cent youth (eighteen to twenty-eight years) (Registo Único de Víctimas – RUV).[9] Although these numbers are significant, they do not represent the multifaceted roles of children and youth during and after the armed conflict. They exclude children and youth who were not direct or indirect victims of the armed conflict. This also creates hierarchies among victims, as discussed by McEvoy and McConnachie (2012), with victims of some crimes receiving more attention than victims of other crimes whose cases JEP has not prioritised.

JEP does not guarantee substantive participation for children and youth outside the categories of victims or perpetrators. Although JEP foundational documents assured a special place to different child and youth victims of the armed conflict, they are inside the preconceived categories of victims. There is also a hierarchy of victims in JEP's prioritisation categories. Finally, JEP has developed outreach programmes and other tools to engage only with children like videos[10] (e.g. *La Receta de la Justicia para sanar corazones* (The justice recipe for healing hearts)) and the JEP webpage for boys, girls and adolescents.[11] JEP has no specific webpage for youth. The presumption is that youth are better prepared to understand JEP's role, but this also means that youth are not targeted through JEP's initial outreach actions.

Those initiatives also contribute to shaping particular ideas of victims that are allowed participation in JEP.

Children and youth at the Colombian Truth Commission (CV)

The Comisión para el Esclarecimiento de la Verdad, la Convivencia y la No Repetición[12] (aka Comisión de la Verdade – CV) is a non-judicial body that aims to understand the causes and consequences of the armed conflict guaranteeing victims' and society's rights to truth and non-repetition and promoting the coexistence of the territories. Children appear in one of its main objectives: '1. Contribute to the clarification of what happened, following the elements of the mandate and offering a broad explanation of the complexity of the armed conflict, to promote a shared understanding in society, especially of the lesser-known aspects of the conflict, such as the impact of conflict on boys, girls and adolescents, and gender-based violence.'

The CV, composed of 12 commissioners, started on 18 November 2018. Its mandate lasted three years and could be extended for another six months. In June 2022 the CV published its comprehensive final report with different volumes focusing on specific issues involving the conflict. There is one focusing on the direct and indirect implications of the armed conflict on boys, girls and adolescents that includes stories of people from 0 to twenty-eight years old.[13] Besides that the CV has other functions like implementing dissemination, pedagogy and active relation strategies with the media and adopting measures for the filing of the information collected.[14]

The CV has developed different activities and spaces to hear from all people affected by the armed conflict to accomplish its mandate. People affected by the armed conflict are not only victims; they also involve everybody that has some perspective to share about the conflict. The CV has more possibility to recognise different experiences of children and youth who were not only victims or perpetrators (as discussed in the Introduction to the book) due to its mandate to engage different voices in different formats. Truth and Reconciliation Commissions (TRC) are facilitated structures that allow the participation of children and youth as peacebuilders: 'scholars suggest that the process of storytelling post-conflict is a positive experience that encourages agency and facilitates participation' (Senehi and Byrne 2006: 238). Specifically 'participation in the TRC process affords youth the space to claim ownership over their transitional justice experience' (Mollica 2017: 375).

Another thing that allows the recognition of youth and children as peacebuilders is the CV presence in the Colombian territory through its

22 Truth Houses (Casas de la Verdad).[15] These Truth Houses are political and social spaces where people can go, give their testimonies and know more about the CV work, and the SIVJNRN as a whole. These houses (which are located in the departments more affected by the conflict) also conduct activities, workshops and seminars with particular groups like women, boys, girls, adolescents (NNA), youth, indigenous, Afro-Colombians and other minorities. The CV is developing outreach activities designed for different groups of children and youth, as recommended by Ramírez-Barat (2012). Although there was not much information about how youth and children could get involved in the Houses, they were created as open spaces without limiting participation to direct and indirect victims of the armed conflict. The Covid-19 pandemic has severely affected and delayed the work of the CV, which also impacted the participation of youth and children in this transitional justice mechanism.

There are clear examples that the CV acknowledges children and youth as peacebuilders (Boys and Girls[16] and Youth[17]) without limitations based on victimhood or hierarchy of victims. In the Boys and Girls section, the CV recognises them as right-holders, considering childhood as a time where boys and girls learn to exercise their rights and citizenship. It states that the Commission will conduct participatory exercises in a responsible, safe and respectful way considering boys' and girls' experiences, dignity, expectations and interests, and guaranteeing their right to express their opinion freely and potentialising their capacity to take responsibility and make decisions. The CV argues that knowing and recognising what happened to boys and girls during the armed conflict is fundamental to build truth, coexistence and non-repetition. The Youth Section also recognises youth as right-holders and the different youths (in the plural) as fundamental actors to build the country exercising autonomy and difference. The CV acknowledges that the youth are in the process of strengthening their physical, intellectual, moral, economic, social and cultural autonomy. Finally the CV affirms that it will promote youth's active participation, showing their stories and the impact of the armed conflict in their lives and considering their testimonies and resistance experiences and their importance to constructing peace. In fact on the part of boys, girls and adolescents in its final report the CV (2023), under the label 'memory as resistance', explains that: 'Young people have concerns about the places where they live and some of them become leaders. In devastated areas by the conflict, young people remember and try to resignify their territory to overcome the ravages of war.'

The CV has conducted participatory outreach activities in many formats that acknowledge children and youths outside the definitions of victims. For example children born from guerrilla parents tend not to be defined as victims of the conflict. They have no possibility of participation in JEP. Nevertheless, they can participate in the CV. In March 2020 a photography workshop was organised with children of former combatants born in the armed conflict. Those children, defined in the article as 'seeds of peace', could photograph what peace and non-repetition means for them.[18] Through photographs the children and youth reflected a future of peace and the importance of arts, sports and music to constructing peace.

Initial activities of the CV also show that children and youth's substantive participation is not restrained to preconceived definitions of victims of the armed conflict. For example, in November 2019 the CV organised an event in Colombia's second-largest city, Medellín, to listen to youth and children (NNA) about how the war, directly and indirectly, has affected their lives.[19] There was the participation of organisations, community and youth leaders, and children. They shared how they have worked to resignify the armed conflict's impacts and new ways to face and take care of their lives. At the end there was an appeal to avoid any children and youth having to face this violence again.[20]

The CV's foundational documents, final report and activities show the broad possibility of substantive participation of children and youth, including people who are not direct or indirect victims of the armed conflict. CV has more opportunities to understand the particularities of children and youth and different subgroups in these categories.

Conclusions

The SIJVRNR recognises different children and youth in the mandates of both the JEP and the CV. This is an essential first step in recognising children and youth as peacebuilders if we compare it to other transitional justice mechanisms employed in the world that lacked child and youth participation (Mollica 2017). However, naming by itself is not sufficient to guarantee substantive child participation and recognising their role as peacebuilders during the implementation.

As the justice component of the SIJVRNR, the JEP does not recognise the experiences of peacebuilding of children and youth outside the categories of victims. Children and youth can participate in the JEP as victims of the armed conflict. It recognises only 'peacebuilder victims', that is, victims who are important to the construction of peace in Colombia. This fact has three problems. First, it excludes other possibilities of recognising children and youth as peacebuilders when they were not victims (Mollica 2017). Second, it reinforces a specific view of what is necessary to be a victim. Third, it creates a hierarchy between victims, considering the cases that it opens (McEvoy and McConnachie 2012). In that sense JEP is a 'transitional justice mechanism [that] can also create silenced and marginal subjects while reproducing structural forms of oppression' (Sanchez Parra 2018, 48).

JEP has adopted child-friendly language and tools to inform children (as recommended by Ramírez-Barat (2012)), reproducing its view of what it means to be a child peacebuilder in the Colombian Peace Process. Youth do not receive the same attention. This shows that this transitional justice process is a top-down one where the authority has a view of what a durable and sustainable peace means and how and which children and youth should participate in it. This situation tends to prevent other forms of children and youth participation that do not fit the category of victims (Billingsley 2018; Lee-Koo 2018).

While the Colombian JEP has a broader approach than other transitional justice mechanisms to considering youth and children as peacebuilders (with their differential approach), it is not enough to fully access their different experiences during and after the armed conflict. In that sense, due to its mandate and territorial structure, the CV has more spaces to recognise different participation by youth and children in their full expressions without the limitation of the victimhood. The CV has organised different outreach activities specifically designed to allow the participation of different categories of children and youth. It has listened to different youth and children's voices (beyond the traditional ideas of victims) and this is reflected in their final report. Further studies should consider how different children and youth feel about this report, considering whether their roles as peacebuilders were duly recognised by this transitional justice mechanism.

This chapter has presented a preliminary analysis of the possibilities of substantive participation for children and youth in the Colombian SIJVRNR system. The JEP's and the CV's foundational bases are promising to understand the active role of children and youth as peacebuilders in the Colombian Peace Process (as recommended by Ramírez-Barat 2012). Different categories of children and youth (considering the differential approach) are present in the Colombian Peace Agreement and these transitional justice mechanisms' foundational documents. However, more studies on these two organs are needed, considering the situation of continuous violence in Colombia, the risk to children and youth (especially activists) and challenges to transitional justice (like opposition to the peace agreement). At the same time we observe a limitation in the substantive participation of children and youth in JEP. CV does not have a preconceived view of participation connected with the ideas of victims. More time is needed to understand whether CV roles can effectively fill the gap of participation in JEP or whether only children and youth victims of the Colombian armed conflict will effectively participate and have their peacebuilding role guaranteed in practice. If some youth and children are excluded from these transitional justice mechanism or if they feel their role has not been duly recognised, this may impact the construction of a sustainable peace in Colombia especially because there are many armed groups that did not negotiate a peace agreement with the Colombian government.

Notes

1 Peacebuilding involves 'the approaches, processes, and interventions' adopted after a conflict to transform 'violent relationships, structures, attitudes and behaviors' (Del Felice and Wisler 2007: 6).
2 For interesting discussion of previous transitional justice mechanisms in Colombia, see Capone 2016.
3 A first version of the agreement was signed on 24 August 2016. However, the agreement was rejected in a referendum. In November, after some changes, the Final Agreement was approved.
4 I acknowledge that the concepts of children and youth have been problematised in many discussions involving childhood studies. In general children are people under 18 years old as stated in the United Nations Convention on the Rights of Right (1989). For an interesting discussion of youth see United Nations Department of Economic and Social Affairs (UNDESA) n.d. Accessed 21 December 2023.
5 'It is important to describe the damages and impacts in territorial, cultural, spiritual, political and organizational, economic, physical, material and, psychological terms, as well as the damage to women, older adults, boys, girls, adolescents, and youth and members of the LGBTI population' (JEP 2018b, 13).
6 Information available at: https://www.jep.gov.co/macrocasos/caso03.html. Accessed 21 December 2023.
7 For more information on the scandal of false positives in Colombia see Krygier 2019.
8 Information available at: https://www.jep.gov.co/macrocasos/caso07.html#container. Accessed 30 March 2023.
9 Retrieved from https://www.unidadvictimas.gov.co/es/registro-unico-de-victimas-ruv/37394. Accessed 30 June 2023.
10 Video available at: https://www.jep.gov.co/Sala-de-Prensa/Paginas/JEP-lanza-video-para-ni%C3%B1os,-ni%C3%B1as-y-adolescentes.aspx. Accessed 21 December 2023.
11 See: https://www.jep.gov.co/ninosyninas/index.html. Accessed 21 December 2023.
12 In English the complete name of the Truth Commission would be Commission to the Establishment of the Truth, Coexistence and Non-Repetition.
13 All documents of the Colombia Truth Commission are available at: https://comisiondelaverdad.co/hay-futuro-si-hay-verdad. Accessed 21 December 2023.

14 A detailed definition of the CV's mandate and functions is available at: https://comisiondelaverdad.co/la-comision/mandato-y-funciones. Accessed 21 December 2023.

15 More information available at: https://web.comisiondelaverdad.co/participe/casas-de-la-verdad-zoo. Accessed 1 December 2023.

16 See https://comisiondelaverdad.co/en-los-territorios/enfoques/ninas-y-ninos. Accessed 21 December 2023.

17 See https://comisiondelaverdad.co/en-los-territorios/enfoques/jovenes. Accessed 21 December 2023.

18 This photographs are available at: https://comisiondelaverdad.co/actualidad/noticias/hijos-de-excombatientes-toman-fotos-comision-verdad-colombia. Accessed 21 December 2023.

19 https://comisiondelaverdad.co/actualidad/noticias/nunca-mas-ninos-y-ninas-en-la-guera-ninas-ninos-adolescentes-hablaron-colombia. Accessed 21 December 2023.

20 https://comisiondelaverdad.co/actualidad/comunicados-y-declaraciones/cuidar-la-vida-de-los-jovenes. Accessed 21 December 2023.

References

Alias, Amirah M. 2015. 'Reinventing the Role of Children and Youth in Post-Conflict Peacebuilding.' *Capstone Collection*. 2787. https://digitalcollections.sit.edu/capstones/2787. Accessed 30 November 2023.

Berents, Helen. 2018. *Young People and Everyday Peace: Exclusion, Insecurity and Peacebuilding in Colombia*. New York: Routledge.

Berents, Helen, and Siobhán McEvoy-Levy. 2015. 'Theorising Youth and Everyday Peace (Building).' *Peacebuilding* 3 (2): 115–25.

Billingsley, Krista. 2018. 'Intersectionality as Locality: Children and Transitional Justice in Nepal.' *International Journal of Transitional Justice* 12 (1): 64–87.

Capone, F. 2016. 'Children in Colombia: Discussing the Current Transitional Justice Process against the Backdrop of the CRC Key Principles.' In *Justicability of Human Rights Law in Domestic Jurisdictions*, edited by Alice Diver and Jacinta Miller, pp. 197–215. Cham: Springer.

Comision de la Verdad. 2023. *Boys, Girls and Adolescents*. https://www.comisiondelaverdad.co/etiquetas/boys-girls-and-adolescents?page=0. Accessed 30 November 2023.

Comisión de la Verdad. n.d. Legado. https://comisiondelaverdad.co/hay-futuro-si-hay-verdad. Accessed 11 December 2023.

Del Felice, Celina, and Andria Wisler. 2007. *The Unexplored Power and Potential of Youth as Peace-builders*. https://repository.ubn.ru.nl/bitstream/handle/2066/56049/56049.pdf. Accessed 30 November 2023.

JEP. 2018a. *Criterios y metodología de priorización de casos y situaciones en la sala de reconocimiento de verdad, de responsabilidad y de determinación de los hechos y conductas. jurisdicción especial para la paz*. Bogotá, 28 de junio de 2018. https://www.jep.gov.co/DocumentosJEPWP/5CriteriosYMetodologiaDePriorizacion.pdf. Accessed 30 November 2023.

JEP. 2018b. *Orientaciones para la elborácion de informes dirigidos a la Jurisdicción Especial para la Paz (JEP)*. Bogotá: 2018. https://www.jep.gov. co/DocumentosJEPWP/6cartilla-guia-rientacion-para-elaboracion-de-informes-cot-62000.pdf. Accessed 30 November 2023.

JEP. 2019. 'Comprehensive System of Truth Justice, Reparation and Non-Repetition (SIVJRNR).' https://www.jep.gov.co/DocumentosJEPWP/4SIVJRNR_EN.pdf. Accessed 30 March 2023.

JEP. 2020. 'La JEP lanza video para niños, niñas y adolescentes.' https://www. jep.gov.co/Sala-de-Prensa/Paginas/JEP-lanza-video-para-ni%C3%B1os,-ni%C3%B1as-y-adolescentes.aspx. Accessed 1 December 2023.

JEP. 2020. *La JEP vista por sus jueces (2018–2019)*. Bogotá: 2020. https://www. jep.gov.co/DocumentosJEPWP/LA%20JEP%20VISTA%20POR%20SUS%20 JUECES.pdf. Accessed 30 November 2023.

JEP. n.d. 'Conozca la JEP.' https://www.jep.gov.co/DocumentosJEPWP/1conozcala jep.pdf. Accessed 29 March 2023.

JEP. n.d. 'Portal de niños, niñas, y adolescentes.' https://www.jep.gov.co/ninosyni-nas/index.html. Accessed 1 December 2023.

JEP. n.d. 'Caso 3: Asesinatos y desapariciones forzadas presentados como bajas de combate por agentes del Estado.' https://www.jep.gov.co/macrocasos/caso03. html#container. Accessed 11 December 2023.

JEP Colombia. 2020. *En la JEP las víctimas somos creíbles*. YouTube, 15 January. https://www.youtube.com/watch?v=LCO6Pu0SZFU. Accessed 30 November 2023.

Koopman, Sara. 2018. 'La paz en plural: Espacio, raza, género y sexualidad en los acuerdos de paz de Colombia.' In *Geografías de Paz*, edited by Yuri Sandoval. La Paz: Universidad Mayor de San Andres.

Krygier, Rachelle. 2019. 'Colombia Is Exhuming Graves of Civilians Allegedly Killed by Soldiers.' *The Washington Post*, 17 September. https://www. washingtonpost.com/world/the_americas/colombia-exhuming-graves-of-civilians-allegedly-killed-by-soldiers/2019/12/17/0d99e428-20e5-1 1ea-b034-de7dc2b5199b_story.html. Accessed 30 March 2023.

Lee-Koo, Katrina. 2018. '"The Intolerable Impact of Armed Conflict on Children": the United Nations Security Council and the Protection of Children in Armed Conflict.' *Global Responsibility to Protect* 10 (2018): 57–74.

Martuscelli, Patrícia Nabuco and Rafael Duarte Villa. 2018. 'Child Soldiers as Peace-builders in Colombian Peace Talks between the Government and the FARC–EP.' *Conflict, Security and Development* 18 (5): 387–408.

McEvoy, Kieran, and Kirsten McConnachie. 2012. '"Victimology in Transitional Justice: Victimhood, Innocence and Hierarchy.' *European Journal of Criminology* 9 (5): 527–38.

McEvoy-Levy, Siobhán. 2001a. *Youth as Social and Political Agents: Issues in Post-Settlement Peace Building*. Notre Dame: Joan B. Kroc Institute for International Peace Studies, University of Notre Dame.

Mollica, Caitlin. 2017. 'The Diversity of Identity: Youth Participation at the Solomon Islands Truth and Reconciliation Commission.' *Australian Journal of International Affairs* 71 (4): 371–88.

Pruitt, Lesley J. 2015. 'Gendering the Study of Children and Youth in Peacebuilding.' *Peacebuilding* 3 (2): 157–70.

Ramírez-Barat, Clara. 2012. *Engaging Children and Youth in Transitional Justice Processes: Guidance for Outreach Programs*. New York: ICTJ.

Republica Colombiana. 1997. Ley 375 de 1997 (Julio 4) por la cual se crea la ley de la juventud y se dictan otras disposiciones. https://www.acnur.org/fileadmin/Documentos/BDL/2008/6470.pdf. Accessed 29 March 2023.

Republica Colombiana. 2011. Ley 1488 de 2011 (Junio 10). *Por la cual se dictan medidas de atención, asistencia y reparación integral a las víctimas del conflicto armado interno y se dictan otras disposiciones.* https://www.unidadvictimas.gov.co/sites/default/files/documentosbiblioteca/ley-1448-de-2011.pdf. Accessed 26 March 2023.

Republica Colombiana. 2016. *Codigo de la Infancia y la Adolescencia.* Ley 1098 de 2006. https://www.icbf.gov.co/sites/default/files/codigoinfancialey1098.pdf. Accessed 29 March 2023.

Republica Colombiana. 2018. Ley Estatutaria N° 1885 1 Marzo 2018. *Por la Cual se Modifica la Ley Estatutaria 1622 de 2013 y se dictan otras disposiciones.* http://es.presidencia.gov.co/normativa/normativa/LEY%201885%20DEL%2001%20DE%20MARZO%20DE%202018.pdf. Accessed 29 March 2023.

Republica Colombiana. 2018, Ley Estatutaria N° 1885 1 Marzo 2018. *Por la Cual se Modifica la Ley Estatutaria 1622 de 2013 y se dictan otras disposiciones.* http://es.presidencia.gov.co/normativa/normativa/LEY%201885%20DEL%2001%20DE%20MARZO%20DE%202018.pdf. Accessed 29 March 2023.

Republica Colombiana. 2018. Ley No. 1922 18 Jul 2018 Por medio del cual se adoptan unas reglas de procedimiento para la jurisdicción especial para la paz. https://www.jep.gov.co/Marco%20Normativo/Normativa_v2/04%20DECRETOS%20Y%20LEYES/7.%20Ley%201922%20reglas%20procedimiento%20JEP.pdf. Accessed 29 March 2023.

Republica Colombiana. 2019. Ley No.1957 6 jun 2019. Estatutaria de la administración de justicia en la jurisdicción especial para la paz. https://urosario.edu.co/sites/default/files/2022–10/ley-1957-del-6-de-junio-de-2019.pdf. Accessed 30 March 2023.

Republica Colombiana. n.d. *Registro Único de Víctimas (RUV).* https://www.unidadvictimas.gov.co/es/registro-unico-de-victimas-ruv/37394. Accessed 11 December 2023.

Salazar, Ángela. 2019. 'La juventud tiene la palabra.' *Comisión de la Verdad.* 10 October. https://web.comisiondelaverdad.co/en/actualidad/blogs/la-juventud-tiene-la-palabra. Accessed 30 March 2023.

Sanchez Parra, Tatiana. 2018. 'The Hollow Shell: Children Born of War and the Realities of the Armed Conflict in Colombia.' *International Journal of Transitional Justice* 12 (1): 45–63.

Senehi, Jessica, and Sean Byrne. 2006. 'From Violence toward Peace: The Role of Storytelling for Youth Healing and Political Empowerment after Conflict.' In *Troublemakers or Peacemakers? Youth and Post-accord Peace Building*, edited by Siobhán McEvoy-Levy, pp. 235–55. Notre Dame: University of Notre Dame Press.

Steinl, Leoni. 2017. *Child Soldiers as Agents of War and Peace: A Restorative Transitional Justice Approach to Accountability for Crimes under International Law*, Vol. 14. The Hague: Springer.

United Nations Department of Economic and Social Affairs (UNDESA). n.d. *Definitions of Youth.* https://www.un.org/esa/socdev/documents/youth/factsheets/youth-definition.pdf. Accessed 1 December 2023.

UNSC. 2019. *Children and Armed Conflict in Colombia, Report of the Secretary-General*, S/2019/1017. https://reliefweb.int/sites/reliefweb.int/files/resources/N2000035.pdf. Accessed 30 November 2023.

UNSC. 2015. *Resolution 2250 (2015) Adopted by the Security Council at its 7573rd meeting, on 9 December 2015*. *S/RES/2250 (2015)*. https://documents-dds-ny.un.org/doc/UNDOC/GEN/N15/413/06/PDF/N1541306.pdf?OpenElement. Accessed 11 December 2023.

5

The challenge of being taken seriously: symbolic violence and youth participation in peacebuilding in Sierra Leone

Catherine E. Bolten

The months leading up to the 2012 presidential elections in Sierra Leone were characterised by popular and political fear about whether the campaign season would be marked by violence perpetrated by 'youth' – a category delineating primarily poor, unemployed men under 40 who are imagined to be potentially dangerous to the social order (Bolten 2020). Prior elections were marked by politicians engaging the services of 'war affected youth' as campaign muscle, deploying into the streets young men who were chronically unemployed because they were displaced, had lost family, or had lost educational opportunities due to the country's decade-long civil war, which ended in 2002. The 2007 elections in particular involved the large-scale incorporation of youth into the entourages of various politicians as 'bodyguards'. Acting with the blessings of their candidates, they harassed and intimidated voters, scared them away from the polls in heavily contested areas and coerced them to vote for a particular candidate in others (Kandeh 2008; Christensen and Utas 2008; Enria 2015). Though these prior elections were declared 'free and fair' by the international community, large questions loomed over the role young people would play in the 2012 elections.

Elections in Sierra Leone had been a particular preoccupation of the international community since 1996, when the United Nations supervised Sierra Leone's first 'free' election in decades in the midst of its civil war. The country exploded into civil war in 1991 after 23 years of repressive dictatorship, and made international headlines for the rebel Revolutionary United Front's (RUF) campaign of amputations, kidnapping children and forcing those children to mine diamonds to fuel their cause (Gberie 2005). A coup in 1992 eventually led to elections in 1996, when the country experienced a peaceful transfer of power from military to civilian rule. The newly elected president Tejan Kabbah was unsuccessful bringing an end to hostilities, and the war continued through multiple failed peace accords before the then-largest deployment of United Nations peacekeepers in history, with over 17,000 international troops finally forcing the RUF to peace talks in

2002 (Olonisakin 2007). The accords mandated international involvement in elections and a Truth and Reconciliation Commission (TRC), whose recommendations for conflict transformation would be binding on all future governments. The United Nations established explicit rules for political participation spanning party registration, campaigning, polling and ballot counting. Heavy emphasis was placed on the importance of peaceful campaigning, with the parties encouraged to participate in 'peace rallies' where they demonstrated their commitment to non-violent, free and fair elections. According to many of my interlocutors who counted themselves as 'youth', the presence of the international community during the campaign season was an opportunity for young people to prove their credentials as 'peace-loving' and 'law-abiding', rather than being seen as 'thugs' who did the bidding of politicians. They believed the only way they could, in the words of one young man, 'ease the minds of the elders' who saw young people only as disruptive forces, was by publicly performing their own peacefulness and desire for free and fair elections, thus 'turning the elders' minds' away from ideas of postwar youth as inherently violent, and therefore useful only as hired muscle. As I will show here, young people did not see the elections necessarily as an opportunity to be taken seriously as active agents in politics and peace; rather, in 'easing the minds' of the elders, they began unwittingly to participate in their own continued marginalisation in larger political processes (see Bourdieu and Wacquant 2004), thus missing an opportunity to establish an active role in public life beyond the elections. Instead, youth were arguing that, should they be given a place at the table, they would comport themselves 'quietly' and in ways that would lay the groundwork for them to be treated as actors of consequence in the future. In essence, their 'participation' was a performance of potentiality, rather than of actuality as peacemakers.

Young people's understanding of their own participation resonates with questions about what comprises 'quality' participation now, or potentially in the future, and in their thinking they reproduce the dominant tropes about their position in society as 'war-affected'. As Altiok asks in Chapter 6, is youth participation 'quality' if it is mute and passive, and soothes the fears of elder generations, thus creating the trust necessary for more active youth involvement in the future? Or is that a deliberate contradiction of 'quality participation', which can occur only if youth make meaningful contributions now; contributions that may 'disturb the peace', in the words of many elders, because it harkens back to the 'boldness' of youth during the war, and thus their disruptive capacity. In Chapter 4 Martuscelli notes that 'transitional justice is political', which means that stakeholders reproduce hegemonic views of armed groups in writing the tenets of peace agreements, severely circumscribing what is imagined to be possible as 'participation' for affected groups. It also raises a greater question about what needs to occur to make the contributions of youth to the peace process sustainable – in short, if the youth who were most profoundly affected by the war must miss their chance at meaningful participation because of prevailing mistrust and dominant political tropes, will the opportunity to create sustainable change based on their experiences be missed?

In this chapter I present two examples of young people's participation in peacebuilding activities during the 2012 campaign season to argue that the desire to increase the quality of youth participation in peacebuilding set forth in the Youth, Peace and Security agenda in United Nations Resolution 2250 (2015) – pushing for participation to be rendered 'meaningful' – in part misses the problem that, cross-culturally, it is not assumed that all people are actors of consequence who should be granted equal standing in public life. 'Meaningful participation', though it acknowledges that the impact of youth participation has been difficult to measure (see McEvoy-Levy 2006: 19; Helsing et al. 2006), fails to address the fact that, in Sierra Leone as in many other places (see McManus 2013; Zvaita and Mbara 2019), young people are treated as unfinished social beings, who have not earned the right to be treated like adults (Bolten 2018; Hoffman 2003; Shepler 2014). On the contrary, they are actors who need adult training and supervision, especially when they reveal their immaturity by claiming space and speaking up – they are *fityay*, or 'uppity' – thereby demonstrating that they fail both to know their place and to respect their elders (Bolten 2020; Mitchell 2015). Youth can be *subjects* of peacebuilding but not its architects, and there is no language for their voice and participation to be integral to peacebuilding processes because they would have to be 'not youth' in order for that to be true. The greatest obstacle for youth being fundamental to peacebuilding, especially in Sierra Leone, is the fact that young people are victims of *symbolic violence*: seeing their own domination as the natural order of the world, and supporting that order (Bourdieu and Wacquant 2004). Youth fail, often unwittingly, to take themselves and each other seriously as political actors, thus reinforcing the system that only 'adults' should organise, lead and mould the peace. A key component of this failure that I address here is youths' inability to mobilise the material cues of 'seriousness' that announce their presence as political actors to *each other* in addition to adults. Indeed young people who have connections, wealth and resources are, by definition, actors of consequence and thus not 'youth' at all; their visibility is part of their public profile as 'the leaders of tomorrow' and not a source of fear (see Cohen 1980; Bolten 2020, 167). It is symbolic violence, of youth gratefully accepting their place at the table as silent observers, and how it reinforces youth as 'serious' actors only if they are subjects of the peace who know their place, that I address here.

Moving from participation to consequence

The last two decades have seen new ground broken on the role of young people in peace processes, whether they are postwar peace accords (see Schwartz 2010) or the 'everyday' work of peace that occurs in arenas from politics (Archibald and Richards 2002) to education (Zembylas 2013) to popular art and fiction (see McEvoy-Levy 2018). Scholars are clear about the need to move beyond a binary description of youth as either violent or possible participants in peace processes to more nuanced questions about what productive youth 'participation' in these processes looks like. Semantics matter, and moving from 'participation' to 'empowerment' (Drummond-Mundal and Cave 2007) or 'inclusion' (Pruitt 2015; Pugh 2016) or even 'meaningful participation' (see Altiok, Chapter 6) signals that, in many ways, even when given a place at the peacebuilding table, youth are still treated as marginal or observers to those processes (see Sommers 2015) by both local and international powerbrokers. Indeed, African scholars have written extensively about how age, even more than gender, is a primary factor moulding one's status in the hierarchy of public life (Oyewumi 1997; Tripp et al. 2008).

The theories animating my examination of what is required for young people to participate meaningfully are symbolic violence and Cynthia Enloe's concept of 'seriousness'. In her analysis of American suffrage movements, Enloe determined that it is not enough for people to organise, gather and be visible to become meaningful participants – doing so merely highlights the fact that they are not integral to the polity they seek to enter (Enloe 2013, 2). Entry to that space must be granted – as suffrage was granted to women and people of colour by white men – by people who already possess power, who determine that outside actors should be treated as agents of consequence and be granted a place at the table (Enloe 2013, 4). A place at the table is only the beginning, as Jenny Lawy (2017) asserts, as one is still not truly consequential until one can raise their voice in that space, have one's voice heard and one's thoughts acted upon. To be *integral* to a process is to be impossible to dismiss or ignore because one's absence would generate a gap in the body politic. It should be clear from American suffrage that being granted a place at the table does not make the person occupying that place integral to the functioning of that process; indeed, their attendance may be only to witness the consequential performance of others so that they themselves 'know their place' (Mitchell 2015).

The TRC bound Sierra Leone to 10 per cent youth representation in political processes (2003). This 'place at the table' has generated passivity among Sierra Leonean youth in many instances. In one example from the 2012 election season, local youth in Makeni, the capital of the northern region, were thrilled that they were given 'delegates' on the nominating committee of one party during the primaries, citing this as an important milestone, even though their delegates were a small minority of the whole (see Bolten 2020, 165). These nods towards integration render them less likely to resist edicts that disempower them than if they were protesting from outside, where they would truly feel ostracised. *Cultural* violence is an insidious consequence of social worlds in which generations of failing to treat certain actors as people of consequence creates a sense of that world as unproblematic. *Symbolic* violence occurs when people who occupy the lower rungs of the ladder of their unequal social world see this position as 'natural' or even 'right', and participate in perpetuating their own subjugation (Bourdieu and Wacquant 2004). In Sierra Leone youth often express their gratitude for being 'allowed to represent ourselves', rather than asserting their integrality to the peace process and indeed to the social world itself. In addition, they see the actions of themselves and their fellows as inconsequential, and fail to support those initiatives *because* they were not started by adults and therefore 'cannot be serious'. As Mamadou Diouf asserts (translated from French), 'At the heart of the margins, young people are often inclined to adopt and reproduce the norms of society' (2005: 37). Indeed youth collaborate in the moments of their exclusion from the world of adults when they themselves initiate, support or reinforce those exclusionary practices.

A new university for the youth of the north

In 2012 I was a visiting professor at a university in northern Sierra Leone, a position I accepted in part to conduct research on the elections. I was invited to participate in a meeting in the town of Kabala, two hours northeast, which was being called to discuss the founding of a new university for students in the far north, a remote and underdeveloped region. Sierra Leone has a long history of skewed formal education opportunities, beginning in the colonial era with administrators favouring the capital Freetown and the Christian south and east of the country for schools and largely ignoring the Islamic north (see Corby 1990; Bolten 2012). The new university was being proposed to correct these imbalances. What emerged from the meeting was a performance that highlighted who the people of consequence were, with everything from the invited guests to the formation of committees and the 'vote of thanks' at the end articulating whose voices and actions mattered and, conversely, who was in the room because the outcome, and not the process, concerned them. It was towards the end of the meeting that the chairman sought the 'youth representative', who was abashed that his opinion was being solicited even on a minor point. However, this was not a bad-faith performance of who the educational heavyweights were in the district, and thus who had a right to be heard. It was, rather, a *good-faith* effort to establish a school for young people, involving the 'experts', with no one realising that the youth would or could have any substantive input on the subject, especially as it pertained to opportunities for a peaceful society. It simply did not occur to anyone, not even the 'youth representative' himself.

The meeting began with introductions, with the regional Minister of Education noting that 'all the key stakeholders are here'. Unlike many meetings that I have attended in Sierra Leone, this was not a roll-call of politicians and wealthy businessmen. Statements were made by the chair of the Head Teachers' Association, the current Inspector of Schools, the retired Inspector of Schools, school principals and vice-principals, administrators and teachers. Much of the content involved individuals taking turns to weigh in on the importance of establishing new educational opportunities for the youth of the district, who had the lowest levels of university attendance in the nation. Because it was a presidential election year and the incumbent hailed from the northern region, this was an opportune moment to demonstrate how the youth of the north wanted to 'come up in the world' to support him. Emphasis was placed on the trend of youth leaving the district for lack of opportunities, with teachers reporting that their favourite students became prostitutes or criminals in Freetown; in essence, even the 'most promising youth' became trouble-makers without education. In everyday speech young people were spoken of as future potentiality, rather than current actuality, and always as a possible threat.

The proposed site for the university was an abandoned international school on a hill overlooking the town, an elite institution educating the children of expatriates until the civil war reached Kabala in 1992, at which point it was evacuated and abandoned permanently. The buildings were wrecked, which concerned the Minister because of the time and resources it would take to repair them. He emphasised that 'for the peaceful development of the north, our youth must have the opportunity to attend university. We must find a way.' Everyone agreed that, if the school could only be established, local young people would be grateful to their elders, they would apply themselves to their educations and the rest would take care of itself. This emphasis on the possibility of young people becoming restless and 'lost' without opportunities echoed the classic discourse of youth who were not kept busy as potential 'trouble-makers' (Honwana and de Boeck 2005; McEvoy-Levy 2006).

After many hours a consensus emerged that the school would generate 'peaceful prosperity' among the youth, and attention shifted to organising committees to govern the process. In creating the Public Relations Committee, the Minister of Education suggested that it have a 'youth representative' to 'talk to the youth' about the new school. There was a brief discussion as everyone asked who that person should be, before a teacher dismissed the conversation with, 'The youth have their own chairman. Let him choose someone.' The comment revealed that there was little knowledge of youth social organisation in the town, and even less concern about who that critical person would be. What was important was that a youth occupied that seat. The room was silent for a moment, and then the Minister asked, 'Do we have a youth representative in the room?' A hand went up tentatively in the back, followed by, 'Here, sir.' The Minister said, 'Let him stand.' The young man stood hesitantly, smoothed down his shirt, and ducked his head, apparently embarrassed at being singled out. The Minister persisted, 'Do you have someone to represent the youth to the process?'

The young man was clearly flustered by the question. 'Sir, I am here on behalf of the youth of this district to make a vote of thanks to everyone for establishing this university for us.' He looked around sheepishly. 'I would like to thank everyone for your efforts towards helping the youth of this district.' The Minister persisted, 'Can you find someone to represent the youth to this process? To talk to the youth?' The young man responded, 'Yes sir. And the youth can help do new construction on this bad road up to the school. We are ready!' A ripple of approving murmurs rose from the crowd, and the Minster was satisfied, exclaiming 'That is good news!' The youth sat down and grinned, looking relieved that he had played a part. The rest of the committees were organised, with the Minister confirming with the youth that he would create a work team to liaise with the Building Committee, and the meeting ended.

What is vital to note about the single young man's participation is that, unlike many ostensible peace processes where youth may be a part of the larger landscape of combatants, refugees, victims and 'war-affected' (see Bolten 2012), this meeting was called solely to address a problem faced by young people. Because this was not a political process by which youth 'participation' was determined by a mandated quota, it did not occur to anyone that youth should be integral to that process, as university is the domain of experts and elders whose responsibility it is to educate the young (see Bledsoe 1992). This was true even as several of the Kabala's secondary school graduates were students at my own adopted university in the city of Makeni, and would likely have had fresh ideas about organising it. This meeting was not a deliberate attempt to shut out the voices of the young while simultaneously raising them as 'the leaders of tomorrow'; rather, only those who were 'not youth' were thought to have voices of consequence that could be heard (Lawy 2017). Even the youth representative himself did not imagine that he had a voice other than expressing gratitude for 'being considered', and offering some helpful manual labour.

The peace union that could not put modalities in place

The phrase 'put modalities in place' is often used by Sierra Leoneans to describe the process of finding money, support and material goods to advance one's cause. It is also a useful metaphor for thinking about what young people do when they are working to become 'not youth', as it captures the activities they undertake to represent themselves and to earn a voice. In essence, when youth 'put modalities in place' to start organisations, join political parties or campaign for office, they are orienting adult observers to their future potential, and requesting investment in that process. If youth can put modalities in place, they are displaying that someone takes them seriously enough to support them publicly as legitimate actors. A failure to put modalities in place means that no funding has been found, that no one sees them as consequential. Without this initial investment, that possibility of seriousness is lost.

In September 2012 I listened to a radio broadcast featuring two members of a new organisation who wanted to promote peaceful campaign conduct among politicians in Makeni. The DJ introduced them, noting that they were Chairman and Secretary of the brand new Makeni Youth Advocacy Union. They were imploring listeners to attend a peace rally they were holding the next day, to which they had invited the main 'stakeholders' in the town – the Paramount Chief, the mayor and the politicians campaigning in their constituency. The youth repeated their cell phone numbers, asking listeners to contact them to volunteer or to gather guests. The DJ extolled the virtues of the two young men, who he noted were neatly dressed and enthusiastic about peace. He emphasised that the blossoming of youth unions in Makeni to further the causes of peaceful society would put them in place to become the leaders of tomorrow. They had one 'modality' in place.

I contacted the secretary and arranged a meeting for that afternoon. He apologised for having nowhere official to meet, but suggested a covered bench near the main square. He arrived with two other members, and I asked them a question about the organisation, which they deflected. The secretary repeated, 'Please, just wait for the chairman to arrive, and he can give you our official position. Right now he is putting modalities in place for the rally tomorrow. He is trying to find a PA [public address] system.' Replicating the hierarchy of other political and civic organisations, the rest of the young people present did not want to overstep their bounds.

The secretary appeared anxious that I would leave before the chairman arrived, assuring me that he was running only slightly late. He repeated several times, 'Please, we are a real union, you just must be patient for the chairman to arrive!' In every apology was a plea that I take them seriously, especially because they were respecting the hierarchy of their own organisation.

Upon arriving, the chairman apologised for his tardiness, as he was unsuccessful getting the public address system, and so was looking for a smaller sum of money for a banner to hang in the central square. He explained, 'You see, this union is entirely our own efforts, and we aren't receiving funding from anyone. We are focusing our efforts on our own constituency inside Makeni because we don't have any funding to expand beyond that. We are hoping that if the stakeholders see that we are doing good work, they will provide us with support so that we can register officially and expand our activities.' He explained that he had sent letters to the town's politicians and had verbal promises to attend from several of them. He was hoping that the mayoral candidates would come so that the residents of the ward could meet them. This was a critical moment for the union.

The chairman seemed exhausted from his efforts, and so I asked why he had chosen this cause and this moment to start a peace movement. He spoke of the previous election, when people voted for candidates they did not know and had never seen, which was typical for party-loyalty voting (see Kandeh 2008; Bolten 2016). Most of the elected candidates won because they had the support of the youth, which they had received on the basis of open pandering to youth hopes and dreams for jobs, political inclusion and a voice in civic life. All of these promises came to nothing, and the candidates abandoned the youth once they were sworn into office, as the chairman explained, 'Closing their doors and pretending they had never seen us before. So, all of the aspirants will give their manifestos, talk about their concerns for the youth, and perhaps promise not to misuse the youth this time around.' The secretary chimed in that they had formed the union to protect themselves against being abused by politicians, because if the aspirants saw that they were organised and working hard, that they would see the power of youth, and not their vulnerability, even as they had no money to fund their efforts. These youth were actively trying to shift popular understanding of youth behaviour during elections away from 'trouble-making' to positive peacebuilding that would match their power at the polls.

The chairman never found the money for a PA system or banner and, in the end, only the five members of his organisation and I showed up for the rally. Though he had received promises from politicians, none bothered to come. As for the other youth, however, the elusiveness of 'modalities' revealed the union as insufficiently important for the attention of their own demographic. He mused, 'If a politician is holding a rally, the youth will attend, as there are tee-shirts and drinks, and they hope that he will include them in his campaign team, or that if they pledge to vote for him, that he will consider them in his policies. But if the youth try to do something for themselves, the other youth do not take them seriously, because we are not powerful. If we had been successful putting modalities in place, maybe we would have had a PA system, and we could encourage the youth to come right now.' Everything he had cited the previous day – youth putting their hopes in established politicians but not seeing the possible power of youth acting together – had come to pass, as none of the young people in his ward took the Makeni Youth Advocacy Union, or its organisers, seriously. Once again it had simply not occurred to other young people to treat their fellows as people of consequence unless they already had the 'modalities' that revealed them as such. Youth, in this case, did not recognise the power they have in their numbers, the possibilities inherent in raising their voices together and the legitimacy they could gain as political actors simply by showing up for each other. Their numbers, as they know from the fears about the 'youth bulge' in the country (GoSL 2003), are impossible to ignore, and yet they perpetuate their own position on the margins.

Conclusions

In emphasising the role of symbolic violence in hampering youth participation in peacebuilding, my goal with this chapter is to shift the conversation around the relative exclusion of youth voices from peace processes, however formal or informal. As is clear from the two examples in this chapter, peacebuilding – and youth involvement in it – does not always occur in the formalised, overt process of sitting down at peace talks or hashing out United Nations resolutions. In fact, the formal delegations, internationally supervised activities and landmark decision-making of peace processes are the exception, rather than the norm. Indeed, in order for peacebuilding to be sustainable, it cannot be limited simply to those large-scale, formal processes, nor can youth involvement be limited to counting their numbers or measuring the 'quality' of their participation in those processes. Peacebuilding as I examine it here, and youth 'participation' in it, occurs in the local meetings where everyday decisions about the future are made, as occurred with the university, and in the margins of public life itself, where one has to look hard for young people because of the often-invisible ways they inhabit this space and its possibilities for peace, as did the Makeni

Youth Advocacy Union. In this sense the work of peace is the work of the everyday, and, if young people are marginalised in everyday life, so will they be in these intimate spaces of peacebuilding.

I emphasise that exclusion is not always deliberate, malevolent or designed to put youth 'in their place', even if that place is one of ostensible inclusion 'at the table'. Rather, we must analyse how people cross-culturally take for granted who are the actors of consequence, whose voices can be heard and carry weight, and what roles can be played by various members of a social world. One of the primary arguments about the origins of the war in Sierra Leone was that it was driven in part by the ability of the Revolutionary United Front to prey on the frustrations of young people who were systematically excluded from decision-making while simultaneously put forward as available labour for violence (Richards 1996; Peters 2006; Hoffman 2011). Politicians using youth as hired muscle resonates with the logic of this social hierarchy, even as the devastation of the decade-long war revealed the unsustainability of this manifestation of patrimony, and the need for an evolution in order for peace to be sustainable, rather than the result of the gerontocracy seizing even tighter control of their position as the only actors of consequence.

In even good-faith efforts to help young people, such as the project to establish a new university, both the young and old took for granted that the young are not partners in this process, only construction labour and grateful beneficiaries of its establishment. In efforts that young people make themselves, such as the youth union, other young people may not show up to claim a place at that table – wherever it is erected in the social landscape – because they do not believe that their fellow youth can lead these efforts, even if they would display the powerful voting block that youth comprise. There simply were not the visual and material cues that union members were people of consequence, therefore there was no reason to treat them as such. For peace to be truly sustainable, much of the change needs to happen within the cultural worldview of consequence, with young people integrated into that vision, rather than merely included in its purview.

References

Archibald, Steven, and Paul Richards. 2002. 'Converts to Human Rights? Popular Debate about War and Justice in Rural Central Sierra Leone.' *Africa: Journal of the International African Institute* 72 (3): 339–67.

Bledsoe, Caroline. 1992. 'The Cultural Transformation of Western Education in Sierra Leone.' *Africa: Journal of the International African Institute* 62 (2): 182–202.

Bolten, Catherine. 2012. *I Did It to Save My Life: Love and Survival in Sierra Leone*. Berkeley: University of California Press.

Bolten, Catherine. 2016. 'I Will Vote What Is in My Heart: Sierra Leone's 2012 Elections and the Pliability of "normative" democracy.' *Anthropological Quarterly* 89 (4): 1019–48.

Bolten, Catherine. 2018. 'Productive Work and Subjected Labor: Children's Pursuits and Child Rights in Northern Sierra Leone.' *Journal of Human Rights* 17 (2): 199–214.

Bolten, Catherine. 2020. *Serious Youth in Sierra Leone: An Ethnography of Performance and Global Connection*. New York: Oxford University Press.

Bourdieu, Pierre, and Loïc Wacquant. 2004 'Symbolic Violence.' In *Violence in War and Peace*, edited by Nancy Scheper-Hughes and Philippe Bourgois, pp. 272–4. New York: Wiley Blackwell.

Christensen, Maya M., and Mats Utas. 2008. 'Mercenaries of Democracy: the "Politricks" of Remobilized Combatants in the 2007 General Elections, Sierra Leone.' *African Affairs* 107 (429): 515–39.

Cohen, Stanley. 1980. *Folk Devils and Moral Panics: The Creation of the Mods and the Rockers*. New York: St Martin's.

Corby, Richard A. 1990. 'Educating Africans for Inferiority under British Rule: Bo School in Sierra Leone.' *Comparative Education Review* 34 (3): 314–49.

Diouf, Mamadou. 2005. 'La Jeunesse africaine: entre autochtonie et cosmopolitisme.' *Horizons Maghrebins* 53 (1): 31–9.

Drummond-Mundal, Lori, and Guy Cave. 2007. 'Young Peacebuilders: Exploring Youth Engagement with Conflict and Social Change.' *Journal of Peacebuilding and Development* 3 (3): 63–76.

Enloe, Cynthia. 2013. *Seriously? Investigating Crashes and Crises as Though Women Mattered*. Berkeley: University of California Press

Enria, Luisa. 2015. 'Love and Betrayal: the Economy of Youth Violence in Post-war Sierra Leone.' *Journal of Modern African Studies* 53 (4): 637–60.

Gberie, Lansana. 2005. *A Dirty War in West Africa: The RUF and the Destruction of Sierra Leone*. Bloomington: Indiana University Press.

GoSL (Government of Sierra Leone). 2003. *Sierra Leone National Youth Policy*. Freetown: Ministry of Youth and Sports. https://www.youthpolicy.org/national/Sierra_Leone_2003_National_Youth_Policy.pdf. Acessed 1 December 2023.

Helsing, Jeff, with Namik Kirlic, Neil McMastern and Nir Sonnenschein. 2006. 'Young People's Activism and the Transition to Peace.' In *Troublemakers or Peacemakers? Youth and Post-accord Peace Building*, edited by Siobhán McEvoy-Levy, pp. 195–216. Notre Dame: University of Notre Dame Press.

Hoffman, Danny. 2003. 'Like Beasts in the Bush: Synonyms of Childhood and Youth in Sierra Leone.' *Postcolonial Studies* 6 (3): 295–308.

Hoffman, Danny. 2011. *The War Machines: Young Men and Violence in Sierra Leone and Liberia*. Durham, NC: Duke University Press.

Honwana, Alcinda, and Filip de Boeck. 2005. *Makers or Breakers: Children and Youth in Postcolonial Africa*. Oxford: James Currey.

Kandeh, Jimmy D. 2008. 'Rogue Incumbents, Donor Assistance and Sierra Leone's Second Post-Conflict Elections of 2007.' *The Journal of Modern African Studies* 46 (4): 603–35.

Lawy, Jenny R. 2017. 'Theorizing Voice: Performativity, Politics, and Listening.' *Anthropological Theory* 17 (2): 192–215.

McEvoy-Levy, S. 2006. 'Introduction: Youth and the Post-Accord Environment.' In *Troublemakers or Peacemakers? Youth and Post-accord Peace Building*, edited by Siobhán McEvoy-Levy, pp. 1–26. Notre Dame: University of Notre Dame Press.

McEvoy-Levy, S. 2018. *Peace and Resistance in Youth Cultures: Reading the Politics of Peacebuilding from Harry Potter to The Hunger Games*. New York: Palgrave Macmillan.

McManus, Laura. 2013. *A Space for Peace: Inclusion of Youth and Peacebuilding in the Post-2015 Development Agenda*. United Network of Young Peacebuilders. https://www.unmultimedia.org/avlibrary/asset/T138/T1381758280/. Accessed 30 November 2023.

Mitchell, Koritha. 2015. 'Keep Claiming Space!' *CLA Journal* 58 (4): 229–44.

Olonisakin, 'Funmi. 2007. *Peacekeeping in Sierra Leone: The Story of UNAMSIL*. Boulder: Lynn Rienner.

Oyewumi, Oyeronke. 1997. *The Invention of Women: Making an African Sense of Western Gender Discourses*. Minneapolis: University of Minnesota Press.

Peters, Krijn. 2006. 'Footpaths to Reintegration: Armed Conflict, Youth, and the Rural Crisis in Sierra Leone.' PhD Dissertation, Wagenigan University.

Pruitt, L.J. 2015. 'Gendering the Study of Children and Youth in Peacebuilding.' *Peacebuilding* 3 (2): 157–70. https://doi.org/10.1080/21647259.2015.1052630.

Pugh, Jeffrey. 2016. 'Peacebuilding among Transnational Youth in Migrant-receiving Border Regions of Ecuador.' *Journal of Peacebuilding and Development* 11 (3): 83–97.

Richards, Paul. 1996. *Fighting for the Rain Forest: War, Youth, and Resources in Sierra Leone*. Oxford: James Currey.

Schwartz, Stephanie. 2010. *Youth in Post-conflict Reconstruction: Agents of Change*. Washington, DC: United States Institute of Peace.

Shepler, Susan. 2014. *Childhood Deployed: Remaking Child Soldiers in Sierra Leone*. New York: New York University Press.

Sommers, Marc. 2015. *The Outcast Majority: War, Development, and Youth in Africa*. Athens: University of Georgia Press.

Tripp, Aili, Isabel Casimiro, Joy Kwesiga and Alice Mungwa, eds. 2008. *African Women's Movements: Changing Political Landscapes*. Cambridge: Cambridge University Press.

Truth and Reconciliation Commission of Sierra Leone (TRC). 2003. *Recommendations of the Truth and Reconciliation Commission*, vol. 2, ch. 3. www.sierraleonetrc.org. Accessesd 1 December 2023.

United Nations 2015. *Resolution 2250 on Youth, Peace and Security*. New York: United Nations. https://documents-dds-ny.un.org/doc/UNDOC/GEN/N15/413/06/PDF/N1541306.pdf?OpenElement. Accessed 30 November 2023.

Zembylas, Michelinos. 2013. 'The Emotional Complexities of "Our" and "Their" Loss: the Vicissitudes of Teaching about/for Empathy in a Conflicting Society.' *Anthropology and Education Quarterly* 44 (1): 19–37.

Zvaita, Gilbert T., and George Chimdi Mbara. 2019. 'Engaging the Values of Local Participation in African Peacebuilding Processes.' *Journal of African Union Studies* 8 (2): 155.

6

Meaningful youth participation? The pitfalls of merging counter-terrorism with the Youth, Peace and Security agenda

Ali Altiok

Fostering youth participation is central to the global Youth, Peace and Security (YPS) agenda. Participation is the first pillar of the landmark YPS Resolution 2250 that the United Nations Security Council (UNSC) adopted in December 2015. Participation is arguably the most important and all-encompassing pillar of the YPS agenda. Participation cut across the four other action pillars of Resolution 2250: protection, prevention, partnership and disengagement and reintegration. Whether it is to improve protection measures or to design more effective disengagement and reintegration programmes, youth participation is considered necessary in the YPS field (Simpson 2018). Young peace practitioners see participation as essential to the development of local, national, regional and global peace and security policies, action plans, strategies and funds, as well as in the design, implementation and monitoring and evaluation of programmes (see, for example, Upadhyay 2022).

The global YPS agenda is also concerned with the quality of participation. Resolution 2250, and the subsequent YPS Resolutions 2419 (2018) and 2535 (2020), emphasise that the participation of youth should be *meaningful*. The desire to move from superficial forms of participation to 'meaningful youth participation' is widespread. Almost all actors engaged in this agenda frequently use the term 'meaningful youth participation' to express their commitment to the global YPS agenda. For young peace advocates 'meaningful' entails an objection to what Hart (1992) described as decorative, manipulative or tokenistic forms of youth participation (see, for example, Jelinkova and de Luliius 2021; Canada YPS Coalition 2021). Young peace advocates use the term 'meaningful' to demand greater influence in decision-making processes. States promote youth participation for significantly different reasons from those of young peace advocates. States' interest in the YPS agenda is primarily rooted in their globalising security concerns (Sukarieh and Tannock 2018). For most states 'participation' is a way to moderate, regulate and control disruptive agency of youth. By qualifying youth participation with the term 'meaningful', states performatively respond to peace advocates' demands, while framing their repressive behaviour to control youth in positive terms. Consequently, meaningful participation becomes new jargon that states and young peace advocates attribute opposing views to. Whose needs shape the address through meaningful participation should be a critical inquiry for peace scholars and practitioners (Altiok et al. 2020).

This chapter delves into how such opposing views on meaningful youth participation unfold, particularly in political decision-making processes. Resolution 2250 urges states to increase youth representation at all decision-making levels, and in conflict prevention, resolution efforts, peace negotiations and implementation of peace agreements. Importantly, Resolution 2250 requests states to foster youth participation in 'institutions and mechanisms to counter violent extremism, which can be conducive to terrorism'. This particular emphasis on the need to foster youth participation in countering violent extremism institutions and mechanisms brings the primary interests of states to the surface.

States primarily view the YPS agenda's call for a greater youth participation from national and international security perspectives. Despite the UNSC being paralysed due to disagreements between the permanent members, the council has consistently reached agreements to broaden multilateral counter-terrorism institutions and policies for over two decades (Altiok and Street 2020; de Londras 2022). States' shared interest in multilateral system through counter-terrorism frameworks subsumes the global YPS agenda's call for greater youth participation. For most states, fostering youth participation is directly connected to counter-terrorism objectives. UNSC's emphasis on fostering youth participation in peace negotiations, implementation of peace agreements and decision-making processes largely works as a cover to legitimise their common strategic interests in broadening multilateral counter-terrorism frameworks.

The common ground states found in the counter-terrorism field also shapes how YPS resolutions tackle youth participation in violence. UNSC's YPS resolutions suggest that fostering youth political participation makes them less amenable to and less likely to participate in violence, particularly in extremist and terrorist forms.[1] With YPS resolutions states posit a monocausal relationship between higher levels of youth political participation and their rejection of violent extremism, despite evidence on the relationship being weak or under-researched (see Ismail and Olonisakin 2021). In fact some studies suggest negative correlation between higher levels of youth political engagement and rejection of violent extremism. Politically engaged young people in Yemen and Palestine are more prone to engage in violence than their peers who are not engaged in politics (Cragin et al. 2015; Robinson et al. 2017).

In the following, the first section elaborates why governments embraced youth political participation within the multilateral counter-terrorism field. The second section discusses the three counter-productive outcomes of linking youth political participation with counter-terrorism measures. Governments aim to enhance the political participation of young people who are at risk of being involving in violence through structured programmes. These structured programmes generate the risk of fostering nepotism, elitism and tokenism. Moreover, when political spaces are created with the objective of countering terrorism, many young people reject participating in politics as they do not want to be instrumentalised by counter-terrorism actors. This exacerbates the political alienation and exclusion of young people. Additionally, counter-terrorism approaches romanticise youth political participation as if it was something necessarily non-violent. This romanticisation enables policy-makers and decision-makers to dismiss and ignore the social, political and cultural meanings attached to youth involvement in violence. The third section focuses on the negative impact of counter-terrorism measures on youth political participation in civic spaces. Many states misuse counter-terrorism measures 'to narrow or shut down the availability of civic spaces for dissenting youth voices' (Simpson 2018, 26). Yet the most recent YPS Resolution 2535 (2020) urged states to protect civic and political spaces. Considering the previous record of states in closing down spaces through counter-terrorism measures, their interest in protecting civic space through the YPS initiatives may have an obfuscating impact. Instead of protecting these spaces for youthful dissent and peaceful protest, governments may potentially use the global YPS agenda to expand their ability to monitor, surveil, suppress and regulate youth political participation in civic spaces. To avoid or minimise these risks, the chapter recommends that the global YPS agenda be liberated from counter-terrorism policy frameworks and measures. The chapter ends with recommendations of what the YPS agenda should do to distance itself from the growing international counter-terrorism policy frameworks and approaches.

The politics of youth political participation

Fostering positive youth political participation was a marginal issue in the peace and security field until the adoption of Resolution 2250 in 2015. The United Nations General Assembly and Security Council largely prioritised the protection or livelihood of young people, particularly in the context of disengagement, disarmament and reintegration and post-conflict reconstruction processes (see UNOY Peacebuilders 2013). The political participation of young people rather gained importance with two institutional development processes, namely the UN Peacebuilding Architecture and the Counter-Terrorism Architecture. These two institutional development processes claimed the importance of youth political participation to maintain international peace and security. Despite these two agendas being motivated by related but different concerns, they followed somehow parallel trajectories in exploring the importance of youth political agency. Although it is worthwhile to compare the differences in how UN Peacebuilding Architecture and the Counter-Terrorism Architecture reached similar conclusions about the importance of youth political agency, due to the limited focus of this chapter I will unpack only how the latter, UN Counter-Terrorism Architecture, embraced youth political inclusion.

United Nations member states first started incorporating youth political participation as a counter-terrorism tool at the UN General Assembly. In 2006, with the adoption of the Global Counter-Terrorism Strategy (GCTS), UN member states asserted that addressing youth unemployment 'could reduce marginalization and the subsequent sense of victimization that propels extremism and the recruitment of terrorists' (UN General Assembly 2006). Thus, providing employment opportunities to young people became a way to address the conditions considered conducive to the spread of terrorism (UN General Assembly 2006, 6).[2]

It took almost ten years for the UN General Assembly to move from a strategy to an action plan. In 2015 member states of the UN General Assembly adopted 'the Plan of Action to Prevent Violent Extremism (PVE)'. The role of youth empowerment became more visible in this document. The Plan of Action acknowledged youth empowerment as one of the six priority areas of the UN Counter-Terrorism Architecture (UN General Assembly 2015). The Plan of Action asserted that politically disenfranchised and excluded young people are vulnerable to radicalisation and recruitment by extremist armed groups or at risk of committing terror attacks due to violent extremist incitement on the internet. To prevent radicalisation, mobilisation and recruitment of young people, the Plan of Action urged governments to '[i]ntegrate young women and men into decision-making processes at local and national levels, including by establishing youth councils and similar mechanisms which give young women and men a platform for participating in mainstream political discourse' (UN General Assembly: para. 52). This policy development made it clear that one of the main motivations of states in enhancing youth political participation is to make them less amenable to and less likely to participate in extremist forms of violence (see also Fett, Chapter 3).

In the meantime addressing the underlying causes of terrorism through youth participation was also embraced by the UN Security Council. In 2014 the UN Security Council adopted the Countering Violent Extremism (CVE) framework under Resolution 2178 (2014a). The CVE put forward youth empowerment as an instrument to 'address the conditions conducive to the spread of violent extremism'. The CVE framework later emphasised the importance of youth participation in 'developing strategies to counter terrorism and violent extremism', as noted in UNSCR 2195 (2014b). These CVE resolutions of UNSC prepared the conditions for states to formalise the YPS agenda, which is evident in the preamble of Resolution 2250 and subsequent YPS resolutions.

Risks of fostering youth political participation under counter-terrorism objectives

The potential of promoting political participation of young people to prevent their involvement in extremist violence or terror acts deserves further scrutiny from the lens of conflict sensitivity. This requires reflecting on the complex social and political factors that may potentially create unintended consequences, including the possibility of exacerbating tense dynamics (Dwyer 2015). As a matter of fact there is some evidence suggesting that fostering youth political participation may encourage more young people to become involved in extremist or terrorist form of violence. This section will elaborate on the risks of forming a correlation between youth political participation and prevention of youth involvement in terrorist or extremist violence.

Programmatisation

Although most young people are excluded from formal political decision-making processes, only a minuscule proportion of youth populations participate in violence (Hilker and Fraser 2009; Sommers 2015). The numbers are even lower for young people's involvement in extremist or terrorist form of violence. None the less, for the sake of argument, let us assume that a subset of that minuscule proportion of the youth population are involved, or are 'at risk' of becoming involved, in extremist forms of violence due to their exclusion from politics. The question then becomes whether offering opportunities for political engagement – projects, events, activities or even civic education training – can satisfy the participation needs of young people and prevent their engagement in violence. Would putting political participation into structured programmes find and recruit young people who are at high risk? It is extremely unlikely that such programmes could and would identify, recruit and fulfil the political participation needs of young people who may potentially be 'violent extremists' or 'terrorists'. Even if the programmes identify and recruit youth who are at risk of engaging in violent extremism or terrorism, would they reject extremist forms of violence because of offered political engage-ment opportunities? How would such political participation opportunities impact conflict dynamics and sensitivity?

There are lessons to be learned, particularly from the evaluations of employment programmes implemented with similar objectives. Izzi's (2013) study showed that youth employment programmes designed to reduce youth participation in violence serve only a tiny fraction of the youth popu-lation. Furthermore, when these programmes are 'perceived as privileging certain groups of young people at the expense of others', they generate the risk of exacerbating conflict dynamics (111). There is no evidence to suggest that the dynamics play out differently or in a less harmful way for the programmes that aim to foster youth political engagement. Many of the young people consulted for *The Missing Peace* study shared that the programmatisation of youth political participation fosters nepotism, elitism and tokenism (Conciliation Resources 2018; Interpeace and Mustakbalna 2017; Life and Peace Institute 2017). For example young people in the Eastern European and Central Asian regional consultations expressed that 'involvement in these platforms [youth councils] is often limited to the youth organizations working with political elite' (Altiok 2017a). Another young person who participated in a focus group discussion in the country of Georgia explained, 'Unfortunately, nepotism is flourishing in today's Georgia. Those who have access to state programmes are mainly those who have close ties with government officials, political organisations and so on' (Conciliation Resources 2018, 15).

Instrumentalisation

Fostering youth political participation as a counter-terrorism tool stig-matises and alienates young people who do engage in politics outside of counter-terrorism fields. This was a sentiment shared widely by young participants of the European Consultations that contributed to *the Missing Peace* study. When young participants were asked to speak about their peace and security challenges, they said that selectively including young people in 'security-related discussions that are almost only on violent extremism … devalue the impact of various forms of violence and security threats young people are concerned about' (Altiok 2017b). Their concerns underlined the exceptionalisation of extremist forms of violence, which leads to the neglect of other forms of violence and security challenges that young people face.

Instrumentalising youth political participation for counter-terrorism purposes also risks turning young people away from engaging in politics altogether. Such an instrumentalisation of youth political inclusion for counter-terrorism objectives particularly pushes marginalised and excluded young people away from politics. As Barzegar and Kharili (2018) observed, 'due to fears of instrumentalization and cooptation [by counter-terrorism actors], many youth populations avoid direct participation in formal political spaces'. Thereby only elite and privileged young people who usually do not disagree with state counter-terrorism measures participate in these policy discussions (for selective inclusion of youth, see Berents, Chapter 7).

This dynamic in counter-terrorism policy-development processes builds an uncontested feedback loop between young people and security actors. While young people who typically come from elite backgrounds speak about marginalisation and exclusion of their peers, security-sector actors legitimise more expansive counter-terrorism measures through youth political inclusion. Youth as a microcosm of society includes individuals who do not mind being tokens or who voluntarily use tokenistic forms of participation for their own personal interest. The counter-productive element in this relationship is that youth participants in counter-terrorism programmes often do not serve as legitimate representatives of concerns of the marginalised and excluded youth. For most young people, '"participation" and "inclusion" are not unconditional: they cannot be a form of co-option or tokenism where young people are used or manipulated by others' (Simpson 2018: 63). In such cases participation is manipulated by unbalanced power dynamics between security institutions and young people, and conditional on serving the interest of states and those in power, rather than to empower marginalised youth.

Romanticisation

The link between youth political participation and youth rejection of extremist forms of violence is weak and underexplored (Ismael and Olonisakin 2021). In fact there is a body of evidence countering the assumptions made about the link between fostering youth political participation and their rejection of violence. This body of literature demonstrates that politically engaged youth are more prone to violence than their peers who are not actively engaged in politics. Mercy Corps' study, based on key informant interviews and focus groups with young people in Afghanistan, Colombia and Somalia found 'civically engaged youth to be more supportive of armed opposition groups, not less' (Mercy Corps 2015, 2). In fact in some cases fostering youth political engagement makes young people more vulnerable to 'radicalisation' of extremist armed groups. Studies conducted by the RAND Corporation in the West Bank and Yemen revealed that participation in non-violent activism does not decrease young people's propensity and radicalisation toward violence (Cragin et al. 2015, 15; Robinson et al. 2017, 36). These studies suggest that young people in Palestine and Yemen see violence as a form of political activism. There are also countless examples of how politically engaged youth similarly saw violent struggle as an extension of their political principles in postcolonial Africa, especially through youth wings (Abbink 2005). Violent youth groups, such as gangs or urban militias, often engage in politics as they 'entertain direct relations with political parties (or armed opposition groups) in post-war contexts or acute social conflicts' (Doudet 2015).

Building global policies and programmes based on sweeping and romantic generalisations that claim that youth political participation prevents youth engagement in violence results in overlooking, disrespecting and ignoring social, political and cultural meanings attached to youth involvement in violence, both as perpetrators and victims. Violence might be seen as a form of expression and communication by young people to resist state institutions that violently ignore them. As a young person from Tunisia said, 'They listen to you only by violence. When I request an appointment to discuss an issue, they [state institutions] close their doors and refuse to accept any initiative of dialogue, they only understand violence' (Deman and Saidani 2017, 17). Violence is seen as an extension of their political activism in civil wars, where young people are exposed to violence perpetrated by multiple parties (Robinson et al. 2017). Violence can also be a coping mechanism for survival and self-defence (Kolar, Erickson and Stewart 2012), or have a reparative function – 'as a salve for humiliation' – to their exposure to violent oppression (McEvoy-Levy 2006, 16). Ultimately youth participation in politics and violence takes the form of complex and multifaceted relationships. This complexity requires us to treat the political agency of young people neither as something inherently peaceful nor as something universally inclined to violence.

Closing civic spaces

Civic spaces are undeniably the most important engagement site where young people exercise their political agency. Civic spaces enable young people to participate in dissent and protest movements, which have been the most popular form of political participation among younger generations in the last two decades (Young 2019). Young people have initiated political transition processes (Arab Spring, Gezi Park, Umbrella Movement,

Qeerroo), protested against socio-economic (Occupy and the Indignados) and racial injustices (Black Lives Matter), set the agenda on climate justice (Fridays for the Future), demanded gun-control laws (March for Our Lives) and raised their voices to reform state security institutions (#EndSARS). Through their key and perhaps leading roles in social movements, young people engaged in various forms of activism that disrupted the status quo and transformed power relations. Young people's ability to organise and mobilise for peace activism is directly connected to their access to protected civic spaces and their ability to exercise their right to freedom of expression, assembly and association without fear of repression and retaliation (Izsák-Ndiaye 2021).

The most recent YPS resolution of UNSC, 2535, urged governments 'to protect civic and political spaces'. How should states' interest in protecting civic and political spaces be interpreted, given that their motivation behind fostering youth political participation is tightly connected to repressive counter-terrorism measures? Counter-terrorism measures globally have been the primary tool governments use to clamp down on civic spaces in the last two decades (Charbord and Ní Aoláin 2018; Young 2019). Considering that most states tend to see the global YPS agenda merely as an extension of counter-terrorism frameworks (Altiok 2021), it is necessary to think critically about the potentially harmful consequences of states' involvement in civic spaces through youth political participation initiatives.

Actions taken by states to protect civic spaces may inadvertently create new risks for the YPS agenda. This includes further expansion of security apparatuses and their legitimacy to monitor, surveil and control youth activism in civic spaces. Governments across the world do intervene in civic spaces to regulate, pacify and pathologise youth political activism that demands systemic positive change (see Grasso and Bessant 2018). States utilise legal mechanisms, particularly anti-terror laws and penal systems, to increase their authority to monitor and heavily punish young people (Mosteyrin and Lopez 2018). Through such legal measures, states discourage and regulate youthful dissent. In some countries governments use counter-terrorism measures to legitimise pre-emptive mass surveillance of young people in schools, religious sites, youth and sport centres through signalling young people's vulnerability to radicalisation (Baburdeen 2018; Coppock, Guru and Stanley 2018). This unlawful state surveillance and monitoring of youth political activism also increasingly takes place in online spaces (Feldstein 2020). Moreover, when governments intervene in civic and political spaces, their interventions do not necessarily support youth activism for peace and democracy. Many governments increasingly protect civic and political spaces for 'regressive forces to flourish alongside progressive ones' (Hayes and Joshi 2020). This provides fertile ground for ultra-right-wing populism to thrive among young people who collaborate with anti-democratic and fundamentalist political parties (Bessant 2018).

As the examples suggest, through diverse repression methods, and constructing simplistic threat and victim narratives, governments may potentially further close civic spaces and securitise informal youth political participation in the name of implementing the global YPS agenda in civic and political spaces. This is a risk that could undermine the legitimacy and accountability of the global YPS agenda and more broadly UN's sustaining peace efforts.

Conclusion

This chapter argues that UNSC member states agreed to foster youth political inclusion through the YPS agenda in order to broaden counter-terrorism measures. This motive is rooted in the assumption that more political engagement opportunities would deter young people from engaging in extremist or terrorist violence. However, providing political participation opportunities for young people as part of counter-terrorism efforts leads to negative consequences. Political engagement initiatives associated with counter-terrorism objectives instrumentalise youth agency in service of legitimising broadening security measures. Programmatic efforts exacerbate disparities privileging pro-state elite youth further. These programmes also disregard the meanings young people attach to violence and undermine the grievances they express through violence. As these negative consequences suggest, drawing clear-cut boundaries between the global YPS agenda and multilateral counter-terrorism frameworks is critical to making youth participation meaningful.

Boundaries between the global YPS agenda and the national and multilateral counter-terrorism frameworks could be drawn in the following ways. Peace advocacy efforts need to concentrate on challenging the policy connections that states built between UNSC's YPS resolution and multilateral counter-terrorism frameworks. This could be achieved through co-ordinated civil society advocacy efforts raising the awareness of states on the negative impact of counter-terrorism measures on youth-focused peacebuilding work. Policy-level connections need to be challenged at the national levels as well. Some UN agencies and governments tend to associate or merge National Action Plans on YPS with National Action Plans on PVE (Upahyay 2022). In the implementation of the YPS agenda at the country level, youth organisations should advocate for the development of distinct action plans focused solely on YPS, rather allowing it to be conflated with counter-terrorism plans or strategies. Implementation of YPS at the national level also means scrutinising the national counter-terrorism laws, frameworks and practices from conflict sensitivity and peace responsiveness perspectives.

Additionally the distinction between YPS and counter-terrorism needs to be made at the programmatic level. Since the adoption of UNSCR 2250 there has been an observable rise in the number of youth-focused peace-building programmes. There is, however, significant lack of clarity on how YPS programmes differ from those implemented by counter-terrorism funds or institutions, particularly under CVE and PVE frameworks. In fact many UN country offices, international peacebuilding organisations and local civil society organisations implement YPS programmes that are funded through counter-terrorism funds, blurring the lines between peace-building work and counter-terrorism engagements. To gain insight into the counter-productive nature of securitised forms of youth engagement programmes, peace researchers and practitioners should closely examine how youth programmes in the peacebuilding field are framed and funded in comparison to counter-terrorism programmes. Examining differences at the programmatic level would reveal the extent to which peacebuilding engagements are superior to counter-terrorist ones regarding the preven-tion of youth engagement in extremist violence, but also with respect to fostering trust, social cohesion and reconciliation. Teasing out these differ-ences would also help the international community gain a more nuanced understanding of the effectiveness of diverging approaches to conflict prevention, which is central to the UN's sustaining peace agenda. These insights would help the UN's 'A New Agenda for Peace' not to repeat the same mistakes.

Lastly advocates of the YPS agenda need to critically reflect on, and, when necessary, push back against, state-led interventions protecting civic spaces under counter-terrorism frameworks. States are the main violator of the rights of young people, especially those who identify as dissenter peace activists, in civic and political spaces. Expecting states to protect civic and political spaces would be naive given states' role in suppressing youth peace activism. Advocates rather need to think about developing tools that can hold states accountable for their repressive interventions in civic spaces to regulate, control or suppress youth political participation. This requires the YPS agenda to challenge repressive counter-terror laws and strategies, and to counter state surveillance practices. The protection of civic spaces from state repression is what makes youth participation meaningful.

Notes

1 The absence of a mutually agreed definition for terrorism and violent extremism poses a challenge to examining this relationship. To date there has been no consensus between states regarding the definition of 'terrorism', and the concept of 'violent extremism' has not been defined in any legal treaty or multilateral policy frameworks (for further discussion, see the Special Rapporteur on the Promotion and Protection of Human Rights and Fundamental Freedoms While Countering Terrorism 2019). States simply use their own definitions of these terms in developing laws, policies and other measures.
2 Despite youth employment receiving very significant attention among donors and governments, evidence suggests that '[e]mployment status does not appear to distinguish recruits from non-recruits' (Izzi 2020, 12).

References

Abbink, Jon, and Ineke van Kessel. 2005. *Vanguard or Vandals: Youth, Politics and Conflict in Africa*. Leiden: Brill.

Altiok, Ali. 2016. *Youth, Peace, and Security in the Arab States Region: a Consultation and High-level Dialogue*. United Nations. https://www.youth 4peace.info/system/files/2017–10/2017.03.08%20-%20Report%20-%20 Arab%20States%20YPS%20Consultation%20%26%20High-Level%20 Dialogue%20-%20FINAL.pdf. Accessed 3 September 2020.

Altiok, Ali. 2017a. *Youth, Peace & Security in Eastern Europe and Central Asia Region: A Consultation and Dialogue*. United Nations. https://www. youth4peace.info/system/files/2017–11/2017.09.06%20-%20Report%20- %20Eastern%20Europe%20and%20Central%20Asia%20Consultation%20 and%20Dialogue%20on%20Youth%2C%20Peace%20%26%20Security.pdf. Accessed 3 September 2020.

Altiok, Ali. 2017b. *Youth, Peace & Security European Regional Consultation*. United Nations. https://www.youth4peace.info/system/files/2017–12/2017.12.21%20- %20Report%20-%20European%20Regional%20Consultation%20on%20 Youth%2C%20Peace%20%26%20Security_0.pdf. Accessed 3 September 2020.

Altiok, Ali. 2021. 'Squeezed Agency: Youth Resistance to the Securitization of Peacebuilding.' In *Securitizing Youth: Young People's Role in the Global Peace and Security Agenda*, edited by Marisa E. Ensor. New Brunswick: Rutgers University Press.

Altiok, Ali, and Jordan Street. 2020. *A Fourth Pillar for the United Nations? The Rise of Counter-terrorism*. Saferworld. https://www.saferworld.org.uk/ resources/publications/1256-a-fourth-pillar-for-the-united-nations-the-rise-of- counter-terrorism. Accessed 11 March 2023.

Altiok, Ali, Helen Berents, Irena Grizelj and Siobhán McEvoy-Levy. 2020. 'Youth, Peace and Security.' In *The Routledge Handbook of Peace, Security and Development*, edited by Fen Hampson, Alpaslan Özerdem and Jonathan Kent. Abingdon: Routledge.

Baburdeen, Fathima Azmiya. 2018. 'Surveillance of Young Muslims and Counterterrorism in Kenya.' In *Governing Youth Politics in the Age of Surveillance*, edited by Maria T. Grasso and Judith Bessant, pp. 48–61. Cham: Palgrave Macmillan.

Barzegar, Abbas, and Nagham El Karhili. 2018. 'Youth Engagement and Violence Prevention: a Review of Transatlantic Experiences.' British Council. https://www.britishcouncil.us/sites/default/files/youth_engagement_and_violence_prevention_report.pdf. Accessed 3 September 2020.

Bessant, Judith. 2018. 'Right-wing Populism and Young "Stormers": Conflict in Democratic Politics." In *Young People Re-generating Politics in Times of Crises*, edited by Sarah Pickard and Judith Bessant, pp. 139–59. Cham: Palgrave Macmillan.

Canada YPS Coalition. 2021. *More than Tokens: Findings*. https://www.canadayps.org/more-than-tokens. Accessed 11 March 2023.

Charbord, Anne, and Fionnuala Ní Aoláin. 2018. *The Role of Measures to Address Terrorism and Violent Extremism on Closing Civic Space*. Report prepared under the aegis of the Mandate of the United Nations Special Rapporteur on the Protection and Promotion of Human Rights while Countering Terrorism. https://www.law.umn.edu/sites/law.umn.edu/files/civil_society_report_-_final_april_2019.pdf. Accessed 20 October 2020.

Conciliation Resources. 2018. *Youth Perspectives on Peace and Security: the Georgian-Abkhaz Context*. https://www.youth4peace.info/system/files/2018–04/3.%20FGD_Georgia%20and%20Abkhazia_CR_0.pdf. Accessed 3 September 2020.

Coppock, Vicki, Guru Surinder and Tony Stanley. 2018. 'On Becoming "Radicalised": Preemptive Surveillance and Intervention to Save the Young Muslim in the UK.' In *Governing Youth Politics in the Age of Surveillance*, edited by Maria T. Grasso and Judith Bessant, pp. 108–22. Cham: Palgrave Macmillan.

Cragin, Kim, Melissa A. Bradley, Eric Robinson and Paul S. Steinberg. 2015. *What Factors Cause YouthtTo Reject Violent Extremism: Results of an Exploratory Analysis in the West Bank*. RAND Corporation. https://www.rand.org/content/dam/rand/pubs/research_reports/RR1100/RR1118/RAND_RR1118.pdf. Accessed 3 September 2020.

De Londras, Fiona. 2022. *The Practice and Problem of Transnational Counter-terrorism*. Cambridge: Cambridge University Press.

Deman, Hilde, and Zeineb Saidani. 2017. 'Youth Consultations on Peace and Security: Findings from Focus Group Discussions and Interviews Including Hard to Reach Youth in Tunisia.' *Search for Common Ground*. https://www.sfcg.org/wp-content/uploads/2017/12/UNSCR-2250-Report-Tunisia-SFCG-FINAL.pdf. Accessed 3 September 2020.

Dudouet, Véronique. 2015. '"Violent Mobilization of Youth Gangs by Political Parties.' In *Understanding a New Generation of Non-state Armed Groups*, edited by United Nations System Staff College and Center for International Peace Operations. Turin. https://gisf.ngo/wp-content/uploads/2020/02/2023-UNSSC-2015-Understandinganewgenerationofnon-statearmedgroups.pdf. Accessed 1 December 2023.

Dwyer, Leslie. 2015. 'Beyond Youth "Inclusion": Intergenerational Politics in Post-conflict Bali.' *Journal of Peacebuilding and Development* 10 (3): 16–29.

Feldstein, Steven. 2020. 'State Surveillance and Implications for Children.' Good Governance of Children's Data Project Office of Global Insight and Policy,

Issue brief no. 1. https://www.unicef.org/globalinsight/media/1101/file/UNICEF-Global-Insight-data-governance-surveillance-issue-brief-2020.pdf. Accessed 3 September 2020.

Grasso, Maria T., and Judith Bessant, eds. 2018. *Governing Youth Politics in the Age of Surveillance*. Cham: Palgrave Macmillan.

Hart, Roger A. (1992). *Children's Participation: From Tokenism to Citizenship*. United Nations Children's Fund. https://www.unicef-irc.org/publications/pdf/childrens_participation.pdf. Accessed 11 March 2023.

Hayes, Ben, and Poonam Joshi. 2020. *Rethinking Civic Space in an aAge of Intersectional Crises: a Briefing for Funders*. Funders' Initiative for Civil Society at Global Dialogue. https://global-dialogue.org/wp-content/uploads/2020/05/FICS-Rethinking-Civic-Space-Report-FINAL.pdf. Accessed 3 September 2020.

Hilker, McLean Lyndsay, and Erika Fraser. 2009. *Youth Exclusion, Violence, Conflict and Fragile States*. London: Social Development Direct. http://linkasea.pbworks.com/f/McLean+Kilker,+Lyndsay+&+Erika+Fraser+April+2009.pdf. Accessed 7 December 2023.

Interpeace and Mustakbalna. 2017. *Palestinian Youth Challenges and Aspirations: A Study on Youth, Peace and Security Based on UN Resolution 2250*. https://www.youth4peace.info/system/files/2018–04/9.%20FGD_Palestine_Interpeace.pdf. Accessed 3 September 2020.

Ismail, Olawale, and Funmi Olonisakin. 'Why Do Youth Participate in Violence in Africa? A Review of Evidence.' *Conflict, Security & Development* 21 (3): 371–99.

Izsák-Ndiaye, Rita. 2021. *IF I DISAPPEAR: Global Report on Protecting Young People in Civic Space*. United Nations.

Izzi, Valeria. 2013. 'Just Keeping Them Busy? Youth Employment Projects as a Peacebuilding Tool.' *International Development Planning Review* 35 (2): 103–17. https://gsdrc.org/wp-content/uploads/2016/03/Izzi_youthemployment-peacebuilding.pdf. Accessed 3 September 2020.

Izzi, Valeria. 2020. *Promoting Decent Employment for African Youth as a Peacebuilding Strategy*. INCLUDE Knowledge Platform. https://idl-bnc-idrc.dspacedirect.org/bitstream/handle/10625/58931/IDL-58931.pdf?sequence=2. Accessed 3 September 2020.

Jelinkova, Eliška, and Sofia de Luliis. 2021. *Meaningful Youth Engagement Checklist*. United Networks of Young Peacebuilders. https://unoy.org/downloads/mye-checklist/. Accessed 11 March 2023.

Kolar, Kat, Patricia Gail Erickson and Donna Stewart. 2012. 'Coping Strategies of Street-involved Youth: Exploring Contexts of Resilience.' *Journal of Youth Studies* 15 (6): 744–60.

Life and Peace Institute. 2017. 'Being and Becoming a Peacebuilder – Insights from 20,000 Hours of Youth-led Dialogues in the Horn of Africa.' https://www.youth4peace.info/system/files/2018–04/20.%20CFR_Horn%20of%20Africa-%20Being%20And%20Becoming%20A%20Peacebuilder_LPI_0.pdf. Accessed 3 September 2020.

McEvoy-Levy, Siobhán. 2006. 'Introduction: Youth and the Post-Accord Environment.' In *Troublemakers or pPeacemakers: Youth and Post-accord Peacebuilding*, edited by Siobhán McEvoy-Levy, pp. 1–26. Notre Dame: University of Notre Dame Press.

Mercy Corps. 2015. *Youth & Consequences: Unemployment, Injustice and Violence.* https://www.mercycorps.org/sites/default/files/2020–01/MercyCorps_YouthConsequencesReport_2015.pdf. 3 Accessed September 2020.

Mosteyrín, Laura Maria Fernandez de, and Pedro Limon Lopez. 2018. 'Controlling Dissent through Security in Contemporary Spain.' In *Governing Youth Politics in the Age of Surveillance*, edited by Maria T. Grasso and Judith Bessant, pp. 48–61. Cham: Palgrave Macmillan.

Robinson, Eric, P. Kathleen Frier, Kim Cragin, Melissa A. Bradley, Daniel Egel, Byrce Loidolt and Paul S. Steinberg. 2017. *What Factors Cause Individuals to Reject Violent Extremism in Yemen?*. Rand Corporation. https://www.rand.org/content/dam/rand/pubs/research_reports/RR1700/RR1727/RAND_RR1727.pdf. Accessed 31 October 2020.

Simpson, Graeme. 2018. *The Missing Peace: Independent Progress Study on Youth and Peace and Security.* United Nations. https://www.youth4peace.info/system/files/2018–10/youth-web-english.pdf. Accessed 3 September 2020.

Sommers, Marc. 2015. *The Outcast Majority: War, Development, and Youth in Africa.* Athens: University of Georgia Press.

Sukarieh, Mayssoun, and Stuart Tannock. 2018. 'The Global Securitisation of Youth.' *Third World Quarterly* 39 (5): 854–70.

The Special Rapporteur on the Promotion and Protection of Human Rights and Fundamental Freedoms while Countering Terrorism. 2019. *Human Rights Impact of Policies and Practices Aimed at Preventing and Countering Violent Extremism, A/HRC/43/46.* United Nations Human Rights Council.

UN General Assembly. 2006. *The United Nations Global Counter-Terrorism Strategy.* https://documents-dds-ny.un.org/doc/UNDOC/GEN/N05/504/88/PDF/N0550488.pdf?OpenElement. Accessed 11 March 2023.

UN General Assembly. 2015. *Plan of Action to Prevent Violent Extremism: Report of the Secretary-General.* https://documents-dds-ny.un.org/doc/UNDOC/GEN/N15/456/22/PDF/N1545622.pdf?OpenElement. Accessed 11 March 2023.

UN Security Council. 2014a. *Resolution 2178 on Foreign Terrorist Fighters.* New York: United Nations. https://documents-dds-ny.un.org/doc/UNDOC/GEN/N14/547/98/PDF/N1454798.pdf?OpenElement. Accessed 11 March 2023.

UN Security Council. 2014b. *Resolution 2195 on Preventing and Combatting Terrorism, including Terrorism Benefitting from Transnational Organized Crime.* New York: United Nations. https://documents-dds-ny.un.org/doc/UNDOC/GEN/N14/708/75/PDF/N1470875.pdf?OpenElement. Accessed 11 March 2023.

UN Security Council. 2015. *Resolution 2250 on Youth, Peace and Security.* New York: United Nations. https://documents-dds-ny.un.org/doc/UNDOC/GEN/N15/413/06/PDF/N1541306.pdf?OpenElement. Accessed 11 March 2023.

UN Security Council. 2018. *Resolution 2419 on Youth, Peace and Security.* New York: United Nations. https://documents-dds-ny.un.org/doc/UNDOC/GEN/N18/173/81/PDF/N1817381.pdf?OpenElement. Accessed 11 March 2023.

UN Security Council. 2020. *Resolution 2535 on Youth, Peace and Security.* New York: United Nations. https://documents-dds-ny.un.org/doc/UNDOC/GEN/N20/182/94/PDF/N2018294.pdf?OpenElement. Accessed 11 March 2023.

UNOY Peacebuilders. 2013. *Agreed Language on Youth, Peace and Security,* 1–34. The Hague: UNOY Peacebuilders. http://unoy.org/wp-content/uploads/2015/03/Agreed-UN-Language-on-Youth-Participation-in-Peacebuilding-2-FLAT.pdf. Accessed September 2020.

Upadhyay, Mridul. 2022. *Assessing Youth Participation in the Implementation of the YPS Agenda*. Interpeace. https://youth4peace.info/system/files/2023–01/Assesing-Youth%20Participation%20in%20Implementation_Mridul%20Upadhyay.pdf. Accessed 11 March 2023.

Youngs, Richard. 2019. *Civic Activism Unleashed: New Hope or False Dawn for Democracy?* Oxford: Oxford University Press.

7

Institutionalising a radical vision: the idea of youth, and the Youth, Peace and Security agenda

Helen Berents

In December 2015 the UN Security Council unanimously passed resolution 2250 on Youth, Peace and Security (hereafter SCR2250), recognising for the first time 'the important and positive contribution of youth in efforts for the maintenance and promotion of international peace and security' (UNSC 2015). SCR2250 was the culmination of years of campaigning by civil society including youth-led organisations, and parts of the UN, to achieve recognition and inclusion of youth in peace and security.[1] More significantly, it moves 'youth' as a category into practices and processes of organisations and institutions. This institutionalisation of youth-inclusive peacebuilding as an agenda – the YPS agenda – is a significant achievement and means youth and their allies have access to increased support, funding and visibility.

The inclusion of youth in peacebuilding is a radical proposition; although it should not be. The voices and perspectives of people most impacted by conflict should be centred in any response. However, structural practices, and the mechanisms of liberal peace (Berents 2018; Mac Ginty 2011), mean that the *meaningful* and *equal* participation of any marginalised or excluded group is inherently radical. For youth, a constituency that has long been characterised as apathetic and disengaged at best, and dangerous at worst, claims to the benefit and necessity of including their voices have been often ignored. Centring youth as knowledge-bearers in their own right, and as having expertise about their own experiences and the context in which they live, poses a challenge to institutions that are often slow to recognise new sites of expertise and to change practices.

Working against the dominant stereotypes of youth as delinquent or passive victims, scholarship and advocacy have worked to position youth as agential contributors to peace, usually at a local level (e.g. Pruitt 2013; Berents 2018; Senehi and Byrne 2006; Berents and McEvoy-Levy 2015). Much of the early scholarship on the inclusion of youth in peacebuilding notes that *despite* their exclusion from formal politics youth are already active in building peace at local levels and sometimes even nationally (McEvoy-Levy 2001; Del Felice and Wisler 2007; Borer, Darby and McEvoy-Levy 2006). Such claims for youth inclusion challenge understandings of how politics and peace should be done.

The emancipatory vision of youth as collaborators and co-constitutors of knowledge and practice described in the literature, and forwarded by some advocates for YPS, runs up against engrained positions and assumptions within the structures and systems of the UN. Cécile Mazzacurati was the Head of the Secretariat on Youth, Peace and Security at the UN (jointly established between the UNFPA and UNPBSO), and co-chair of the Global Coalition on YPS. In reflecting on the agenda she notes the discomfort it can present:

> There is a discussion on young people that everyone is comfortable having. It is: young people need education, they need employment, and they should be empowered. Everyone is happy to have that discussion. The discussion that young people are leaders already, and young women need space, and about opening up the doors of power where important discussions are held, is a discussion that a *lot* of people are not comfortable with ... So it's important to try to keep the political edge of the agenda. It [the agenda] is not a nice conversation about how young people need our help. (in interview, 2019)

Mazzacurati clearly articulates the need to maintain the critical focus of the agenda. Yet this is an ongoing challenge for YPS advocates. Tensions and dilemmas in the 'inclusion' of marginalised constituencies persist across UN peacebuilding efforts (Nadarajah and Rampton 2015; Berents and Mollica 2022; Basu, Kirby and Shepherd 2020).

Some of these tensions and lessons can be seen in the Women, Peace and Security (WPS) agenda. Reflecting on twenty years of WPS, Basu, Kirby and Shepherd note that, alongside the many positive gains for women and gender equality enabled by the agenda, the increasing institutionalisation of the agenda has

> included, among others, the assimilation of the more 'radical' aspects of gender politics into the 'business-as-usual' organizational culture at these organizations; and related to this, the instrumentalization of women's inclusion in the arena of international peace and security, wherein the argument for increasing their participation is made on the basis of operational effectiveness and not gender equality. (2020, 8)

Such reflections are valuable for those invested in the YPS agenda also as they offer a cautionary tale for the still-nascent YPS agenda.

This chapter traces the tensions and opportunities of the emergent Youth, Peace and Security agenda that sits between an agential vision for youth inclusion and the sometimes-depoliticising effects of institutionalising an agenda. Claims by youth peace activists for inclusion are radical, their demands and articulations for not just participation but for partnership challenge the usual forms of acknowledging young people. However, by being 'brought in' to an institutional process, there is a risk that these demands are diluted or co-opted. The 'political edge' of the agenda of youth activists and their allies can be blunted by the institutionalisation of such claims.

Attention must be paid to the consequences and implications of connecting a radical vision to the mechanisms and institutions of international governance. This chapter asks: how does the formalisation of an agenda of YPS configure the role of youth and what spaces are opened or closed for the radical position of inclusion of youth as full social and political actors? To address this question, it draws on a critical document analysis of key resolutions, declarations and associated statements that relate to the formal YPS agenda since 2015, and interviews conducted in 2019–20 with individuals involved in efforts to pass the first UNSC YPS resolution including both youth and adult civil society and UN representatives. It also is informed by observation of high-level meetings and public webinars on aspects of YPS.[2] It highlights three sites of tension: discursive commitments to youth 'participation', claims to seriousness and legitimacy in including youth, and finally who is included and excluded in the idea of the 'good youth' who is encouraged to participate in institutional processes. Together these threads highlight the need for continued critical attention as the YPS agenda evolves, and for scholars and practitioners to keep the political project of youth inclusion in focus as the agenda is institutionalised and operationalised.

Partnership and (de)politicising discourses of youth

The first tension relates to the idea of partnership. Rhetoric for partnership with youth has been strongly evident in advocacy efforts for UNSC2250; however it is helpful to examine the way in which the idea of partnership manifests in the formal discourse around the resolution and its implications.

Language matters when considering representation and inclusion. The way in which youth are positioned within the formal documents of the YPS agenda shapes the ways in which they are able to be included and the nature and extent of that inclusion. As Shepherd argues, discourse analysis can help uncover the ways in which the '"conceptual apparatus" regulating knowledge is produced and reproduced' (2015, 889). Discursive contestations over the role and place of youth contribute to the fundamentally contested nature of youth inclusion. The YPS agenda presents the most recent intervention in this space, and, given the weight it is being given in the international arena, its construction of youth and their capacities is significant.

SCR2250 is a milestone resolution for the UNSC. In its aims it is ground-breaking in recognising youth as positive contributors to peace and security; and in its language it draws on other (radical) documents, in particular the Amman Youth Declaration on Youth, Peace and Security (2015) and SCR1325 (2000), the foundational resolution for the Women, Peace and Security agenda. Here I explore how this language is reflected, and in some cases muted, in SCR2250 to demonstrate the ways that youth and their roles are positioned in the institutionalising of the agenda.

As part of the strategy of moving towards a UNSC resolution, advocates and Member States worked to bring together youth peacebuilders and other stakeholders in a high-level forum in August 2015 (see Figure 7.1 for timeline of key events leading to UNSC 2250). Hosted by the Republic of Jordan, and organised by the UN through the UN Youth Envoy and UNPBSO, and through the Global Coalition members including Search for Common Ground and UNOY, among others, the 'Global Forum on Youth, Peace and Security' was framed as a consensus-building exercise that included youth as central participants. Over two days almost six hundred representatives participated in panels, presentations and breakout discussions, and at the conclusion the organisers presented the Amman Youth Declaration on Youth, Peace and Security.[3] The Forum and Declaration were influential in building momentum and support for a UNSC resolution a few months later. Unusually for a UNSC resolution, SCR2250 actually picks up a significant amount of language from the Amman Youth Declaration.

The Amman Youth Declaration on Youth, Peace and Security uses the word 'partner/ship' eight times in four pages. All references call on inter-national agencies, national governments and local authorities to partner with youth or youth-led organisations. This language is active; it positions young people in their aspirational position as 'equal' and 'crucial' partners (Amman Youth Declaration 2015). It also locates the onus of a lack of partnership with the organisations and mechanisms themselves rather than with the young people who are positioned as engaging in peacebuilding work despite lack of recognition: "Yet, our efforts remain largely invisible, unrecognised, and even undermined due to lack of adequate participatory and inclusive mechanisms and opportunities to partner with decision-making bodies (Amman Youth Declaration 2015)." The Amman Youth Declaration is calling for an understanding of partnership with youth that sees them as leaders in their own right, and equal. It is a radical position.

Partnership as a concept makes its way into SCR2250 as one of the five pillars of the resolution, which is an apparent achievement. However 'Partnership' in SCR2250 (paras 14–16) manifests as largely institutional partnership. For example, the UNSC 'urges' Member States

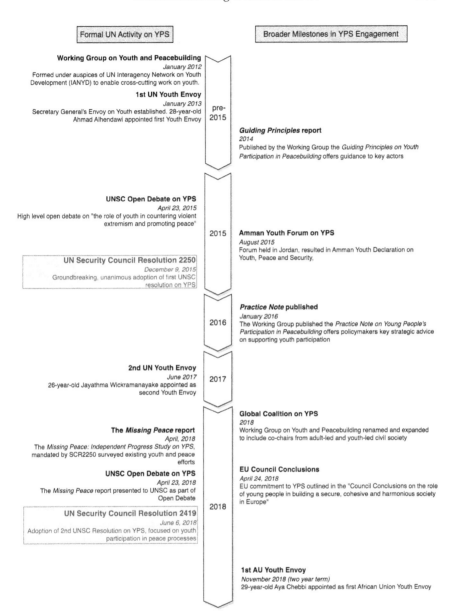

Figure 7.1 Timeline of key milestones in the YPS agenda

Figure 7.1 (continued)

to fund programmes run by organisations including UN bodies and 'other relevant bodies' that 'take account of the needs and participation of youth' (para. 14). 'Partnership' also manifests explicitly in relation to the Peacebuilding Commission's role in addressing the rise of violent extremism 'among youth' (para. 15). The only time young people are engaged directly is as part of a list of local community actors who can help address the conditions 'conducive to violent extremism':

> including by empowering youth, families, women, religious, cultural and education leaders, and all other concerned groups of civil society and adopt tailored approaches to countering recruitment to this kind of violent extremism and promoting social inclusion and cohesion. (para. 16)

The only other place 'partner/ship' appears in SCR2250 is in the 'Disengagement and Reintegration' pillar where it positively echoes of some of the calls from the Amman Youth Declaration around including youth in addressing employment and social opportunity.

This shift in language from the youth-co-authored Amman Declaration to the UNSC resolution is notable because the more radical nature of the calls of the youth represented in the Amman Declaration for 'partnership' has all but disappeared. While the Amman Declaration called for youth to be 'crucial' and 'equal' partners SCR2250 calls for institutions to 'take account of' youth 'needs'. Naturally a youth declaration and a UNSC resolution have different objectives, audiences and parameters. A UNSC resolution must provide direction and requirements for Member States and other parties, it is a document to *institutionalise* the agenda, and such a product is the process of political negotiation and compromise. However, the softening or erasing of the more radical calls for partnership with youth evidences a reluctance to challenge or change the very mechanisms and opportunities the Amman Declaration identifies as inadequate for young people's participation and partnership.

Limited framings of youth, precluding their presence as 'equal partners', also manifest in language that curtails and conditions their inclusion. SCR2250 is notable for how much language was adapted from the first resolution on Women, Peace and Security (WPS) SCR1325 (2000). Yet what is evident in SCR2250 is the conditionality of youth participation, in a way that was not caveated for women. In SCR2250 calls for action are caveated five times with the phrase 'as appropriate', all in relation to consultation and participation of youth. Four of these five instances directly echo phasing in SCR1325 (2000) that formalised the WPS agenda, none of which is caveated.

Illustratively paragraph 15 in SCR1325 reads: 'Expresses its willingness to ensure that Security Council missions take into account gender considerations and the rights of women, including through consultation with local and international women's groups'. In the YPS resolution, SCR2250, an almost-identical call is made: 'Stresses the importance of Security Council missions taking into account youth-related considerations including, *as appropriate*, through consultation with local and international youth groups' (italics added).[4] While age-bound definitions of youth vary, SCR2250 defines youth as those eighteen to twenty-nine years old. Crucially, 'youth' here are actually legally (young) adults in the jurisdictions of most Member States, yet their conditional participation is normalised, making evident an underpinning dismissal of young adults' capacity. This has significant symbolic implications, but also practical ones in terms of shaping the legal obligation on Member States by enabling wide-ranging discretion to determine what counts as 'appropriate'.

The conditionality attached to young people's engagement in politics broadly, and peacebuilding specifically, reflects ingrained assumptions about young people's participation and adultist (Checkoway 1996) ideas about youth's competence. How youth are discursively positioned with respect to their participation and partnership within the formalised agenda reflects the tension between the diverse ways that youth are already engaged in this space in their own contexts, and ideas of youth participation that are institutionalised with potentially limiting effects.

Seeking and claiming legitimacy

A second tension for the YPS agenda is the issue of getting others to *take youth seriously*. As Bolten describes in Chapter 5, drawing on Cynthia Enloe's work on 'seriousness', treating youth seriously requires recognition by those already with power that their inclusion is *integral*. Having youth, peace and security on the UNSC agenda is evidence of a seriousness of regard for youth. Yet, until July 2020, despite two previous resolutions, YPS was not a regular agenda item of the UNSC (and instead depended on whichever country was serving as President to agree to include it). In fact it was a question of seriousness that had prevented its inclusion, with Russia and China arguing that perhaps YPS was not *really* within the mandate of the Security Council at all. Illustratively, in 2018 at a UNSC Open Debate on YPS, Russia argued that there were other UN bodies better suited to 'youth' issues such as 'education, employment, sustainable development and human rights' (UNSC 2018). By repositioning and limiting the issues that youth can or should be involved in to those often associated with youth, Russia implied that youth and their concerns were beneath the serious work of the UNSC, and also not matters of international peace and security. Following Enloe, taking youth seriously requires that 'we see it *matters*', and that 'something matters when we start to uncover its *consequences*' (2011, 11). Keeping youth off the UNSC agenda allowed the consequences of youth exclusion to remain institutionally invisible.

This institutional visibility shifted in July 2020, when the third YPS resolution was passed. SCR2535 includes a request for a biennial report by the Secretary-General on the YPS agenda (covering all three resolutions). The inclusion of YPS on the regular agenda – even if biennial rather than annual (like the WPS agenda) – is a clear success of advocates for the issue to be given sufficient seriousness and legitimacy.[5]

Youth peacebuilders and advocates instrumentalise the agenda for legitimacy too. This legitimacy granted by the institutionalisation of the agenda is used by youth peacebuilders to position themselves as actors who can speak in this space. As Solvi Karlsson, Co-Co-ordinator of UNOY in 2015 when SCR2250 passed, noted:

> What matters about it is that it's a recognition of the UN Security Council that young people matter. It's a tool, it's an instrument. And I'd say it's an instrument we've used fairly well … as a community, we've managed to take it and claim a space with it... It's given us some legitimacy.

Echoing this, youth peacebuilders also argue that the formalisation of a YPS agenda addresses recognition 'that was lacking' and:

> 2250 has been able to solve that political problem. So, I at times look at it as a political tool, because the UN [and members] there have been able to recognise that young people, they are not just victims and perpetrators, but they are contributors to peace and security, and they are on the front line in solving conflict. (Mohammed Foboi, West and Central Africa Regional Co-ordinator UNOY)

The resolutions of the YPS agenda, in particular SCR2250, have allowed youth peacebuilders to claim space and make a case for being taken seriously; SCR2250 has meant young people can 'get a foot in the door' (fieldnotes, 2020), and 'the piece of paper tells the government they have to listen' (Foboi, in interview). While institutionalising youth peacebuilding can lead to narrowing of the spaces where youth can be seen to participate, youth themselves are also instrumentalising the agenda for their own ends. These manoeuvres are often less visible to viewpoints more attuned to the level of institutions, but demonstrate how the agenda can both co-opt youth but also be co-opted by them.

Narrowing the space of participation: the 'good youth'

The third tension that surrounds YPS concerns the idea of participation and the assumptions and practices which permit or preclude certain youth from that participation. One key feature of the YPS agenda is its call for 'meaningful participation' of youth, and it is true that the UN and other regional bodies are making significant investments and efforts to implement mechanisms, processes and programmes to better include youth and ensure their participation. Despite this, cautions persist in relation to which youth are included and how they are included.

One critique of institutionalising youth inclusion in political processes is that it is predicated on a neoliberal framing of youth, which individualises their contribution and reinforces the idea of participation as not-political. Sukarieh and Tannock argue that 'the ideal of "youth as peacebuilders" has joined other ideal roles of youth (as active citizens, change agents and entrepreneurs) as ideological models for interpellating young people into supporting the contemporary global economic order' (2018, 855). Such a critique misses the myriad ways in which youth resist this interpellation and contest the structures and conditions of their participation; however, the broader caution is valid and significant.

The neoliberal lens of youth participation, across a wide range of political and social spaces, sees young people framed as participating 'based on individual actions, entrepreneurship and job market participation are privileged, while approaches that are more collective and concerned with challenging systemic issues are downplayed or ignored' (Hartung and Pruitt 2017: 119). Fett, in Chapter 3, demonstrates how historic youth-diplomacy efforts by the US government were deliberately framed to depoliticise youth participation. Kwon demonstrates how global youth conferences, including the Amman Youth Forum, are presented as spaces where youth participation is necessary, and an opportunity to enact their right to global citizenship:

> [Y]outh actively negotiated these global political spaces but were ultimately restricted by the structure and culture of engagement found in UN confer-ences. Unsurprisingly, these global youth conferences were institutionalized spaces of power that offered young people limited opportunities for involve-ment in actual politics and they reinforced participation as a depoliticized practice of consensus. (2018: 6)

The sometimes tokenistic inclusion of youth reflects the ways in which an agenda can be 'institutionalised' without disrupting existing power relations and functioning of institutions. As one interviewee noted, when a youth delegate speaks it is promoted as a reflection of how 'youth-sensitive' these processes are but 'they're not'. Rather, this interviewee argues, 'it requires changing how the UN works. Creating a meaningful space for youth requires very much larger reforms, they want to call it reforms, but I want to call it transformations.' Given the context, such transformation is unlikely, which makes it all the more crucial to maintain critical reflection on the ways in which youth are able to appear and participate.

While it is encouraging to see youth included more widely, and invited to participate in high-level forums such as Amman, or to speak at the UN Security Council,[6] these young people are required to participate in particular, contained ways. Attending to how youth appear in formal political processes 'reveals that often their voice functions to reinforce existing, sanctioned messages' (Berents and McEvoy-Levy 2015, 121; see also Berents 2016). At more than one high-level YPS event in 2019–20, I observed youth peacebuilders from the audience contest the discourse being presented by senior UN or government representatives on the stage about their inclusive practices. Often the young peacebuilder will argue that the representative is ignoring them because they are saying something they do not want to hear. These exchanges are managed through polite deferral or offers to speak further in other avenues. Since the Covid-19 pandemic required all meetings and high-level events to be held online, space for this contestation has shrunk, with online events often restricting and siloing 'engagement' within chat functions (frequently denying participants the use of voice and video through setting controls), while sanctioned speakers appear within the formal programme. These contestations make visible the politics that guide the accepted presence of the 'good youth' in these forums, and raises concerns about the ways in which institutionalising an agenda narrows the space for different youth to participate and benefit.[7]

The consequences of prescribed roles for youth are also exacerbated by the reality that it is often the same young people being asked to participate. As one interviewee noted, 'I've been going for five years to [these high-level events] with young people, 80 per cent are the same people ... It tells you something about the system.' Similarly, Mohammed Foboi argued:

> So these are things we need to keep talking, need to look at the bottom to top approach, and go down the trenches and meet the hard to reach youth ... We must not mistake that because someone is able to attend one or two conferences abroad, or if someone has a university degree, that is a representation of the young people.

This critical pushback against the embedded institutional practices that can result in tokenistic or non-representative engagement with young people is vital. Gizem Killinç, the Co-Co-ordinator of UNOY (2016–20), argues that 'there is a risk it is very much on the surface ... you're just hearing a lot of rhetoric around youth participation is important ... and we must make sure we go beyond that'. As well as being crucial to maintain the critical edge of the agenda, if the goal of the formal agenda is wide adoption and inclusion, then reaching 'hard-to-reach' youth is also important from an instrumental point of view.

There are material realities facing youth peacebuilders as well. Competition for funding, negotiation of access and limited resources shape how youth navigate their advocacy. For youth activists this negotiation of their identity between an entrepreneurial model that speaks to the political agenda of their context and a commitment to their goals is common. For example young people in Kenyan student environmental clubs developed a political identity that is hybrid: 'straddl[ing] two seemingly incongruous positions: a commitment to a neoliberal agenda of self-making and a commitment to environmental politics' (Muthoni Mwaura 2018, 66). These kinds of 'sites of straddling' should be kept in focus by critical YPS scholarship and practice. While the institutionalisation of the YPS agenda is inherently and unavoidably a process of neoliberalisation and operationalisation through entrepreneurial frameworks of self; it also holds within it the possibilities for young people to enact their commitments to community, family and collectives.

Conclusions

The claim that youth deserve to be included in peace and security is a radical idea. As the past decades of scholarship and activism have attested, the dominant assumptions of youth as delinquent or passive victims miss the ongoing, constructive and crucial work that youth have been doing around the world in their communities and beyond. The establishment of a formal international agenda on Youth, Peace and Security is a momentous accomplishment, and attests to the commitment and dedication of many people – youth and adult. However, institutionalising the inclusion of historically marginal(ised) groups, such as youth, carries risks. The process of 'bringing in' youth to institutional processes and systems can function to depoliticise their agency, limit the scope of their inclusion and exclude those who are not deemed the 'good youth'. To return to Cécile Mazzacurati's observation, discussed in the introduction to this chapter, that the YPS agenda is 'not a nice conversation about how young people need our help' is a crucial reminder of the necessity and urgency of ensuring the 'political edge' is not lost.

There is also a risk, if the YPS agenda becomes the primary prism through which youth peace work is viewed and engaged, that we lose sight of spaces that are outside the structures, funding, focus and evaluation of the formal agenda. This includes youth who don't 'fit' the idea of the 'good youth' who are included and can participate, and also youth who as Gizem Kilinç noted 'are creating their alternative spaces because they don't trust their authorities or the actors that are supposed to be protecting them'.

Engagement and participation by youth can sometimes become framed as 'a dichotomous framework of engagement versus disengagement pushes young people who refuse the burden of reconstituting current political institutions ... into conceptual boxes marked "expressive", "apolitical", "antipolitical", "disengaged"' (Bowman 2019, 301). Such frameworks miss the multiple and varied ways in which youth already participate in these spaces. The institutionalisation of a commitment to youth-inclusive peace and security practices offers many opportunities, but it also risks discursively narrowing the space of participation, and limiting which youth can participate and the manner of their participation. Scholars and practitioners working with youth on peacebuilding have offered a radical vision of youth participation and inclusion, as co-constitutors of knowledge, as equal partners, and as deserving of meaningful engagement. There are opportunities to provoke the agenda to be more representative of this more radical vision. As the YPS agenda continues to evolve as it heads towards its first decade of existence, advocates, allies and academics should, in the words of the UNSC, remain actively seized of the matter.

Notes

1 These efforts were co-ordinated and highly effective. In 2012 the Inter-Agency Working Group on Youth and Peacebuilding (Working Group) was established under the auspices of the UN's Inter-Agency Network on Youth and Development (IANYD) (created in 2010 to co-ordinate efforts across the UN's organs and bodies). From 2012 the Working Group expanded its efforts to position itself beyond the UN as a global focal point for strengthening the role of youth in peacebuilding. Since 2018 the Working Group has renamed itself as the Global Coalition on Youth, Peace and Security. The Working Group or Global Coalition has been co-chaired by a representatives from the UN, the INGO Search for Common Ground and, since 2013, the youth-led peacebuilders' network United Network of Youth Peacebuilders (UNOY). See Berents 2022 for discussion on the advocacy efforts that led to the first UNSC Resolution.
2 Ethics approvals for this research were obtained from the Queensland University of Technology Faculty of Law Review Panel on 12 February 2019 (#1900000047) and the QUT Human Research Ethics Committee on 11 June 2020 (#2000000226). Interview participants had the opportunity to review their interview transcripts, and choose whether to be identified by name or quoted anonymously.

3 Speaking to several individuals who were involved in drafting the Amman Declaration, they noted that, while they had the best intentions, and undertook significant efforts to 'socialise' the document and seek feedback, for various reasons this was not as successful as they had hoped. While this does not diminish the final result, or the achievement of the forum, it is a valuable reminder that, while processes may appear inclusive and democratic, sometimes they do not in effect fully function as intended.

4 See also the comparison of use of 'as appropriate' elsewhere in the two resolutions: 1325 para. 1 / 2250 para. 1 on 'inclusive representation at all levels'; 1325 para. 8 / 2250 para. 2 on negotiating and implementing peace agreements; and 1325 para. 7 / 2250 para. 14 on Member States increasing 'financial, technical and logistical support'. The fifth use of 'as appropriate' refers to youth participation in supporting quality education for peace (2250 para. 12) which does not appear in SCR1325.

5 In 2022 the 2nd UN Secretary General's Report on YPS was released – this was the first mandated by the biennial reporting requirement (the first report, in 2020, had been requested by the second YPS Resolution SCR2419 (2018)). However, it is relevant to note that, while the report was released and publicly accessible in March 2022, advocates were unable to get it tabled and discussed in session at the UNSC. It was 12 December 2022 when the UNSC held an Arria-formula meeting to discuss the 2nd SG's report. Arria-formula meetings enable an SC member (in this case Ghana and incoming Ecuador) to invite other members and interested parties to meet outside Council chambers. This delay and the use of the Arria-formula meeting evidences the challenges of and resistance to formalising YPS within the UNSC.

6 *The Missing Peace*, the progress report mandated by SCR2250, was presented to the UN Security Council in an Open Debate on 23 April 2018. Alongside the adult report author, Graeme Simpson, three young women briefed the Security Council: the Secretary General's Envoy on Youth, Jayathma Wickramanayake, and two young women civil-society members, Sophia Pierre-Antoine and Kessy Ekomo-Soignet. This was significant as it was the first time three young women had been the briefers for the UNSC. Since then there has been an effort to include youth briefers at all YPS-related UNSC meetings. The 2nd SG's report on YPS (2022) notes that an unspecified number, with no demographic notes, of '"Young briefers participated in thematic discussions on the climate crisis and country-specific discussions on Colombia, Haiti, Nigeria and Somalia' (para. 58), which points to efforts made to address one of the actions that the 1st SG's report on YPS (2020) calls on the UNSC: to 'expand', but perhaps not yet 'systematiz[e]' youth inclusion (para. 74.c).

7 Beyond the space of formal and high-level events, David Duriesmith notes how agendas can function to exclude 'problematic' young people; in his research he notes how young men are positioned as a potential problem and must 'fix' themselves rather than be brought into broader discourses where their insights can be included (2019). Relatedly, Lewis et al, Chapter 10, highlight the structural barriers and ways the lives of young people of colour in the US are deemed problems, and excluded.

References

Altiok, A., H. Berents, I. Grizelj and S. McEvoy-Levy, (2020). 'Youth, Peace and Security.' In *The Routledge Handbook of Peace, Security and Development*, edited by F. Hampson, A. Ozerdem, and Jonathan Kent. Abingdon: Routledge.

Basu, S., P. Kirby L.J. Shepherd. (2020). 'Women, Peace and Security: a Critical Cartography.' In *New Directions in Women, Peace and Security*, edited by S. Basu, P. Kirby and L.J. Shepherd, pp. 1–28. Bristol: Bristol University Press.

Berents, H. (2016). 'Hashtagging Girlhood: #IAmMalala, #BringBackOurGirls and Gendering Representations of Global Politics.' *International Feminist Journal of Politics* 18 (1): 513–27.

Berents, H. (2018). *Young People and Everyday Peace: Exclusion, Insecurity and Peacebuilding in Colombia*. New York: Routledge.

Berents, H. (2022). 'Power, Partnership, and Youth as Norm Entrepreneurs: Getting to UN Security Council Resolution 2250 on Youth, Peace, and Security.' *Global Studies Quarterly* 2 (3): 1–11.

Berents, H., and S. McEvoy-Levy (2015). 'Theorising Youth and Everyday Peace(building).' *Peacebuilding* 3 (2): 1–14.

Berents, H., and C. Mollica. (2022). 'Reciprocal Institutional Visibility: Youth, Peace and Security and 'Inclusive' Agendas at the United Nations.' *Cooperation and Conflict* 57 (1): 65–83.

Borer, T., J. Darby and S. McEvoy-Levy. (2007). *Peacebuilding after Peace Accords: Violence, Truth and Youth*. Notre Dame: University of Notre Dame Press.

Bowman, B. (2019). 'Imagining Future Worlds alongside Young Climate Activists: a New Framework for Research.' *Fennia* 197 (2), 295–305.

Checkoway, B. (1996). *Adults as Allies*. Omaha: Kellogg Foundation.

Del Felice, C., and A. Wisler. (2007). 'The Unexplored Power and Potential of Youth as Peace-builders.' *Journal of Peace and Development*, 11: 1–29.

Duriesmith, D. (2019) 'Engaging or Changing Men? Understandings of Masculinity and Change in the New "Men, Peace and Security" Agenda.', *Peacebuilding* 8 (4): 418–31.

Enloe, C. 2013. *Seriously! Investigating Crashes and Crises as if Women Mattered*. Sa Francisco: University of California Press.

Hartung, C., and L. Pruitt. (2017). 'Brexit, Bono and the Entrepreneurial Self: Young People's Participation as "Global Citizens". In (Eds.), *Young People, Citizenship and Political Participation: Combating Civic Deficit?*, edited by M. Chou, J.-P. Gagnon, C. Hartung and L. Pruitt, pp. 105–22). London: Rowman and Littlefield Publishers Inc.

Kwon, S.A. (2019). 'The Politics of Global Youth Participation.' *Journal of Youth Studies* 22 (7): 926–40.

Mac Ginty, R. (2011). *International Peacebuilding and Local Resistance: Hybrid Forms of Peace*. Rethinking Peace and Conflict Studies. New York and Basingstoke: Palgrave Macmillan.

McEvoy-Levy, S. (2001). *Youth as Social and Political Agents: Issues in Post-settlement Peace Building*, 21st ed. Kroc Institute Occasional Paper. Notre Dame: University of Notre Dame.

Muthoni Mwaura, G. (2018). '"Professional Students Do Not Play Politics: How Kenyan Students Professionalise Environmental Activism and Produce Neoliberal

Subjectivities.' In *Young People Re-generating Politics in Times of Crises*, edited by S. Pickard and J. Bessant, pp. 59–76. Cham: Springer.

Nadarajah, Suthaharan, and David Rampton. (2015). 'The Limits of Hybridity and the Crisis of Liberal Peace.' *Review of International Studies* 41 (1): 49–72.

Pruitt, L. (2013). *Youth Peacebuilding: Music, Gender, and Change*. Albany: SUNY Press.

Senehi, J., and S. Byrne. (2006). 'From Violence toward Peace: the Role of Storytelling for Youth Healing and Political Empowerment after Social Conflict.' In *Troublemakers or Peacemakers?: Youth and Post-accord Peace Building*, edited by S. McEvoy-Levy, pp. 235–58. Notre Dame: Notre Dame Press.

Shepherd, L.J. (2015). 'Constructing Civil Society: Gender, Power and Legitimacy in United Nations Peacebuilding Discourse.' *European Journal of International Relations* 21 (4): 887–910.

Simpson, G. (2018). *The Missing Peace: Independent Progress Study on Youth and Peace and Security*. Progress Study on Youth, Peace and Security. United Nations.

Such, E., O. Walker and R. Walker. (2005). 'Anti-War Children: Representation of Youth Protests against the Second Iraq War in the British National Press.' *Childhood* 12 (3): 301–26.

Sukarieh, M., and S. Tannock. (2018). 'The Global Securitisation of Youth.' *Third World Quarterly*, 39 (5): 854–70.

United Nations Security Council. (2015). *Resolution 2250 on Youth, Peace and Security*. United Nations. S/RES/2250 (2015).

United Nations Security Council (2018). *Open Debate: Maintenance of International Peace and Security: Youth, Peace and Security*. United Nations. S/PV.8241.

8

Youth and transitional justice: interrogating formal and informal sites of engagement

Caitlin Mollica

While youth are increasingly recognised as political actors with diverse interests, institutional representations often adhere to marginalising ideas *about* youth (Altiok et al. 2020; Schnabel and Tabyshalieva 2013). As noted in the *Missing Peace: Independent Progress Study on Youth, Peace and Security*, transitional justice processes offer youth a vehicle for active participation in pursuing accountability for human rights violations, as well as a forum to tell their stories and to address their trauma (Simpson 2018: 103). However, the political nature of these practices, which produces narrow parameters for the character of youths' participation, often creates conditions where youth are visible, but their agency and ownership are denied. Youths' significant demographic presence in post-conflict communities makes their stories essential to the realisation of successful reconciliation processes. Without their stories, the conflict narratives that Truth and Reconciliation Commissions (TRC) construct reveal incomplete 'truths', which perpetuate the maintenance of social and political environments where the aims of reconciliation, most notably community healing and interpersonal restoration, remain unfulfilled. Karen Brounéus observes that 'reconciliation is a societal process' that involves not only 'mutual acknowledgement of past suffering' but also 'the changing of destructive attitudes and behaviours into constructive relationships towards sustainable peace'. Thus it necessitates an inclusive approach, which takes seriously a broad range of voices (2008: 3).

Rebuilding inclusive interpersonal relationships through the acknowledgement of experiences and justice claims is critical to a holistic reconciliation agenda. This agenda recognises the symbiotic relationship between successful transitional justice and sustainable peace and highlights the active role that traditionally marginalised individuals such as youth could play in its realisation if political space and opportunity were ceded or transformed (Parrin et al. 2022). Meaningful fulfilment of the aims of reconciliation requires widespread recognition of youths' stories as told from their perspectives. More commonly, however, TRC processes demonstrate a tendency to homogenise or recharacterise their stories in the formal conflict records to serve a politicised agenda and to reinforce idealised perceptions about what youths' political participation *should* entail (Mollica 2024). This has broad social and political implications for the capacity of transitional communities to rebuild in ways that ensure responsive, sustainable peace. Simply put, the reconciliation stories of youth are essential for a reconciliation agenda that contributes to lasting peace following violence and instability. Yet youth and their voices are often unacknowledged, misappropriated or ignored in pursuit of a form of accountability that reflects a politicised, 'popular' and linear *truth*.

Accountability is increasingly conceived expansively to recognise the contributions of legal and non-judicial responses to human rights violations (Olsen, Payne and Reiter 2010, 25). Within this framework non-judicial mechanisms exist across an accountability spectrum; from formal mechanisms (sanctioned by the state), such as TRCs, to informal activities (derived within the community) including art projects and healing circles. The notion of acknowledgement *as* accountability is common across this spectrum and manifests through different forms of storytelling, either oral or visual. Accountability through acknowledgement occurs when individuals or groups provide or seek to elicit admissions of responsibility (either shared or whole) for past harmful acts committed against others that resulted, either directly or indirectly, in the denial of an individual's human rights (Govier 2011, 36). Acknowledgement, as such, is a powerful tool of justice particularly when it occurs in a public forum where broad debate and dialogue facilitates transparency and ownership. Underpinned by a broader community-centred, sustainable peace agenda, this approach seeks to 'diffuse knowledge' about human rights violations with the aim of ensuring they are 'never again' repeated (Lundy and McGovern 2008, 272).[1] By conceptualising *justice* beyond the stringent legal structures, accountability processes that prioritise acknowledgement create opportunities for the development of transitional justice processes capable of addressing a wide range of complex justice needs and voices. Yet within formal mechanisms, an over-reliance on political storytelling, and the pursuit of a unifying narrative, often marginalises the very voices these processes aim to include.

Informal mechanisms offer individuals an opportunity to tell their stories unfiltered, as they are not constrained by the politics of formal transitional justice mechanisms. Mechanisms such as art function to complement and challenge formal transitional justice processes and thus are sites of transformation, where resistance to the status quo is revealed and enacted. The fluid and open character of art 'reveal[s] depth, complexity, and the affective and embodied dimensions' of conflict stories, which are often excluded from procedurally driven justice practices (Cole 2014, 317).

When employed together, formal and informal practices produce a rich tapestry of voices that reflect the complexity and ambiguity of conflict experiences. As such, in transitional justice contexts, multi-mechanism approaches, which recognise the complementarity of informal and formal sites of storytelling offer opportunities to address the silences and exclusions that are (re)produced when diverse conflict experiences are whittled down to a linear interpretation.

Reconciliation expressed through art when employed in isolation acts as a site of resistance for traditionally marginalised individuals. The creativity and free expression enabled by art have the potential to 'challenge and disrupt' formal conflict narratives and to elicit reflection and exploration of whose voices are represented by transitional justice practices (Jeffery 2020). As a justice tool, art provides a mechanism for those excluded from formal processes to assert ownership over their stories. These mechanisms 'signal presence, highlight absence, and' expose 'toler[ated] silences' in ways that 'challenge and disrupt' the politicised status quo of formal mechanisms, which often limits the pursuit of holistic and inclusive justice, as they fail to recognise the diverse ways that individuals experience violence and its aftermath (Cole 2014, 317). To that end, youth are increasingly engaging with art and other non-institutional forms of transitional justice to reframe the boundaries of accountability and create spaces for their diverse voices. As this chapter demonstrates, art serves as a forum where innovative ideas about justice and reconciliation emerge through creative storytelling. It enables a meaningful connection between past and future generations through dialogue and provides a forum for the diffusion of knowledge that is underpinned by inclusivity, political agency and a commitment to transparency.

Drawing on examples of formal (TRCs) and informal approaches (art) this chapter examines the relationship between youth and storytelling within the transitional justice field. Utilising discursive examples from the South African TRC, this chapter first demonstrates that, within the formal structures the pursuit of a singular, often politicised story impacts how youth participate and the ways their voices are represented. While youth are increasingly visible throughout these practices, their stories are often silenced or reappropriated to fit the desirable politicised narrative. It then moves to examples of youth-led art projects in Timor-Leste and Kenya to reveal art's capacity to complement and contest this exclusion and mischaracterisation, and to highlight how youth's participation in informal justice spaces enhances the possibility for transformation and sustainable peace. While it is often considered contradictory, I argue that substantively engaging youth in transitional justice practices requires that both forms of narratives be produced, disseminated and valued. Youths' political participation doesn't exist and thus cannot be meaningfully understood in isolation as it is a product of constructed and realised interpersonal interactions. As such, both formal and informal narratives add value to our understanding by revealing the perceived and actualised stories of the roles youth occupy in a post-conflict context. This chapter suggests that the outcomes and benefits of each approach, generally conceptualised as distinct processes, are complementary, and thus should be recognised as mutually reinforcing mechanisms within a broader holistic process for pursuing justice and sustainable peace (Olsen et al. 2010).

Navigating frameworks for participation

The nature of youth's participation in transitional justice is continually evolving. Yet to understand the embeddedness of the challenges that youth encounter in their pursuit of substantive engagement with formal mechanisms it is useful to examine their historical origins. Beginning in 1996, the South African TRC was the first to hold special hearings on children and youth, and thus offers valuable insights. The relationship established between the South African TRC and young people was underpinned by the responsibilities and obligations outlined in the UN Convention on the Rights of the Child (UNCRC) which was ratified by South Africa in 1995 (South African TRC 1998, 251). The engagement of young people was guided by two central but at times competing ideas. First, that children's and youths' voices should be honoured by 'giving them an opportunity to express their feelings and relate their experiences'; and, second, that those under eighteen are 'entitled to special protection by government and society' (South African TRC 1998: 251). These two guidelines generated significant debate during the TRC planning process amongst government and community representatives with respect to the testimony of individuals under eighteen years old. Furthermore, they substantially influenced how the TRC process engaged with the stories of those over eighteen.

While the first obligation recognises the importance of young people's agency and their voices, the protectionist rhetoric which underpins the second obligation generates operational challenges with respect to the realisation of the first mandate. Most notably there were concerns amongst the Commissioners and civil society that 'the formal structures of the hearings might intimidate children and subject them to additional trauma' (South African TRC 1998, 251). Following a consultation process with international stakeholders and South African NGOs the decision was made to have 'NGOs and other professional people working with children testify on their behalf' and to allow testimony only from young people over the age of eighteen (South African TRC 1998, 251). This consultation presented significant challenges to the realisation of youth's agency in these contexts as it failed to elicit dialogue or engage with the testimony of individuals who may self-identify as youth or to recognise their capacity as decision-makers (Berents and Mollica 2020). While the institutional framework allowed testimony only from those technically deemed to have reached adulthood, their stories were presented as representing those of children and youth without reflecting the problematic homogenisation that this classification may produce. Thus the process enabled participatory conditions where youth were visible but without political agency, particularly on a decision that would directly impact how their stories were employed. While the final report notes that 'the Commission' made 'extensive efforts to involve children directly in the hearings and in the collection of data before the hearings' (South African TRC 1998, 251), the translation and dissemination of these stories within the formal process was reliant on third parties, rather than empowering those under 18 to speak. This decision produced an institutional and rhetorical joining of children's and youths' experiences, as the stories were universalised. Moreover, the reliance on institutionalised classifications to determine who speaks resulted in a demarcation between children, youth and adults that failed to consider how the individuals telling their stories self-identified.

The reliance on a protectionist framework for managing children's engagement with the TRC had significant implications for how youths' stories were represented. Throughout the final report they were employed to represent a collective experience, which cast children and youth as interchangeable, and through the narrow victim/perpetrator lens. The report notes for example that 'the security establishment engaged in the informal repression of children by hunting down "troublesome" youth' (South African TRC 1998, 256). In addition, as the final report notes, the Commission prioritised the testimony of youth over eighteen years old as it 'felt that those testifying as adults had ... the opportunity of applying an adult perspective to memory and the articulation of their experiences' (South African TRC 1998, 250). These claims throughout the South African TRC process laid the foundations for the common mischaracterisations *about* young people, that persist within the practice of TRCs today, namely that they do not have the capacity to speak for themselves with political agency, and that their experiences have greater value when told through the lens of adulthood (Mollica 2020). This provides significant insights regarding the maintenance of marginalising conditions within formal transitional justice practices, as it exposes a hierarchy of voices that privileges and assigns authority to adults or more specifically those considered by society to have reached adulthood.

Alongside these characterisations the report of the South African TRC classifies youth as the 'hope' and 'heroes' of South Africa's future (South African TRC 1998, 300). This dual classification, which highlights their agency and resilience, echoed emerging trends within the international discourse surrounding young people in post-conflict contexts, which emphasised their role as social actors with individual rights (Machel 1996). Yet prioritising the future in this rhetorical classification assigns meaning to youth identity that fails to adequately recognise their contributions to the present (see Eng and Hughes, Chapter 1). These classifications assign meaning and visibility to the roles of youth in transitional contexts, yet they often fail to reflect their diverse voices or acknowledge the constantly shifting character of youth's experiences, which is often informed by their role *as* youth, as well as their engagement with their cultural communities. Instead they prioritise the beliefs of international actors and the normative traditions established around children's rights during this period. In these contexts youth embody externally constructed notions of the *ideal* political actor rather than being empowered to be political actors. The South African case highlights an absence of recognition within institutions of the evolving and transitional nature of the youth identity and the impact of this on how youth experience conflict and reconciliation. Rigid adoption of institutional classifications, such as those outlined in the UNCRC, which move between childhood and adulthood without acknowledging the transition phrases within and between these spaces, produces mechanisms that are unrepresentative of the voices of this unique demographic. Representing the stories of youth requires an acknowledgement of the evolutionary nature and impact of this transitional phrase. While commonly understood as those between the ages of fifteen and twenty-four, classifications of youth and their stories should also consider those who self-identify as youth (Berents and Mollica 2020). Within the formal structures of transitional justice, inconsistencies in distinguishing between youth, adolescents and children creates challenges for the operationalisation of an inclusive agenda (Fisher 2013). Constructed definitions of who constitutes youth vary widely between institutions, and often intersect or are subsumed by notions of 'the child'. This has broader implications for the reconciliation goals of transitional states, as the failure to include the heterogeneous and fluid voices of youth challenges the inclusiveness, which transitional justice strives for to facilitate sustainable peace.

The South African TRC reveals a tension between the ways in which international actors, local political representatives and young people (both children and youth) construct representations of children and youth in formal reconciliation processes. The behaviour of the state highlights the resilience of the norms associated with the moral responsibility to protect, which are derived from international human rights instruments, such as the UNCRC. This convention facilitated the creation of a universal understanding of 'the child' which prioritised 'welfare over their autonomy' (Huynh 2014: 42). The emphasis on welfare informs perceptions of young people that are underpinned by a narrow protectionist mandate, which detracts from demonstrations of agency and ownership. While the institutionalised, formal narrative of the final report privileged this homogenising, protectionist framework, the testimony (direct voices of youth) revealed patterns of behaviour that reflect differentiated experiences. Direct participation through first-hand testimony highlighted claims of agency, political engagement and community, thus challenging the Commission's focus on their vulnerability and primary status as victims (South African TRC 1998, 30). As a member of a local youth organisation told the hearings on their experiences as victims and witnesses of Apartheid, 'as young Afrikaners, we are proud of the role that we play in this community' (South African TRC 1998: 227). As such the South African case reveals that, in transitional justice contexts, international organisations and local governments often grapple with displays of agency and the reconciliation stories of youth, particularly when they do not fit the institutionalised notions of young people embedded in the CRC.

Conceptual implications for formal transitional justice mechanisms

Youth are critical actors for the future prosperity and peace of post-conflict communities. As such their substantive inclusion in transitional justice is imperative, as it acknowledges their unique conflict experiences, while also 'enabling their full participation' and contributions to broader efforts for 'improving [access] to justice, accountability and reconciliation' (Parmer et al. 2010). UN Resolution 2250 on Youth, Peace and Security, codified for the first time youth's importance, noting that they are critical stakeholders to the 'fourth dimension of justice', namely the design and implementation of transitional justice mechanisms (Simpson 2018). Youth's capacity and their contributions are also evident in a growing body of scholarly work which centres the relationship between youth and transitional justice mechanisms (Mollica 2020; Ensor 2014; Karabegovic 2018; Martuscelli, Chapter 4). This empirical scholarship notes the diversity and complexity of youths' experiences and concludes that when youth are empowered to substantively participate in transitional justice they are 'able to find inspiration from past experience' which leads them to 'contribute to the community' and to take ownership over the future (Betancourt and Ettien 2010).

Despite this, in transitional justice contexts youths' lived experiences continue to be represented through the narrow political discourse of influential actors, including local governments and the international community (Mollica 2017). These political discourses, which prioritise the stories of victimhood, deviance, marginalisation and exclusions, perpetuate a static approach to the implementation of transitional justice mechanisms. In doing so they prioritise the restoration of traditional ideas about belonging, citizenship and accountability to the state. The origins of this can be traced back to the South African TRC, which established narrow participatory precedents, which continue to inform the mandates and structures of TRCs today, most notably the Commissions of Sierra Leone and the Solomon Islands (Mollica 2017). As argued throughout this chapter, the development of a more holistic narrative of youths' experience requires recognition of how their stories are communicated through formal and informal sites of knowledge. This will ensure that youth are not only seen, they are also heard and taken seriously as political actors (Bolten, Chapter 5).

Acknowledging the capacity of youth to contribute as political actors remains a critical challenge for practitioners of transitional justice. While the scholarly discourse on young people is slowly shifting to reflect agency, voice and diversity, institutional reconciliation narratives about youth's experiences remain largely static, narrow and one-dimensional. The over-reliance on linear narratives, which reflect a political compromise, rather than the often uncomfortable and messy realities of the conflict, restrict youth's role within these mechanisms (Jeffery and Mollica 2017). As a result, representations of youth as 'social shifters' or as 'an entry point for unravelling the ways in which processes of change invoke people's agency' remain largely conceptual (Özerdem and Podder 2015: 5).

The challenges associated with acknowledging youth and their contributions are evident in the final report of the South African TRC. Within the formal TRC process youth's stories were often mobilised to represent the politics of the transitional community, rather than reflecting their capacity as political actors. Youth are perceived as assets, employed to project unity, to give a face to the harm or to highlight the willingness of a country to look toward the future (McEvoy-Levy 2011). Despite their best intentions, TRCs which pursue the active participation of youth continue to produce reconciliation narratives *about* their experiences that are unhelpful, inaccurate and counter-intuitive to the aims of healing and restoration. While formal processes such as TRCs continue to evolve in ways that close the gap between discursive representation and actual political engagement, informal transitional practices offer an important and emerging avenue for youth's substantive participation that was underutilised during the South African Transitional Justice process.

Youth as arbiters of accountability in informal spaces

When youth engage in transitional justice their contributions represent a nuance and sophistication not often attributed to young people in these contexts. Their participation in transitional justice using methods such as memorialisation focuses accountability at the community level, thus pursuing inclusivity. The *Missing Peace* notes that youth's engagement with transitional justice can shift the practice 'away from elite-led and externally driven processes and approaches' that often prioritise a politicised version of the scale and extent of the violence (Simpson 2018). Creating an open dialogue that extends beyond elite voices to those traditionally marginalised by formal justice produces a more holistic understanding of the violence and the harms experienced (Mollica 2017). Through engagement with informal and non-judicial forms of transitional justice, youth are empowered to take ownership of how they experience accountability. Informal approaches to justice create opportunities for youth to exercise their political will, and to talk with 'each other and their leaders about a violent and often controversial past, and to face and reflect on uncomfortable truths and realities' (McEvoy-Levy 2011, 173). This allows for a broad, visible acknowledgement of the diverse ways in which youth experience conflict and its aftermath.

The use of art for memorialisation is employed by youth in transitional justice contexts to circumvent and supplement the stories told through the formal justice mechanisms. As demonstrated above, these practices create narrow participatory boundaries, which often act as gatekeepers to accountability. This gatekeeping, which produces a linear, often politicised conflict narrative fails to reflect the nuance associated with youth's positioning in conflict and reconciliation. Youth activists, therefore, utilise art to disseminate their stories of violence in ways that democratises the reconciliation process. By utilising a highly visible medium, youth can challenge and reframe the boundaries of justice to prioritise transparency as a form of accountability (Kurze 2019, 64–5).

Broadly speaking, the use of art as activism and deliberation for accountability has received growing recognition and legitimacy within the transitional justice field (Kurze and Lamont 2019; Rush and Simic 2014; Jeffery 2020). Youth have demonstrated that they are adept at employing art to navigate complex sites of justice. In Tunisia, for example, street art was used effectively by youth activists as a way of communicating a message about past violence to both the state and the broader community (Chaffee 1993: 4). Street art was also a common feature of youth's approach to accountability and resistance in Timor-Leste, as murals were used by youth to express their displeasure regarding the continued violence and lack of accountability in the years following independence (Arthur 2015; Ordzhonikidze 2006). These examples suggest that, in the transitional justice context, youth's voices are visible through informal mechanisms, revealing new spaces for accountability. Youth are utilising the public space and graffiti to negotiate and reframe the parameters of accountability for past human-rights abuses, particularly those political in nature.

Youth occupy a unique space in transitional justice due to the evolving nature of their place within a community. While in formal processes this status is problematised as a challenge for youth to overcome, within informal justice sites it offers opportunities for engagement (Özerdem and Podder 2015, 4). It ensures that they are perfectly positioned to translate past historical violence into substantive responses, as well as opportunities for relationship-building through participation. This contribution is highlighted in *The Missing Peace*, which acknowledges that 'young people's' contributions to the design and implementation of transitional justice practices can 'transform the very shape and orientation of these instruments from dealing with the past to shaping the future' (Simpson 2018). Youth are uniquely positioned to be key strategic stakeholders in the implementation of a forward-looking, holistic approach to justice that prioritises the restoration of interpersonal relationships in its pursuit of sustainable peace.

Holistic approaches recognise that accountability following violence requires political buy-in and ownership from a wide range of community stakeholders. Ramírez-Barat argues that the success of transitional justice mechanisms is determined by 'their impact not only on the individuals they affect directly, but also on the broader societies in which they operate' (2011, 3). The substantive participation of youth, therefore, is a central consideration for ensuring successful transitional justice outcomes. Youth are key strategic actors for this approach to transitional justice as they are 'less constrained by tradition and the weight of the past', and thus can look past and let go of the social norms and political structures that produced the conflict conditions (Ensor 2014: 241). Art, which promotes a form of memorialisation by initiating dialogue, and evoking empathy, provides an 'alternative way of delivering the message of international criminal law' to individuals traditionally excluded from the conversation (Akenova cited in Jeffery 2020, 341).

Increasingly art and the spaces where art is created have been employed by youth to demonstrate their political will. In their doing so, art has become an effective mode of communication for ensuring that future generations learn from the past, while looking to their futures. This is evident in Timor-Leste, where the Arte Moris (Living Art) centre was established in 2003 to help young people connect with their country's history of violence (Arthur 2015; Ordzhonikidze 2006). The aim of Arte Moris was to establish a place where young people could go and 'use art as a building block in the psychological and social reconstructions of a country devastated by violence' (Ying Hooi 2020). This connection to the future is essential for ensuring that youth meaningfully engage with the transitional justice process. In these contexts art acts as a mechanism for 'outreach' as not only does it 'translate and communicate' core ideas, it also serves as a forum for 'dialogue and consultation' between generations (Jeffery 2020). Intergenerational dialogue that is consultative and inclusive can encourage political buy-in and attachment to the stories of the past, which ensures that meaningful lessons are learnt. The link between the past and the future is a critical imperative, as youth themselves have acknowledged that in transitional contexts they are often 'lost', and they cannot 'think of the long-term perspectives as [they] are not sure about [their] own futures' (Simpson 2018). An emphasis on the future, and youth's place within that future, should thus be a key strategic priority when operationalising transitional justice mechanisms as it will empower youth to take ownership over their futures.

Where youth are concerned, memorialisation through art has also become a space for collective healing, and the restoration of positive interpersonal relationships. Since 2003 multiple art centres have emerged throughout Timor-Leste. These have become important sites of visibility for youth, as they provide youth with opportunities to engage in a dialogue about how the past will inform their future. As Ying Hooi explains, youth 'will never stop' producing art about the violence, they 'will keep doing what [they] do [and] hopefully [they] can influence more of our people especially young brothers and sisters to also appreciate arts for the future of Timor Leste' (2017). The art scene in Timor-Leste, as such, provided an entry point into conversations about the past for youth that they might otherwise be excluded from. Furthermore, the artistic spaces have become forums for youth to publicly contribute to a conversation about how the past impacts the future identity of post-conflict nations.

This dynamic is also evident in the Kenyan youth-led initiative Picha Mtaani, which uses street art to empower youth to participate in national reconciliation efforts. Their stated mission is to bring 'rural and urban youth' and the broader community together to 'forgive, make peace, heal and move forward', by creating opportunities for reflection on how the past can impact the future. This transitional justice initiative had a positive impact on the success of transitional justice in Kenya and has facilitated widespread engagement amongst Kenyan youth as by the end of 2010 the project had mobilised twenty thousand young people to take part in the nation's first peace brigades (Chuma and Ojielo 2012, 33).

When youth are empowered to heal and engage in accountability dialogues through informal justice mechanisms, their participation has a

positive impact on community reconciliation. In addition, youth's participation in transitional justice through art has demonstrated the importance
of prioritising accountability mechanisms that are accessible to diverse
and far-reaching communities. Through art youth have not only shifted
the discourse on deliberation and negotiation within transitional justice
contexts, but they have also highlighted the importance of approaches to
memorialisation that acknowledge the past, whilst connecting it to the
future.

Conclusion

Institutional engagement via TRCs with youths' voices, and most importantly their interpretations of their stories, has the potential to provide a
form of public acknowledgement, which encourages local youth *buy-in*
and ownership of conflict narratives. This buy-in by youth is essential as
it lends legitimacy to the politicised storytelling process amongst the individuals ultimately responsible for carrying forward its legacy for future
generations (Ladisch 2018). Maintaining the legacy of these stories ensures
that the lessons embedded are imbued with significance and meaning to
empower subsequent communities to (re)build interpersonal relationships
that maintain peace, through the fulfilment of the *Never Again* proposition that has come to define the transitional justice field. However, the
generation-crossing potential of TRCs, and their capacity to contribute to a
legacy of building positive interpersonal relationships for sustainable peace,
is rarely borne out. As demonstrated in this chapter and elsewhere (Mollica
2024), current institutional processes silence youths' distinctive voices and
mediate the boundaries of their participation, to maintain the politicised
status quo regardless of the broader implications for the realisation of the
reconciliation agenda and thus sustainable peace. To overcome these challenges and to complement the stories *about* youth reproduced by formal
mechanisms, youth have turned increasingly to informal mechanisms, such
as art.

Informal mechanisms such as art are increasingly employed by youth
to reclaim the meaning of their stories and conflict experiences. As the
examples in this chapter demonstrate, expressions of youths' reconciliatory
voice through art challenge the established norms of storytelling associated
with formal mechanisms such as TRCs. By supplementing, and at times
contesting, the stories that TRCs construct, art offers opportunities for
youth to exert ownership and agency over their participation, both during
conflict and during efforts to build and maintain peace through the restoration of interpersonal relationships. Assertive participation through art in

the reconciliation dialogues occurring throughout transitional communities also expands the participatory nexus, empowering individuals to share expressions of trauma when words are insufficient. Art, therefore, subverts the traditional modes of verbal participation, which currently dominate TRC processes. In doing so, it creates more inclusive parameters for a wide range of stakeholders to engage in reconciliation through acknowledgement. The inclusive potential of art as a mechanism for justice and sustainable peace in these contexts is reflected in the increased recognition of art as a central, expected and complementary tool in transitional justice (Labor 2018; Jeffery 2020). Art and informal mechanisms more broadly facilitate increased visibility of the nuance and complexity often associated with youth's relationship to past human rights violations. As such, they enable a more responsive reconciliation dialogue, where youths' ownership of the constructed narrative is legitimised and enacted through retelling and public visibility.

Young people's stories represent a site of tension for political science and transitional justice discourses. On the one hand, their participation through informal mechanisms challenges the political hierarchies and agendas embedded in the stories that formal mechanisms construct. By amplifying youth's voices informal mechanisms reveal the complex interplay between agency and vulnerability, trauma and resilience. These alternative discourses are constructed and enacted in ways that contest and complement the linear simplicity of narratives, which emphasise their role as solely victims or perpetrators. On the other hand, youth develop identities and pursue belonging within transitional communities by engaging with the 'social, cultural, and historical traumas' (Hamber 2009) and associated webs of meaning that find form through institutionalised dialogue. Perceptions of how youth participate, which are mediated through political agendas, while problematic and marginalising, nevertheless offer important insights into the character of youth's interactions within these communities. While formal mechanisms continue to grapple with how to engage meaningfully with youth's distinct voices, informal mechanisms produce important knowledge for the facilitation of more responsive and inclusive reconciliation discourses.

Creating positive pathways to more inclusive justice that can facilitate sustainable peace, therefore, necessitates the implementation of transitional justice processes where stories that are constructed across formal and informal mechanisms exist together rather than in silos. Ultimately, pursuing sustainable peace through transitional justice requires a multifaceted approach to accountability, which empowers widespread, substantive participation from diverse voices including youth. When reconciliation processes are open and inclusive, they are better able to contribute to sustainable peace, due in part to their capacity to elicit buy-in from youth who are often responsible for keeping the legacy of reconciliation discourses alive for future generations.

Note

1 Across Latin America in the 1990s storytelling served as a key mechanism for 'victims of state violence to create a shared story about violent events that had previously been silenced' (Lundy and McGovern 2008). Advocates of 'truth-telling' suggest that by revealing and acknowledging violence, and the circumstances in which violence manifests, it is possible to prevent it. In Guatemala this was reflected in the title of the report by the Recovery of Historical Memory Project (REHMI), *Guatemala Never Again! The Official Report of the Human Rights Office, Archdiocese of Guatemala* (1999).

References

Altiok, Ali, Helen Berents, Irena Grizelj and Siobhán McEvoy-Levy. 2020. 'Youth, Peace and Security.' In *The Routledge Handbook of Peace, Security and Development*, edited by Fen Hampson, Alpaslan Özerdem and Jonathan Kent, pp. 433–47. Abingdon: Routledge.

Archdiocese of Guatemala 1999 – Catholic Church. Archdiocese of Guatemala. Oficina de Derechos Humanos. 1999. Translated by Siebentritt, Gretta Tovar. *Guatemala: Never Again! The Official Report of the Human Rights Office of the Archdiocese of Guatemala*. Guatemala: Latin America Bureau.

Arthur, Catherine Elizabeth. 2015. 'Writing National Identity on the Wall: The Geração Foun, Street Art and Language Choices in Timor-Leste.' *Cadernos de Arte e Antropologia* 4 (1). https://journals.openedition.org/cadernosaa/842.

Berents, Helen, and Caitlin Mollica. 2020. 'Youth and Peacebuilding.' In *The Palgrave Encyclopedia of Peace and Conflict Studies*, edited by Gëzim Visoka and Oliver P. Richmond. Cham: Palgrave. https://doi.org/10.1007/978-3-030-11795-5_95-1.

Betancourt, T.S., and Ettien, A. 2010. *Transitional Justice and Youth Formerly Associated with Armed Forces and Armed Groups: Acceptance, Marginalization and Psychosocial Adjustment* (No. 2010-17). UNICEF Innocenti Research Paper. UNICEF.

Brounéus, Karen. 2008. *Reconciliation: Theory and Practice for Development Cooperation*. Uppsala: Uppsala University.

Chaffee, Lyman G. 1993. *Political Protest and Street Art: Popular Tools for Democratization in Hispanic Countries*. Westport: Greenwood Press.

Chuma, Aeneas, and Ozonnia Ojielo. 2012. 'Building a Standing National Capacity for Conflict Prevention and Resolution in Kenya.' *Journal of Peacebuilding & Development* 7 (3): 25–39.

Cole, Catherine M. 2014. 'At the Convergence of Transitional Justice and Art.' *International Journal of Transitional Justice* 8: 314–22.

Ensor, Marisa O. 2014. 'Youth Culture, Refugee (Re) Integration, and Diasporic Identities in South Sudan.' *Postcolonial Text* 8 (3 & 4): 1–19.

Fisher, Kirsten. 2013. *Transitional Justice for Child Soldiers: Accountability and Social Reconstruction in Post-conflict Contexts*. London: Palgrave Springer UK.

Govier, Trudy. 2011. *Forgiveness and Revenge* (2nd dition). New York: Routledge.

Hamber, Brandon. 2009. *Transforming Societies after Political Violence: Truth, Reconciliation, and Mental Health*. London: Springer.

Huynh, Kim. 2015. 'Children and Agency: Caretakers, Free-rangers, and Everyday Life.' In *Children and Global Conflict*, edited by Kim Huynh, Bina D'Costa and Katrina Lee-Koo, pp. 35–64. Cambridge: Cambridge University Press.

Jeffery, Renee. 2020. 'The Role of the Arts in Cambodia's Transitional Justice Process.' *International Journal of Politics, Culture and Society*, 34: 335–58.

Jeffery, Renee, and Caitlin Mollica. 2017. 'The Unfinished Business of the Solomon Islands TRC: Closing the Implementation Gap.' *The Pacific Review* 30 (4): 531–48.

Karabegović, Dženeta. 2018. 'Aiming for Transitional Justice? Diaspora Mobilization for Youth and Education in Bosnia and Herzegovina.' *Journal of Ethnic and Migration Studies* 44 (8): 1374–89.

Kurze, Arnaud. 2019. 'Youth Activism, Art, and Transitional Justice: Emerging Spaces of Memory after the Jasmine Revolution.' In *New Critical Spaces in Transitional Justice: Gender, Art, and Memory*, edited by Arnaud Kurze and Christopher K. Lamont, pp. 63–89. Bloomington: Indiana University Press.

Kurze, Arnaud, and Christopher K. Lamont (editors). 2019. *New Critical Spaces in Transitional Justice: Gender, Art, and Memory*. Bloomington: Indiana University Press.

Labor, Jonalou S. 2018. 'Role of Art Education in Peace Building Efforts among Out-of-School Youth Affected by Armed Conflict in Zamboanga City, Philippines.' *Journal of International Development* 30 (7): 1186–202.

Ladisch, Virginie. 2018. *A Catalyst for Change: Engaging Youth in Transitional Justice*. New York: International Centre for Transitional Justice.

Lundy, Patricia, and Mark McGovern. 2008. 'Whose Justice? Rethinking Transitional Justice from the Bottom up.' *Journal of Law and Society* 35 (2): 265–92.

Machel, Graça. 1996. *Impact of Armed Conflict on Children*. U.N. Doc. A/51/306, 26 August 1996. https://undocs.org/A/51/306.

McEvoy-Levy, Siobhán. 2011. 'Children, Youth and Peacebuilding.' In *Critical Issue in Peace and Conflict Studies: Theory, Practice and Pedagogy*, edited by Thomas Matyok, Jessica Senehi and Sean Byrne, pp. 159–76. Lanham, MD: Lexington Books.

Mollica, Caitlin. 2017. 'The Diversity of Identity: Youth Participation at the Solomon Islands Truth and Reconciliation Commission.' *Australian Journal of International Affairs* 71 (4): 371–.88

Mollica, Caitlin. 2020. 'Tales of Progress: Creating Inclusive Reconciliation Narratives Post-conflict.' In *Multi-Level Reconciliation and Peacebuilding: Stakeholder Perspectives*, edited by Kevin P. Clements and SungYong Lee, pp. 152–70. New York: Routledge.

Mollica, Caitlin. 2024. *Agency and Ownership in Reconciliation: Young People and the Practice of Transitional Justice*. New York: SUNY Press.

Olsen, Tricia D., Leigh A. Payne, and Andrew G. Reiter. 2010. 'The Justice Balance: When Transitional Justice Improves Human Rights and Democracy.' *Human Rights Quarterly* 32 4: 980–1007.

Ordzhonikidze, Sergei. 2006. *Speech of the Director General of the United Nations Office at Geneva, at the Opening of the Exhibition Entitled 'Art from Timor Leste'*, 15 March. https://www.ungeneva.org/en/news-media/press-con ference/2006/03/speech-director-general-unog-opening-exhibition-entitled-art. Accessed 6 December 2023.

Özerdem, Alpaslan, and Sukyana Podder. 2015. *Youth in Conflict and Peacebuilding: Mobilization, Reintegration and Reconciliation.* Basingstoke: Springer.

Parmar, Sharanjeet, Mindy Jane Roseman, Saudamini Siegrist and Theo Sowa, eds. 2010. *Children and Transitional Justice: Truth-telling, Accountability and Reconciliation.* Cambridge, MA: Human Rights Program, Harvard Law School.

Parrin, Anjli, Graeme Simpson, Ali Altiok and Njoki Wamai. (2022). 'Youth and Transitional Justice.' *International Journal of Transitional Justice* 16 (1): 1–18.

Ramírez-Barat, Clara. 2011. *Making an Impact: Guidelines on Designing and Implementing Outreach Programs for Transitional Justice.* New York: International Centre for Transitional Justice. https://idl-bnc-idrc.dspacedirect. org/server/api/core/bitstreams/f1b61ae7-e3cb-45dd-90b7-4d0a34a3ddb6/ content.

Rush, Peter, and Olivera Simić. 2014. *The Arts of Transitional Justice.* New York: Editorial Springer.

Schnabel, Albrecht, and Anara Tabyshalieva (eds) 2013. *Escaping Victimhood: Children, Youth and Post-conflict Peacebuilding.* New York: United Nations University Press.

Simpson, Graeme. 2018. *The Missing Peace: Independent Progress Study on Youth, Peace, and Security.* New York: UN.

South African TRC. 1998. *Truth and Reconciliation Commission of South Africa Report.* 7 vols. Truth and Reconciliation Commission. https://www.justice.gov. za/trc/report/.

Ying Hooi, Khoo. 2017. 'How Arts Heal and Galvanize the Youth of Timor Leste.' *The Conversation*, 12 June. https://theconversation.com/how-arts-heal-and-gal vanise-the-youth-of-timor-leste-73927. Accessed 6 December 2023.

Part III

Sustainable peace: youth leading the way

Introduction to Part III

Helen Berents, Catherine E. Bolten and Siobhán McEvoy-Levy

In March 2019 one hundred and fifty youth climate activists, including Greta Thunberg, authored an open letter in *The Guardian* calling for climate change to be recognised as a global crisis. They demanded that decision-makers should 'take responsibility and solve this crisis', stating: 'You have failed us in the past. If you continue failing us in the future, we, the young people, will make change happen by ourselves' (Global Co-ordination Group 2019). Young climate activists have been leading and advocating for change outside of formal structures manifested as continuous youth-led protests and globally networked activism. While the global mobilisations of the Fridays for Future and School Strike for Climate movements are highly visible and much reported, young people's action for a solution to the insecurity and violence posed by the climate crisis occurs in context-specific ways around the world. Young leaders work in their communities and local contexts to effect change. Some of these have received media attention, including the indigenous activist in Brazil Artemisa Xakriabá; Mari Copeny who campaigned against the water crisis in Flint, Michigan, in the US; Autumn Peltier, who at thirteen was named the Chief Water Protector for the Anishinabek Nation; and Ridhima Pandy, who sued the Indian government over inaction on climate change; but many more work to make change where they live despite lack of attention and support.

The work of global youth climate activists is a highly visible case of the ways in which youth organise and advocate, demonstrating the potential of youth-led activism and engagement. From globally organised protests to local, relational community peacebuilding, and across myriad issues, youth are often leading efforts for peace and security. Complex terrains navigated by youth, the marginal(ised) contexts where youth work and the constantly negotiated relations of uneven power, positionality and identity characterise much peace work undertaken by young people. The chapters in this section reveal the myriad ways in which young people build peace and sustainable worlds in their communities every day, outside of the formal institutions of power, and often addressing concerns that are either forgotten or dismissed as marginal to 'peace' by those in power. It is young people especially who see arts, the environment and everyday activities such as a cup of tea as building blocks to a peaceful, sustainable future, and they pursue these in creative ways, literally generating peace from the ground up.

While institutions and processes may be designed to bring young people in to 'participate', as contributions to the previous section examined in varying contexts, the chapters in this section reveal how young people engage in peacebuilding, advocacy and engagement through other spaces. Despite attention on young people's activities for peace being relatively recent, youth have never been absent from conflict prevention, peacebuilding and conflict resolution efforts. Evidence shows how young people's peacebuilding work is ever-present in conflict and post-conflict contexts (Borer et al. 2006; Berents 2018; Berents and McEvoy-Levy 2015; McEvoy-Levy 2006; Pruitt 2015; Özerderm and Podder 2015; Schwartz 2010; Schnabel and Tabyshalieva 2013; Simpson 2018). Youth leadership in peacebuilding reframes what peace means and where it happens, it draws attention to a broader range of ways of doing peace.

The invisibility of much of this work – whether because it occurs at levels below or outside of institutional processes, or whether as a consequence of assumptions about young people's competencies or dispositions – has implications for both scholarly and policy work. If youth are not seen, not considered and their activities not recognised as contributory, then their exclusion can be framed as inevitable. As the *Missing Peace* report highlights, 'we often fail to ask why the majority of young people remain peaceful … This limits the visibility and understanding of youth perceptions of peace and security and, in turn, significantly curbs financial, technical and political support for their work' (Simpson 2018, 35). Support for youth leadership in peacebuilding, beyond statements and speeches, is required to address the ways in which their exclusion has become naturalised through persistent invisibility.

However, young peace leaders navigate highly uneven power relations, and position their advocacy and identities in intersectional and complex ways. They often have to navigate assumptions and stereotypes held by adults about the legitimacy of their leadership or the nature of their participation (UNOY and SFCG 2017; Simpson 2018; Lee-Koo and Pruitt 2020). These encounters with institutional and structural processes have consequences for young people's ability to ensure support for their work, safety for their activities and legitimacy of their contributions to their communities and beyond. Gendered assumptions about competency or the appropriateness of participation pose particular challenges (Pruitt 2015; Lee-Koo and Pruitt 2020) and the persistence of binary assumptions of young women's vulnerability and young men's predisposition to violence frustrate efforts

(Bolten 2012; Simpson 2018; Altiok 2021). Their peacebuilding work is often grounded in relational frames that emphasise intersectionality as a foundational frame of the work they do (Lederach 2020; Our Generation for Inclusive Peace 2020).

Despite these obstacles, or perhaps at times because of them, young people's leadership, their contributions to peacebuilding, conflict resolution and ensuring safety for their communities, is a 'world-building' project (Nordstrom 1998; see Bowman 2019 for use of this idea in relation to climate action specifically; de Leon and Bighorn, Chapter 14; de Visser, Chapter 13). In the face of violence, devastation, insecurity and risk, young people are responsive, creative and dedicated. The idea of world-building seeks to create liveable lives, 'unmaking' violence (Nordstrom 1998), responding to trauma and imagining peace for future generations.

Together these different aspects of young people's advocacy and activism raise important questions about the nature of leadership: how it is recognised by institutions, and how young people's leadership conforms to or exceeds these expectations. It also prompts reflection on the intergenerational tensions and opportunities that are opened when young people's leadership is taken seriously. Chapters in this section show the ways in which relational understandings of identity and place inextricably underpin and inform youth peacebuilders' work. They also reveal the ways in which young people navigate, resist and work beyond structures that reinforce harmful stereotypes that exclude youth and delegitimise their peace leadership. Young people seek diverse ways of leading that open space for possibilities and promises in collectively building sustainable peace. That their concerns, organising tactics and perspectives on the world around them are simply *different* from those of their elders should be recognised as a strength of the work that they do, rather than as a flaw. If the young will inherit this earth, their contributions to building a world in their image of the good must be embraced.

Angela J. Lederach's chapter attends to the reciprocal, multi-species and intergenerational relations of care undertaken by campesino youth in Colombia. Her chapter draws on twenty-two months of ethnographic research with communities in the conflict-affected territory of Montes de María to explore the efforts undertaken to reweave the social and ecological fabrics of their communities after conflict. The continued stigmatisation and political, social and ecological insecurity facing campesino communities in the region is recognised by youth. The shared, underlying sense of urgency to create liveable conditions for youth in the campo (countryside) animates the collective struggle to 'build peace from and for the territory' across generations in Montes de María. Lederach's careful attention to the ways in which youth establish roots (*arraigarse*) and establish young people as 'generational successors' (*relevo generacional*), highlights the ways in which youth peacebuilding in situations of ongoing insecurity and dispossession is engaged and understood as situated, relational and reciprocal.

The chapter by Jaimarsin Lewis, Siobhán McEvoy-Levy, Karayjus Perry, Trinity Perry and Julio Trujillo is a collaboration between three out-of-school Black and biracial teenagers, a Latino university undergraduate student and a white college professor in the US Midwest. It highlights the challenges facing youth who are out of school but not in employment or further education, and the racialised injustices of exclusion in the US. Using Participant Action Research (PAR), sustained relationship building and other paid opportunities, the authors show that marginalised young people face a world of pressures that complicate the transition from school to college and constrain their agency. Yet, as they are close witnesses to the causes and consequences of a lack of peace, marginalised youth are also often urgently involved in peace(building) on their own terms. By focusing on the lives of BIPOC youth in the United States, this chapter asks readers to reflect critically on what 'peacebuilding' is, who it is for and how more inclusive and emancipatory approaches to peace can be imagined and enacted.

In their chapter Katrina Lee-Koo and Lesley Pruitt demonstrate that, despite persistent marginalisation, young women do lead for peace. Drawing on interviews with young women leaders in Asia and the Pacific, they explore the challenges young women face and their leadership in peacebuilding efforts. Young women's leadership is pivotal to sustainable peacebuilding, including through enhancing gender equality and women's human rights and ensuring young people's contributions. Young women adopt creative ways to support each other and to build peace: ways that Lee-Koo and Pruitt argue respond to, resist and challenge their exclusion from peacebuilding. Gendered forms of exclusion can be addressed, and young women's leadership can be better recognised and supported to ensure sustainable peace in their broader communities.

Emmily Koiti, Bush Buse Laki and Chara Nyaura, three young peacebuilders from South Sudan, discuss the creation of their organisation Sixty-Four Children from One Mother (64–1M) as well as a platform they have created for amputees to tell their stories and raise awareness of their rights, and a process called 'Taking Tea Together'. These efforts demonstrate the importance of relationship-building as a key peacebuilding activity and underscore how peacebuilding processes can rest on local innovation, direction and ownership with flexible international accompaniment. The chapter exemplifies the challenges of navigating power relations, building legitimacy for youth-led peacebuilding and strengthening local capacity for youth. Youth leadership for peace, this chapter argues, can be best supported by all actors listening and acting together.

Writing on behalf of Global Unites, the organisation he first founded in Sri Lanka, Prashan de Visser reflects in his chapter on the importance of recognising the unique insights and contributions of youth movements, the obstacles they face in realising their vision and the reasons that youth movements might fail. Global Unites draws together existing organic youth peacebuilding movements from Afghanistan to Zimbabwe for training, reflection and mutual aid, teaching member organisations to use their collective strength to address the particular challenges of youth extremism through peaceful change-making. It offers a blueprint for generational change, as the 'youth' of today are the parents of tomorrow's youth.

Justin de Leon and Jordan Bighorn push peace studies scholars and practitioners to confront the absence of attention on indigenous approaches to peace and mediation. Native youth in North America face the challenge of imagining and creating a decolonial future amidst the realities of the settler present. Turning to Native teachings is a world-building project for the authors, for Native youth, and beyond. De Leon and Bighorn highlight the devastating reality of intersecting violences and oppression facing Native youth. Drawing from experience with Lakota traditions, they outline seven poles – point of a circle, conditions of creation, crying for a vision, ceremony of performance, travelling without moving, consummated transformation and the circle complete. These poles offer a roadmap forward for peacebuilders looking for new horizons built on Indigenous principles of reciprocity and balance, and, at the same time, a letter for Native youth, an offer of a new worldview. Together the chapters by Lewis et al. and by de Leon and Bighorn challenge the tendency to see peacebuilding as something that is done 'over there', instead drawing attention to the disproportionate impact of ongoing violence and insecurity on marginalised youth within settler-colonial states in the Global North and young people's leadership in resisting, surviving and building peace.

Together chapters in this section reveal how youth peacebuilding is grounded in identity and place, shaped by the contestation of young people's exclusion from formal spaces and the creation of alternative understandings of peace work. Young people's peacebuilding is a 'world-building' endeavour, grounded in lived experience and committed to visions of intersectional, intergenerational efforts for peace.

References

Altiok, Ali. 2021. Squeezed Agency: Youth Resistance to the Securitization of Peacebuilding.' In *Securitizing Youth: Young People's Role in the Global Peace and Security Agenda*, edited by Marisa E. Ensor. New Brunswick: Rutgers University Press.

Berents, Helen. 2018. *Young People and Everyday Peace: Exclusion, Insecurity and Peacebuilding in Colombia*. New York: Routledge.

Berents, Helen, and Siobhán McEvoy-Levy. 2015. 'Theorising Youth and Everyday Peace(building).' *Peacebuilding* 3 (2): 115–25.

Bolten, Catherine. 2012. '"We have been sensitized": Ex-combatants, Marginalization, and Youth in Post-war Sierra Leone.' *American Anthropologist* 114 (3): 494–506.

Borer, Tristan Anne, John Darby and Siobhán McEvoy-Levy. 2006. *Peacebuilding after Peace Accords: The Challenges of Violence, Truth and Youth*. Notre Dame: University of Notre Dame.

Bowman, Benjamin. 2019. 'Imagining Future Worlds alongside Young Climate Activists: a New Framework for Research.' *Fennia* 197 (2): 295–305.

Global Co-ordination Group of the Youth-led Climate Strike. 2019. 'Climate Crisis and a Betrayed Generation.' Letters, *The Guardian*, 1 March. https://www.theguardian.com/environment/2019/mar/01/youth-climate-change-strikers-open-letter-to-world-leaders. Acessed 1 December 2023.

Lederach, Angela J. 2020. 'Youth Provoking Peace: an Intersectional Approach to Territorial Peacebuilding in Colombia.' *Peacebuilding* 8 (2): 198–217.

Lee-Koo, Katrina, and Lesley Pruitt, eds. 2020. *Young Women and Leadership*. New York: Routledge.

McEvoy-Levy, Siobhán, ed. 2006. *Troublemakers or Peacemakers? Youth and Post-accord Peace Building*. Notre Dame: University of Notre Dame Press.

Our Generation for Inclusive Peace (OGIP). 2019. 'Inclusive Peace, Inclusive Futures: Exploring the Urgent Need to Further the Women, Peace and Security and the Youth, Peace and Security Agendas.' *OGIP Policy Papers*. October. https://6d688fb3-adb9–4734-accd-733d8f3078ce.filesusr.com/ugd/286f6c_50e48e22c4064cbab1cbeb27aa86b652.pdf. Accessed 1 December 2023.

Özerdem, Alpaslan, and Sukanya Podder. 2015. *Youth in Conflict and Peacebuilding: Mobilization, Reintegration and Reconciliation*. Basingstoke: Palgrave Macmillan.

Pruitt, Lesley. 2015. 'Gendering the Study of Children and Youth in Peacebuilding.' *Peacebuilding* 3 (2): 157–70.

Schnabel, Albrecht, and Anara Tabyshalieva. 2013. *Escaping Victimhood: Children, Youth and Post-conflict Peacebuilding*. New York: United Nations Press.

Schwartz, Stephanie. 2010. *Youth and Post-conflict Reconstruction: Agents of Change*. Washington, DC: United States Institute of Peace Press.

Simpson, Graeme. 2018. *The Missing Peace: Independent Progress Study on Youth and Peace and Security*. United Nations. New York: Progress Study on Youth, Peace and Security, UN.

United Network of Young Peacebuilders (UNOY) and Search for Common Ground (SFCG). 2017. *Mapping a Sector: Bridging the Evidence Gap on Youth-driven Peacebuilding: Findings of the Global Survey of Youth-led Organisations Working on Peace and Security*. The Hague: UNOY and SFCG.

9

'We lived the river through our bodies': environmental care, intergenerational relations and sustainable peacebuilding in Colombia

Angela J. Lederach

'¿Si no soy un campesino joven, quién soy yo?' (If I am not a campesino youth, who am I?), Miguel asked, pain and frustration inflecting his voice. He swayed back and forth in a hammock as we debriefed the public presentation that a well-respected campesino leader had given earlier that morning. Miguel had travelled several hours by foot, moto and bus from the rural, high region of the Alta Montaña (High Mountain) to the bustling city of Sincelejo, Colombia, in order to attend a forum on Campesino and Indigenous alternatives to 'development', hosted by the local peacebuilding organisation, Sembrandopaz. The elder campesino leader, who had been at the forefront of organising one of Colombia's largest social movements, mourned the 'loss of campesino youth' in the northern territory of Montes de María. He echoed a common sentiment shared among campesino elders, NGO workers and state bureaucrats engaged in peacebuilding across the region. Armed conflict, forced displacement and violent dispossession as well as the economic and ecological devastation wrought by the war had, indeed, driven youth from rural communities to urban cities over the last several decades. For the older generation, the 'loss' of young people represents one of the most devastating consequences of the Colombian armed conflict – one that threatens to undermine the continuation of campesino ways of living and being in the world.

Like his elder, Miguel emphasises the need for a 'relevo generacional' (generational successor) who can guarantee the future of campesino life. As one of the co-ordinators of the Jóvenes Provocadores de Paz (JOPPAZ, Youth Peace Provokers) movement in the Alta Montaña, Miguel explicitly works to 'maintain youth in the territory' in the face of economic, political, social and ecological insecurity (JOPPAZ 2016). The shared, underlying sense of urgency to create liveable conditions for youth in the campo (countryside) animates the collective struggle to 'build peace from and for the territory' across generations in Montes de María. However, as Miguel's reaction suggests, narratives that focus solely on the *absence* of campesino youth deny recognition for the agentive actions that young people have taken to resist the multiple and compounding forms of violence that threaten campesino life in the wake of war. When elder campesinos mourn the 'loss' of campesino youth, they not only erase Miguel's most salient identity as a campesino youth, they also foreclose the possibility of creating intergenerational relations of solidarity and care – necessary for the formation of a *relevo generacional*.

In this chapter I argue that the everyday labour of caretaking social and environmental relations of solidarity regenerate a sense of self and place for campesino youth living in the wake of violence and dispossession. I place Miguel's pressing question, 'who am I?' as the central starting point for ethnographic inquiry into how youth understand and build sustainable peace in Colombia. For Miguel the social processes of belonging that shape his identity as a campesino youth are deeply tied to embodied practices of place-making. I centre Miguel's critique of the harm enacted when analytic attention focuses solely on youth who have migrated to urban cities and turn my attention to the lives of young people who, against all odds, have stayed in the campo.

I contend that meaningful participation in an intergenerational peace movement generates a sense of agency, desire and pride for young people living in the wake of violence in Colombia. The JOPPAZ did not emerge as an isolated movement but instead forms the youth wing of the wider campesino movement known as the Peaceful Movement of Reconciliation and Integration of the Alta Montaña (Peaceful Process). The word *provocar* in Colombian Spanish means both to desire and 'to agitate', reflecting the interplay between affect and mobilisation. Rather than mourning youth as 'lost' to the campo, the integration of young people as socio-political actors in a wider, intergenerational movement affirms campesino youth as belonging to the territory. The mutual legitimacy that emerges from intergenerational organising validates the contributions that young people make to peace, allowing youth to establish and sustain their roots (*arraigarse*)[1] in a context of dispossession. In becoming 'generational successors' of the movement, Miguel – and the six hundred young members of JOPPAZ – engage in a 'regenerative struggle' to guarantee the future of campesino lives and livelihoods (Alfred 2005, 20).

While much of the peace studies literature focuses on transformation, this chapter draws on Indigenous theories of resurgence to argue that, in a context of dispossession and mass violence, intergenerational relationships, which allow for the continuation of cultural and ancestral claims to place, play a vital role in the ways in which youth envision and build sustainable peace (Alfred 2005; Corntassel 2012; Daigle 2018; de Leon and Bighorn, Chapter 14; Hatala et al. 2019). In the first section I draw on Miguel's life history to illustrate the multiple forms of violence and dispossession that young people in the Alta Montaña have endured – and continue to endure.

I pay particular attention to how young people understand and experience violence as more-than-human. Section two offers a thick account of a river-mapping process that the youth in JOPPAZ carried out to further illustrate the framework of relationality – across species and generations – that undergirds JOPPAZ's approach to sustainable peace. In the concluding section I argue that intergenerational movement-building works against the 'representational rhetorics' that structure and naturalise processes of dispossession in Montes de María in ways that deepen possibilities for sustainable peace (West 2016, 12).

While situated in the historical and socio-political context of a rural, northern territory in Colombia, this chapter offers broader insight into the ways in which youth who are 'securitised as threats' work to disrupt and transform the compounding violence of racism, social stigmatisation, environmental degradation and armed combat (see Lewis et al., Chapter 10). In the Alta Montaña young people are at the forefront of campesino resurgence (Alfred 2005; de Leon and Bighorn, Chapter 14). The daily work of caretaking social and ecological relations that breathe life into the campo empower youth to reclaim stigmatised bodies and territories as beautiful. Through regenerating multi-species and multigenerational relations of care that were harmed during the war, youth cultivate sustainable futures of dignified life (*vida digna*) in the campo.

'The Montaña has taken me in': violence, displacement and return

As a strategic corridor with access to major highways and the Caribbean Sea, the Alta Montaña became a base for multiple – and competing – armed factions during the war.[2] In response, the state and paramilitaries legitimised violence against campesinos through the discourse of criminality. As a result, campesino identities and territories became synonymous with armed insurgency. Direct violence, including massacres, false positives[3] and selective assassinations as well as more nefarious forms of state violence such as militarised checkpoints and arbitrary detentions, eventually led to the massive displacement of entire communities (CNMH 2017).

'In the middle of this situation, my family displaced. I was born in a popular neighbuorhood,'[4] Miguel explained as we walked through a shallow stream on the way to his palm-thatched home, nestled in the valley of the Alta Montaña. 'I grew up with a lot of gangs, a lot of drugs … I don't think any of those kids that grew up with me are alive today,' he paused as we both reflected on the violent fates that met so many of his young friends. 'Thank God my parents left with me because if not,' he lingered on the thought as his voice grew quiet, 'Well, who knows where I would be.'

Miguel's life history lays bare the uneven forms of violence levelled against campesino youth across the physical locations of rural communities and urban neighbourhoods – without collapsing the distinction between the two. 'I was 15 when my parents decided to return to the Montaña,' Miguel continued, 'This was tragic, it was difficult … When I was in the city, I was one of the ones who would say: "Look at those people from the mountains,"' he explained, reflecting on the ways he had internalised the racist tropes levelled against campesinos. Even after physically returning to the campo, Miguel struggled to find a sense of place and self. As Paige West (2019) has shown, 'representational rhetorics' that construct the campo – and campesinos – as lacking and violent create the very structures of dispossession (12). The armed conflict not only displaced Miguel and his family from their land but also dispossessed Miguel of his identity as a campesino.

Soon after Miguel graduated from high school, JOPPAZ began organising in the Alta Montaña. During JOPPAZ's first general assembly Miguel was elected as a representative of the co-ordinating committee. Although Miguel first experienced the campo as 'tragic', his involvement in community peacebuilding changed his relationship with the territory. 'The experience of visiting the communities, of talking to youth … had a big impact on me,' he reflected. 'One lives in the territory but doesn't even know it.'

For Miguel, 'knowing the territory' required more than simply residing in the campo. The process of coming to know the territory entailed embodied movement through the vast landscapes of the Alta Montaña, knowledge of the ancestral history held within the territory and socio-political formation through participation in an intergenerational peace movement. 'In these youth processes, one realises how people are living,' Miguel explained, 'And this opens one's thoughts and gives one ideals – that, *here*, this is one's journey, to help your people … that, *here*, this is the path. This is what animates me now to continue.' For Miguel the work of community peacebuilding helped him to re-establish roots in a context of dispossession. '*Here*.' – he reiterates, anchoring his life project into the landscapes of his ancestors – he has found his path, that which animates him to continue in the campesino struggle for liberation. 'Before, I wanted to leave for the city,' Miguel continued,

> I said, well, now I've finished studying, I'm going to get out of these hills … but my thoughts changed when I entered the youth process. One begins to realise that our parents' situation wasn't really the best in the city. And this raises one's consciousness … I always say that the Montaña has opened its arms and has taken me in, in a beautiful way. I didn't expect it, but thank God, the Montaña has taken me in, in a beautiful way.

There is no singular story of the armed conflict, forced displacement and return in the Alta Montaña. Some people were displaced for extended periods of time, others were displaced sporadically and periodically – returning when direct confrontations between armed groups decreased – and still others remained 'resistant', living side by side with the armed groups that operated in and around the region for decades. Despite the distinct trajectories that shaped young people's experiences of the war, youth in JOPPAZ emphasise their shared experience of being 'lost' (*perdido*) and 'uprooted' (*desarraigado*) as a result of political and environmental violence. For youth who 'resisted' displacement to urban cities, witnessing the land erode under their feet also left them 'uprooted' even as they remained in place. For youth across the Alta Montaña the armed conflict radically reconfigured the social and ecological landscapes of the territory they call home.

At the height of the armed conflict a fungus known as the *phytophthora cinnamomi* spread through the region, eventually killing over 90 per cent of the old-growth avocado forests that knit the dense ecology of the Alta Montaña together. Dramatic changes in waterways, loss of shade for subsistence farming, displacement of native species and the eradication of the primary income-generating crop altered the social, economic and ecological relationships foundational to life in the campo (Lederach 2023). While many in the Alta Montaña assert that the fungus first arrived as part of a military eradication strategy, other campesino leaders echo the state's description of the *phytophthora cinnamomi* as a 'natural disaster' (Unidad de Víctimas 2014). Despite these differences there is widespread agreement that the forced displacement of campesinos from the Alta Montaña as a result of the armed conflict prevented campesinos from caretaking the avocado forest, which enabled the devastating spread of the fungus. As a casualty of war the avocado figures centrally into youth narratives of the war. For young campesinos in the Alta Montaña violence and peace are understood and experienced as more-than-human.

'The land felt so battered that this affected the avocado trees to the extent that today there are more than seven thousand hectares of avocado that are dead,' Naún, one of the co-ordinators of JOPPAZ, explained. 'The land felt alone without its people … It is important that one lives in a way that the earth feels that they are living of it, they go hand in hand, so that while we are working the earth, we are also, at the same time, protecting her.' As Naún underscores, the violent severing of the reciprocal relations of care between campesinos and the campo disrupted the social and legal orders that previously governed collective life in the Alta Montaña (Lederach 2017). In this way the death of the avocado exemplifies West's (2019) definition of dispossession as 'a theft of sovereignty over lands and bodies' (24). In response JOPPAZ locates environmental care as vital for building sustainable peace. 'The violence that our communities have lived through requires that we fight to build peace from here,' Jocabeth Canoles, a co-ordinator of JOPPAZ, explained,

> The territory is where we live, here is where we feel good, and therefore we must accommodate the territory so that we can live in peace. The war has also been violent to the land, and we must reconcile with her.

Jocabeth, Naún and Miguel narrate and experience the land as *living*, *feeling* and *animate*. The land cries out – not figuratively, but literally – experiencing the violence alongside campesinos. In his work in Bajo Atrato, Colombia, Daniel Ruiz Serna (2017) similarly found that the armed conflict 'affected a heterogeneous set of non-human agents that are a fundamental part of the experiences that indigenous, black, and campesino communities sustain in the places they inhabit' (90). For Ruiz Serna (2023) this requires a reconfiguration of how the territory is understood and defined (11). In contrast to definitions of territory as a singular, physical location, Ruiz Serna (2017) advocates for an affective understanding of territory as 'experience bound to specific places' that generate 'feelings and meanings' (95). Multi-species analysis centres the ways in which the forced displacement of people from their land unravels the ecological webs of relationships in which human communities are entangled (de la Cadena 2015; Kirskey and Heimreich 2010; Todd 2016). A multi-species lens, therefore, affords a more accurate reflection of campesino theories of violence and peace (Lederach 2023; Lyons 2016; Ruiz Serna 2023).

In the aftermath of war and forced displacement, caretaking the social and ecological landscapes of the campo enables youth to re-establish their identities as campesinos. As Zoe Todd (2016) writes, the daily works of tending to multi-species and multigenerational relations 'resist and refract colonial attempts to erase and obliterate Indigenous legal orders' (50). In the Alta Montaña where the armed conflict dispossessed not only young people of their relationship to the land but also campesino ways of knowing the land, intergenerational knowledge transmission is vital for the ways in which youth reclaim a sense of self and place.

In contexts of colonial violence and systemic racism, where dispossession extends across multiple generations, 'land education' creates what bell hooks (2009) has called a 'culture of place', through critical, decolonial praxis (McCoy, Tuck and McKenzie 2016; Twance 2019). Land-based education derives from a framework of relationality that understands the territory 'as a system of social relations and ethical practices' (Wildcat et al. 2014, ii). The embodied movement through places that hold social, political and historical meaning facilitates youth processes of 'learning with and from' the land (Simpson 2014, 14). In the Alta Montaña intergenerational practices of placemaking and *memoria viva* (living memory) emplace youth, allowing them to deepen their relational and affective ties with the territory. By disrupting ongoing processes of dispossession, the practices of inter-generational knowledge transmission and land-based education reflect the 'regenerative struggle' at the heart of JOPPAZ's work for sustainable peace (Alfred 2005, 20).

'To know our territory is to build peace': living memory and environmental relations of care

From October to November 2016, JOPPAZ carried out a river-mapping project of the Palenquillo River – the main body of water that runs from the peaks of the Alta Montaña to the Caribbean Sea. During the planning phase the young people explicitly developed the river-mapping process as an exercise of 'living memory'. Prior to mapping the river, the youth identified community allies who would accompany them each day. The allies helped the youth identify not only native flora and fauna but also histories, memories, place names, *décimas* (traditional songs), stories and legends held within the river. The elders also noted the dramatic changes in waterways that they had witnessed over their lifetimes.

Standing knee-deep in the Palenquillo before a group of Afro-Colombian campesino elders, Miguel began the day's river-mapping exercise, 'My name is Miguel. I am from the Alta Montaña. I am a Youth Peace Provoker.' With an audio recorder in his hand, Miguel continued,

> We have been walking this river for the last fifteen days. We are seeking your support, as allies, those who live here, those who know this area ... We ask that you accompany us, that you point out different points of the river, places where there is sedimentation, erosion, where there are swimming holes ... That you tell us the histories, myths, stories ...

Miguel then turned the recorder to the community's traditional healer who had begun speaking. 'Where there is water, there is mystery,' the elder began, pausing before continuing his reflection, 'In the past, they used to say that there was something mysterious in the river, that there was a *bruja* [sorceress] who bathed here, a *mojana* [water spirit][5] ... She had a gourd [*totuma*] made of gold ... I believe that we have the very best river in Colombia.' Miguel and the two other youth nodded in agreement. Another elder stepped forward, leaning into the recorder, 'You see,' he explained further, 'for us, the *aguacateros* [avocado farmers], this arroyo has always been life.' And with that, we began our journey through the lifeways of the Palenquillo.

   Mango, banana and old-growth trees lined the banks of the river as the rays of morning light streamed through the gaps between the trees. As we walked, the elders pointed out medicinal trees and plants, told stories of the river and identified community landmarks that told the history of the campesino struggle for liberation. With the support of their elders, the youth learned about the collective land recuperations that had established campesino communities along the river. They also documented the names of large farms that elite landowners still occupied. The youth took handwritten notes and marked place names, flora and fauna into the GPS. Every ten metres the youth measured the depth of the water and wrote descriptions of the clarity and strength of the river's current.

   Walking slowly and with intentionality, we noted when the rock beds beneath our feet turned to sand and tracked the integrity of the banks of the river. At one point we glimpsed the slight rustling of the trees in the canopy above: a troop of howler monkeys moved quickly, quietly, high above us. We craned our necks, looking upwards into the expansive canopy as we counted each life. The youth rested their hands on each other's shoulders, caring not only for their steps, but for one another, as they took in the nearly imperceptible movements of life overhead and underfoot.

   When they finished mapping the Palenquillo, the youth returned to their communities to present what they had learned and offer suggestions for how to care for the precious body of water. In a co-authored essay that the youth published titled, 'To Know Our Territory Is to Build Peace', they explain the significance of mapping the Palenquillo for peacebuilding. 'To know the river is to know our history, memory, and enchanted places,' the essay begins,

> We lived the river through our bodies: we saw it with our eyes, we felt it, we stepped in it, we bathed in its rich pools. We also lived its pain, the contamination, the erosion, the felling of trees … Everything is connected: the river, the trees, the soil, the plants and animals, human life. We need each other to survive … We must care for what is ours, we can no longer think only of today, but of the future where our children will live. (Vigías Ecológicas 2016)

River-mapping created a space for intergenerational knowledge transmission through land-based pedagogies that infused the territory with social meaning. As they moved through the river, listening to the ancestral stories of their elders, the youth deepened affective and reciprocal relations with the territory. Through the retrieval of place names, the history of the campesino struggle for land and attention to the multiple lives that sustain and are sustained by the Palenquillo, the youth learned to sense the river's joy, pain, desire and love. River-mapping created a process of emplacement, as the youth grafted themselves into the wider campesino struggle for liberatory peace. By attuning themselves to the life of the river, the youth came to know and live the territory through their bodies.

In the process of becoming generational successors (*relevo generacional*), youth who participate in JOPPAZ are not merely passive recipients of their elders' knowledge – nor are they located solely in a distant and abstract future. Instead they form a vital part of the campesino movement as political actors working to regenerate the social and ecological relations that breathe life into the campo. In *Wasáse: Indigenous Pathways of Action and Freedom*, Taiaiake Alfred (2005) argues that regenerative political action does not seek to return to a romanticised past. Instead, he writes, 'regeneration means we will reference ourselves differently, both from the ways we did traditionally and under colonial dominion' (34). In this way Alfred offers an understanding of Indigenous regeneration as the interplay between social reproduction and transformation – one that locates the critical retrieval of Indigenous cultural practices and histories as the groundswell for transformative change.

'We, the youth, are not only the future,' Jocabeth explained to me one day, reflecting on why they had chosen the word *provocar* – provoke – for the name of the movement. 'You see, as the *relevo generacional* [generational successors] we are the future, but we are also the present.' Meaningful participation in an intergenerational peace movement cultivates a sense of agency, desire and pride for young people who have endured the compounding violence of war, social stigmatisation and dispossession in rural Colombia. The multiple valences of meaning embedded in JOPPAZ's name, which includes both action and desire, capture the prefigurative political praxis that animates JOPPAZ's contributions to sustainable peace in Colombia. As Jocabeth suggests, youth reclaim a sense of self and place through regenerating multi-species and multigenerational relations of care that sustain their territory. In doing so they bring campesino futures of dignified life into being in the present.

'The campo is beautiful': youth identity, territory and sustainable peacebuilding

Miguel sat across from me wearing a bright green T-shirt and baseball cap. The fan whirred behind us, drawing the cool evening air from the back patio into the concrete house. *Vallenato* music blared from the neighbours' stereo, intermingling with the night songs of frogs and crickets. The JOPPAZ co-ordinators had a training on the rights of campesino youth with the Defensoría del Pueblo (Ombudsperson) the next day. Miguel had chosen to stay the night in El Carmen, making the journey from his house in the heart of the Alta Montaña to the urban centre of El Carmen a day early in order to arrive to the meeting on time. He spent the evening walking me through his life history. The recorder sat between us on a plastic, white table. As we neared the end of the interview, I asked Miguel about the significance of *'relevo generacional'* – what the term meant to him. He paused for a while, reflecting on the question, before responding, 'I sometimes remember that forum in Sincelejo,' he looked up from the table to make eye contact with me, making sure I remembered the forum, 'the one where the *señor* said that there are no campesino youth,' I nodded, assuring him that I remembered the forum.

> Afterwards, I had to ask myself, well then, *yo, que soy* [me, what am I]? You see, it's not a lie, there are many youth that do not like the campo, there are many youth thinking about displacing to the city ... But, for me, the campo is beautiful ... I lived in the city and now I am living in the campo, and I never want to leave the campo. Here, I live well.

For Miguel the discursive circulation of narratives that portray the campo as lacking young people renders the lives of campesino youth invisible. In doing so the discourses of 'lost youth' erase Miguel's most salient identity. Miguel did not always embrace his identity as a campesino. Instead the violent processes of dispossession dislocated him not only from the campo but also from his deepest sense of self. Miguel's lived experiences challenge simplistic narratives of the rural/urban divide that locate urban cities as places of opportunity – and the campo as deficient. Instead his life history lays bare the uneven forms of violence leveled against campesino youth who are 'securitised as threats' across the physical locations of rural *veredas* and urban *barrios* – without collapsing the distinction between the two (see Lewis et al., Chapter 10). Miguel exposes the ways in which social stigmatisation renders youth in the campo deficient, while simultaneously locating campesino youth living in the urban margins as criminal threats. As Emmily Koiti, Bush Buse Laki and Chara Nyaura underscore in Chapter 12, these discourses naturalise young people as 'vulnerable, helpless, drunkards, unproductive, or troublemakers', in ways that drown out – rather than amplify – the voices of young people who are at the forefront of building sustainable peace. In response to these dynamics Lewis et al. (Chapter 10) call for analysis of the intersectionality of youth insecurity in order to interrogate and dismantle the compounding forces of symbolic and structural violence that naturalise some youth as embodied threats – and therefore not deserving and capable of speaking about security and peace.

For young people born in the midst of the war in Colombia, reclaiming a sense of self and place emerges through intergenerational solidarity.

Miguel learned to live, feel, and 'know the territory' as a place of abundant life and possibility through intergenerational peacebuilding, land-based pedagogies and environmental care. Narratives that focus on the *lack* of campesino youth in rural communities, however, foreclose the possibility of forging the kinds of intergenerational relationships that are vital for youth emplacement in a context of dispossession. In contrast, processes of living memory (*memoria viva*) and intergenerational movement-building empower youth to reclaim stigmatised bodies and places against the forces of social marginalisation. Through caretaking social and environmental relations in the territory, JOPPAZ organisers like Miguel destabilise the 'representational rhetorics' that structure and legitimise violent dispossession to reclaim the campo as a space of beauty (West 2016). In doing so they also reclaim their identities as campesino youth as beautiful and worthy of dignified life.

For youth in the Alta Montaña sustainable peace requires analysis of political and environmental violence as interlocking and mutually reinforcing processes. By tending territorial relations of reciprocal care across generations and species, JOPPAZ organisers are engaged in a regenerative struggle to cultivate futures of dignified life in the campo. By working to transform the systemic inequalities that have led to the persistence of violence in Colombia, youth movements like JOPPAZ play a key role in building sustainable peace. As this chapter has shown, cultivating a 'culture of place' in the wake of violence and dispossession also requires intergenerational relations of care and solidarity (hooks 2009). For Miguel knowing the territory – and, therefore, knowing oneself – is at the heart of campesino peacebuilding. 'This identity, this *sentido de pertenencia* [sense of belonging] for our region and for ourselves, we must create,' Miguel explained, reflecting on the significance of sustainable peace:

> In the beginning, we called ourselves campesinos. But then afterwards they called us 'the displaced,' and after that 'the victims' and now they call us 'survivors'. We have not asked to be called any of these three things, neither displaced, nor victims nor survivors. This is not who we are. We are campesinos. And this is what we must struggle for, to *rescatar* [reclaim] our identity.

Notes

1 JOPPAZ frequently invokes the term *arraigarse*, 'to establish roots', to describe its work. This is used in direct contrast to how they describe forced displacement and the death of the avocado forest as an experience of becoming 'uprooted' (*desarraigado*).

2 These included the Revolutionary Armed Forces of Colombia (FARC), United Self-Defence Forces of Colombia (AUC, also known as the paramilitaries), Popular Liberation Army (EPL), National Liberation Army (ELN) and Workers Revolutionary Party (PRT) as well as the Colombian Marine Infantry.
3 'False positive' refers to a military practice used during the armed conflict whereby soldiers killed civilians and then dressed them in guerrilla fatigues to fulfil quotas aimed at showing that the state was 'winning the war'.
4 'Popular neighbourhood' is frequently used to describe the settlements that emerged on the margins of urban centers as a result of forced displacement.
5 The *mojana* is a shapeshifting water spirit, sometimes known as the Mother of Water.

References

Alfred, Taiaiake. 2005. *Wasáse: Indigenous Pathways of Action and Freedom.* Toronto: University of Toronto Press.
Basso, Keith. 1996. *Wisdom Sits in Places: Landscape and Language among the Western Apache.* Albuquerque: University of New Mexico Press.
CNMH. 2017. *Un bosque de memoria viva, desde la Alta Montaña de El Carmen de Bolívar.* Informe del Centro Nacional de Memoria Histórica y del Proceso Pacífico de Reconciliación e Integración de La Alta Montaña de El Carmen de Bolívar. Bogotá: Centro Nacional de Memoria Histórica.
Corntassel, Jeff. 2012. 'Re-envisioning Resurgence: Indigenous Pathways to Decolonization and Sustainable Self-determination.' *Decolonization: Indigeneity, Education and Society* 1 (1): 86–101.
Daigle, Michelle. 2018. 'Resurging through Kishiichiwan: the Spatial Politics of Indigenous Water Relations.' *Decolonization: Indigeneity, Education and Society* 7 (1): 159–72.
De la Cadena, Marisol. 2010. 'Indigenous Cosmopolitics in the Andes: Conceptual Reflections Beyond "Politics."' *Cultural Anthropology* 25 (2): 334–70.
Hatala, Andrew R., Darrien Morton, Chinyere Njeze, Kelley Bird-Naytowhow and Tamara Pearl. 2019. 'Re-imagining *miyo-wicehtowin*: Human–nature Relations, Land-making, and Wellness among Indigenous Youth in a Canadian Urban Context.' *Social Science and Medicine* 230: 122–30.
hooks, bell. 2009. *Belonging: A Culture of Place.* New York: Routledge.
JOPPAZ (Jóvenes Provocadores de Paz). 2016. *Jóvenes Provocadores de Paz de la Alta Montaña Charter* (unpublished).
Kirksey, Eben, and Stephen Helmreich. 2010. 'The Emergence of Multispecies Ethnography.' *Cultural Anthropology* 25 (4): 545–76.
Lederach, Angela. 2023. *Feel the Grass Grow: Ecologies of Slow Peace in Colombia.* Stanford: Stanford University Press.
Lederach, Angela J. 2017. '"The Campesino Was Born for the Campo": A Multispecies Approach to Territorial Peace in Colombia.' *American Anthropologist* 119 (4): 589–602.
Lyons, Kristina. 2016. 'Decomposition as Life Politics: Soils, Selva, and Small Farmers under the Gun of the U.S.-Colombian War on Drugs.' *Cultural Anthropology* 31 (1): 56–81.

McCoy, Kate, Eve Tuck and Marcia McKenzie. 2016. *Land Education: Rethinking Pedagogies of Place from Indigenous, Postcolonial, and Decolonizing Perspectives.* New York: Routledge.

Ruiz Serna, Daniel. 2017. 'El territorio como víctima: Ontología política y las leyes de víctimas para comunidades Indígenas y Negras en Colombia.' *Revista Colombiana de Antropología* 53 (2): 85–113.

Ruiz Serna, Daniel. 2023. *When Forests Run Amok: War and Its Afterlives in Indigenous and Afro-Colombian Territories.* Durham, NC: Duke University Press.

Simpson, Leanne Betasamosake. 2014. 'Land as Pedagogy: Nishnaabeg Intelligence and Rebellious Transformation.'*Decolonization: Indigeneity, Education and Society* 3 (3): 1–25.

Todd, Zoe. 2016. 'From a Fishy Place: Examining Canadian State Law Applied in the Daniels Decision from the Perspective of Métis Legal Orders.' *TOPIA: Canadian Journal of Cultural Studies* 36: 43–57.

Twance, Melissa. 2019. 'Learning from Land and Water: Exploring mazinaabikiniganan as Indigenous Epistemology.' *Environmental Education Research* 25 (9): 1319–33.

Unidad Para la Atención y Reparación Integral de las Víctimas (Unit for the Attention and Integrative Reparation of Victims). 2014. *Fase de diagnostico del daño de la comunidad campesina de la Alta Montaña de El Carmen de Bolivar.* Bogotá: Unidad Para la Atención y Reparación Integral de las Víctimas.

Vigías Ecológicas. 2016. 'Conocer Nuestro Territorio Es Construir Paz: Jóvenes Montemarianos Mapean El Arroyo Palenquillo.' Sembrandopaz (blog). https://sembrandopazcolombia.wordpress.com/2018/01/18/featured-content/. Accessed 1 December 2016.

West, Paige. 2016. *Dispossession and the Environment: Rhetoric and Inequality in Papua New Guinea.* New York: Columbia University Press.

Wildcat, Matthew, Mandee McDonald, Stephanie Irlbacher-Fox and Glen Coulthard. 2014. 'Learning from the Land: Indigenous Land Based Pedagogy and Decolonization.' *Decolonization: Indigeneity, Education & Society* 3 (3): i–xv.

10

Reimagining 'peacebuilding': out-of-school BIPOC youth as researchers and advocates for sustainable peace

Jaimarsin Lewis, Siobhán McEvoy-Levy, Julio Trujillo, Karaijus Perry and Trinity Perry

Dedicated to the memory of David

Youth who are out-of-school, but not yet either in college or in a career, have important contributions to make to peacebuilding praxis. Too often, though, they are simply the subjects of peacebuilding or completely ignored. In the US BIPOC youth are more likely than white youth to be pushed out of school, criminalised by school systems and not to be in college (e.g. Annamma 2017; Kena et al. 2015). They are thus more likely to be excluded from knowledge-production processes and from potential influence on policy (as opposed to easier to reach school attenders and highly educated college graduates). This dynamic contributes to the 'racial silence' in peace studies (Azarmandi 2018). In this chapter we report on a university community outreach initiative, located in a Midwestern US city, that attempts to address this exclusion by engaging BIPOC youth in thinking about and prescribing for peace. The chapter is a collaboration of three out-of-school Black and biracial teenagers, a Latino university undergraduate student and a white college professor who were part of this initiative. More inclusive peacebuilding requires methods that can expand the circle of those viewed as the producers of knowledge about peace and that brings their insights to a wider audience recognising them as agents of peacebuilding. In the first part of the chapter we show how a space was created for racial and ethnic-minority youth to contribute to knowledge production through a combination of Participant Action Research (PAR), sustained relationship building and other paid experiential learning opportunities (a process we call PAR Plus). PAR Plus is a critical-relational framework, rooted in a Freireian pedagogy, where educational institutional resources are used to create a space of co-learning in dialogue across class, racial, age and other differences (Freire 2021; Darder 2017). The second part of the chapter presents the findings of a PAR study that the youth designed and implemented, and the third part discusses the impact of the project on the youth involved.

The chapter shows that marginalised young people face a world of pressures that fog and often minefield the transition from school to college and constrain their agency. The pressures are multiple and interlocking and lead to survival-mode planning based on lack of money, family demands, conforming to gender stereotypes, guilt and self-blame, police and school discrimination, and anticipated threats of crime and violence. Yet, as they are close witnesses to the causes and consequences of a lack of peace, marginalised youth are also often urgently involved in peace(building) on their own terms, from supporting vulnerable family members to getting non-violence training, to 'speaking truth to power' in academic forums. Defining peace in practical terms, they are reimagining peacebuilding towards more inclusive and emancipatory forms. We conclude that creating widely accessible alternative spaces for youth knowledge production about peace is necessary (but not sufficient) to support any effort towards sustainable peacebuilding. In addition more flexible access to education, skills building for advocacy and sustained intergenerational partnerships are needed to lay further groundwork for structural transformation that will address deeply embedded injustice.

Creating a space for peacebuilding research and action: a PAR-Plus approach

Participation Action Research (PAR) is an empirical research methodology that involves co-researchers who are members of the population being studied and operates 'beyond a vision of research as the sole domain of officially credentialed university researchers' (Irizarry and Brown 2014, 64). It is a collaborative approach, aiming to give power to communities to raise their voices in society, and that emphasises research-based action for 'sociopolitical justice and equity' (Torre and Fine 2006; Irizarry and Brown 2014, 65). A PAR approach recognises that young people, like all people, have valuable knowledge, especially about their own lives. PAR potentially provides a means for marginalised people to better understand and account for the multiple variables that shape their lives and even 'enter into discourses of power' (Irizarry and Brown 2014, 65), to challenge negative stereotypes in research and in society. The PAR methodology aspires to 'humanise' social-science research and create safe spaces where communities' members can work together 'toward more fully realising their human potential' (Irizarry and Brown 2014, 65). Thus envisioned, PAR supports positive peacebuilding (Kaye and Harris 2017; Lancaster et al. 2018).

The realities of PAR are of course rather messier than the theory suggests, and criticisms of PAR as a methodology have noted a lack of rigorous deconstruction of the actual process of PAR and the overstatement of its 'emancipative' potential (Cooper 2006, 467). Engaging with these criticisms we next offer a detailed summary of how our project unfolded and the roles of the different participants, then a summary of the findings of the PAR study the youth conducted, before a discussion of what we see to be modest but real 'emancipative' outcomes for the youth researchers.

The five authors of this chapter began work together in the autumn of 2018 as part of a university–community youth-engagement initiative begun by the Desmond Tutu Peace Lab at Butler University in partnership with the Martin Luther King (MLK) Community Center in Indianapolis, Indiana. Directed by Siobhán McEvoy-Levy, the Peace Lab was an innovative undergraduate 'think tank' focused on peace and justice issues broadly defined and Julio Trujillo was one of two inaugural interns for the lab. Together McEvoy-Levy and Trujillo designed an initiative to engage community youth and university students in meaningful learning experiences related to peace and social justice that were relevant to them. It was envisioned that, alongside university undergraduates, teenagers from the surrounding community would participate in dialogues and study tours and develop research and activism projects that taught them new skills while also positively emphasising their existing skills and knowledge; and they would have a platform to express their ideas and have their voices heard. PAR Plus is the name we gave to this combination of PAR, sustained relationship building and experiential learning, which created a space for the five authors of this chapter to work together over the course of two years.

Julio Trujillo was the lead youth researcher: a twenty-one-year-old Latino undergraduate student of political science and criminology, he had built a relationship with young people in the neighbourhood while working as a summer camp mentor at the MLK Center. He identified three Black and biracial youth who were invited to be co-researchers and members of the Peace Lab Think Tank; two sixteen-year-olds, Jaimarsin Lewis and Karaijus Perry, who at the time were working part-time and irregularly attending high school, and eighteen-year-old Trinity Perry who was studying for her GED while working full-time at the community centre. Trujillo, the lead youth researcher was close in age to the other youth and was supporting a young child while completing college. Nevertheless, he was in a relatively privileged position, being close to finishing a degree at the private university. His much older white professor, originally from Northern Ireland, had financial and career security and was perceived to be, in the words of one of the teenage researchers, 'a powerful person'. Hierarchies of power and privilege are important to acknowledge (Nelson and Wright 1995) and in practice they were negotiated in multiple ways. For example, as the most privileged collaborator, McEvoy-Levy directly acknowledged the teens' own wise understanding of the spectrum of privilege involved and at the same time admitted her own feelings and experiences of powerlessness in many situations. Taking time for frequent conversations not only about the work but also about our lives and histories over meals was important for sustained relationship-building. Both tangible transfer of resources (stipends and experiences) to the teen researchers and recognition of mutual benefit, including the public and private recognition of how their collaboration helped the university and its researchers, were other ways in which the power differential was acknowledged and negotiated. The research part of this initiative took place over ten months from August 2018 to May 2019. But during and after the research project, all of us participated in other activities of the Peace Lab, attended lectures, workshops and films related to mass incarceration and other social justice issues, participated in dialogues between other minority youth and a majority white group of university students, participated in the Annual Re-enactment of the Selma-Montgomery Voting Rights March in 2019, attended academic conferences and travelled with the students to the Legacy Museum and Peace and Justice Memorial in Montgomery, Alabama, and to the Freedom Center Underground Railroad Museum in Cincinnati, Ohio. In addition to their expenses being covered for these activities, the youth were paid for their time during all phases of the project (an hourly living wage funded by the Peace Lab/University with additional support from the MLK Center). Importantly, the project was made possible by the access provided by the MLK Center's Executive Director Allison Luthe. The Center employs a 'co-active coaching' approach to community youth work that is not about 'fixing' people and 'toxic charity' but about 'walking alongside' people as they make goals for themselves (Luthe 2018; Lupton 2011). These ideas guided our work throughout.

All of the authors of this chapter were involved in the initial discussions about a topic for a collaborative research project and various options were weighed. We discussed how research on communities of colour often problematically emphasised the negative and talked about exploring what 'peace' meant in the teenagers' lives and community, what an 'empowering' focus would be and what topics could do harm. Ensuring 'participants' choice and design of research methods improves the likelihood that data collection is done in ways that are sensitive to local contexts and peoples, thus preventing insensitive or even psychologically destructive research' (Cooper 2006, 467). A number of topics generated in dialogues between larger groups of teens and college students hosted by the Peace Lab were considered as foci, including: gun violence, drugs, suicide and sexual assault.

The university-based members of the team encouraged the youth co-researchers to avoid issues that might be retraumatising or incriminating to the interviewees or might raise suspicions among the clients of the MLK Center that we were involved in law enforcement or social welfare surveillance. In the end the youth researchers settled on a topic that connected to the theme of what 'peace' meant in their lives and was directly relevant to them – the barriers to college/work transitions for racial and ethnic-minority youth. This choice of topic is also not surprising because there is persistent societal commentary and media coverage of how, in a globalised world, post-secondary education is needed for social mobility and more than 90 per cent of US youth aspire to obtain a college degree (Anderson 2018). Statistics, none the less, reveal persistent disparities in the completion rates of higher education. In 2014, 41 per cent of European Whites in the twenty-five to twenty-nine age group held a college degree (four years) compared with 22 per cent of African-Americans and Latinas, Latinx, and Latinos at 15 per cent (Kena et al. 2015). Additionally, students from lower-income groups are six times less likely than their higher-income counterparts to earn a bachelor's degree by the age of twenty-five (Bailey and Dynarski 2011). Students with parents who did not attend higher education also struggle. For example, first-generation student test-takers scored 20 per cent below the general population (Duncheon 2015). As already noted, all of the young people in the research team were Latino, black or biracial; furthermore, none of their parents had graduated from college.

Led by Trujillo, the teenagers completed the required university ethics course, were introduced to research methods and designed a questionnaire based on their chosen topic: the barriers to college and career aspirations of racial and ethnic-minority youth. The use of methods such as photo-voice, creative writing, and community resilience-mapping were suggested and we worked together on a separate pop-culture memoir-writing project (McEvoy-Levy et al. 2020). But for the research project the youth asserted that they wanted to do interviews, perceived as a more serious and college-level approach to research than some of the other suggested methods. Their questionnaire notably posed mostly practical questions. They asked about the respondent's attitudes to school, whether or not they liked their teachers, if they had received career planning or college preparation, if they wanted to attend college and if they saw anything stopping them from going to college or getting their 'dream job'. Thus, in the choice of topic and approach, the young researchers were highlighting what peace meant to them – access to education, job security and career success. What is interesting, as will be shown in part two of the chapter, is that many of the original issues of violence brought forward in earlier dialogues, but rejected as themes for the PAR project, emerged anyway in the research on college and career aspirations, illustrating the intersectional complexity of insecurity in the young lives being studied.

Using convenience and snowball sampling, the youth team (aged sixteen to twenty-one) interviewed their friends, co-workers, family members and youth workers. Four interviewees were female and nine were male and they were aged between fourteen and forty. They were interviewed at the community centre, in a nearby park and in their homes. The youth researchers completed a total of thirteen one-hour interviews which they documented with both audio recordings and handwritten notes. McEvoy-Levy did not participate in the community interviews that the team conducted. As a white, European professor, who was thirty years older, she was an 'outsider' whose presence would have disrupted the PAR space; she played a role as supporter to the process by advising Trujillo when requested. The interview transcripts were first coded by Trujillo using the online tool Nvivo 12. Then the transcripts and codings were reviewed and analysed by him with the rest of the youth research team. At the end of the project McEvoy-Levy interviewed each of the youth researchers about their experience (discussed in part three) and with the close involvement of all involved wrote this chapter with Trujillo. The chapter has been revised in several rounds after it was reviewed and commented on by all of the young researchers. In this way we tried to prevent the recolonisation of the youth voices and insights by the main writers of the chapter, but it must be acknowledged this was imperfect. We agreed collectively to dedicate the chapter to the memory of one of the interviewees who was a friend of youth researchers and who tragically was shot and killed shortly after the project was completed.

Intersectional insecurity and the aspirations of marginalised youth

We turn now to the findings of the study that the youth designed and implemented. The names of all interviewees in this section are pseudonyms. A dominant theme of the interviews was that of the multiple, intersecting barriers preventing youth from fulfilling their career and college aspirations, including poverty, family demands or needs, (threat of) violence and lack of information about college or career options. Although some interviewees noted that school was not strict or challenging enough, and several referenced not having enough money for college, participants often blamed themselves for making poor choices and even when the choices they'd made were actually about survival and supporting others and were constrained and dictated by outside structures and systems. This cultural or symbolic violence (see also Bolten, Chapter 5) was interwoven with direct and structural violence in the experiences of interviewees. For example, Dom (age nineteen) emphasised the interlocking threats of crime and violence, the cost of college, pressure to conform to a tough masculine image, at times perceived to be at odds with getting an education, and the pressure of family and personal relationships.

> *Do you want to go to college?*
> Dom: 'Yes. I want to go to college because if my girl goes, then I'll ask myself what do I do? I have to go.'
> *Is there anything stopping you from going to college?*
> Dom: 'The environment. The environment I live in, most are not thinking about going to college. I would not want to pay because it is expensive and most of the time my family needs money.'
> *What is stopping you from getting your dream job?*
> Dom: 'My environment – gangs, drugs, violence. It affects me. I have to prepare myself if someone tries to get me, before they get me. Myself – thinking I cannot get it [dream job]. It is hard to explain. Sometimes I don't want people to think that just because I'm going to school and stuff [that] I am soft.'

Present-day money pressures (rather than the future cost of college) and family obligations were large distractions from focusing on school and getting access to scholarships among the young interviewees as well. Dom explained: 'I have to choose between my education and my family. They call me asking for money.' JJ (nineteen) said: 'Things at home get in the way. They take my focus. Makes me worry about everything else instead of me.' Such pressures prompted one of the youth workers to advocate leaving home to go to college while also recognising the difficulty many have in making that break. Steve said, 'College is a physical and emotional way out. This is why I promote for people to go away for school. If you stay in town and go to school, you will still have the distractions at home.'

While acknowledging the distraction of family worries and obligations, the young people also blamed themselves for 'not going to school. Not going to class' (Elon, fifteen). JJ saw college as a route to 'a good life' and wanted "to study architecture or sports'. When asked what the barriers to living that dream were, he said: 'I stop myself. I am not motivated. I am my number one motivation for myself. I have to keep myself up – keep going and don't give up. I just want to quit. My patience [is the problem]. Really myself.' When asked if he wanted to go to college, Ravon (male, aged sixteen) first said: 'No. I got my own goals.' But when asked what prevented him from going to college, Ravon said: 'Myself. It's out of my budget.' The idea expressed – that he is to blame for not being able to afford college *and* that he has made 'choice' about that – again illustrates symbolic violence or the cultural or psychological violence of internalised self-blame.

Michael (fourteen) said 'I want to succeed' but perceived he would be stopped by 'giving up, or going to jail'. This idea was echoed by David (fourteen) who said 'You cannot do anything without school, that or jail.' Julian (seventeen) said that the only thing stopping him from going to college was 'nothing but me, by not doing good in school or getting locked up and doing drugs'. Another interviewee, James (male, aged twenty), said that young people should listen to older people in the community 'Because if you don't you will end up dead or in jail.' The issue of conflicts with peers was brought poignantly into view in the case of David, one of the youngest of the interviewees, who was aged fourteen at the time of the study. He went to a private school, unlike all of the other participants who attended public schools and he felt the difference: 'Private school is all white people. They privileged,' he said in the interview. David reported that his teachers helped him and 'make sure I turn in all my work. They are strict on me.' He didn't like that the football coach was pressuring him to play and that the 'grading scale is sometimes too high'. College seemed far off and at 'four years [might be] too much responsibility'. But he didn't think anything was stopping him from attending college. Yet his private school access did not insulate him from violence on the streets. Later, David moved to another part of the city; he was shot and killed, aged sixteen, during a conflict with other young people. This tragic outcome for one of the participants in our study highlights how direct violence forms a significant part of the complex insecurity of youth on the margins in the American city: it leads to carrying firearms and to far-ranging legal consequences as well. Because of legal consequences, the danger of such violence is often referred to obliquely. For example, Manny (aged seventeen) talked about further education as a means of acquiring economic and thus physical security:

> I want to get my education ... I want to have things that are big. I want to win. Live in a mansion by yourself with nobody fucking with you. I had this thing that helped me. Twenty-first Century [scholarship] but I lost it when I was incarcerated.

Like Manny, others had already experienced how arrest and jail time meant exclusion from school and loss of career options, though, looking back, older interviewees also recounted how other interlocking factors were involved. For example, when asked what stopped him from going to college, youth worker Steve said: 'I caught a gun charge at fourteen. A lot of things could have stopped me [from going to college]. I grew up in a single-parent home, many things could have stopped me. College is an abstract thing. We don't know what it takes. I don't know if I understood [what it meant] to be a college student.' Steve recommended that all students received one-to-one mentorship: 'Probably impossible to pull off [but] it is important to pair students with staff. Kids fall through the cracks [when] they do not have a connection.' Essence, another youth worker, noted, 'I got expelled for selling drugs. It messed me up [in the school-college trajectory] to get my life back.' Providing further insight into the potentially intersecting factors leading to her expulsion, she recommended attention to the psychological impact of violence and abuse: 'I wish schools helped with trauma; help with sexual trauma and physical trauma [and provided] different forms of support groups.' In the study only four of the interviewees were female but those young women were more likely to reference sexual assault as well as to say that motherhood, or other forms of caretaking and work, had taken them out of school, further showing that insecurity was experienced in differentially gendered ways.

The emancipative impacts of PAR Plus

Living in a city like ours as a young person of colour means living in a state of insecurity or non-peace – complex intersections of direct, structural and cultural violence shape choices and opportunities. Preparing for potential assault, you may take a gun to buy a phone and taser on a trip to visit a peace and justice memorial, as some of the authors of this chapter have done. This is risking legal consequences or even death as well as challenging norms of educational settings. But even schools can be risky places, where, as also happened to one of our authors, a fight with other youth can lead to jail, expulsion from school, probation, the loss of a university scholarship and educational uncertainty. Just *observing* this fight became an arrest warrant and, two years later, the loss of a job opportunity, for his friend. For some of our authors, being illegally evicted, working without health insurance and being profiled by law enforcement are intimate experiences. While they live in the college's neighbourhood, their presence on campus is 'discouraged' by university police. When university students have their drug stash stolen in a break-in, and call the police so they can make an insurance claim, one of our authors was picked up on the street as the suspect, because he is young and black. Our PAR Plus project could not transform such systemic injustices but it did challenge the 'pedagogy of pathologization' (Annamma 2017) they had already experienced, and had a modest emancipative impact on the youth researchers.

First, the PAR project was at least able to demystify the research process. Advocates for 'decolonising' or 'emancipatory' methodologies interpret traditional social-science research as researchers observing indigenous people through 'imperial eyes' (Smith 1999) and note that much of traditional research looks at local people through 'research eyes' (Bensimon et al.

2004) which can be dehumanising and do harm. University researchers are presumed experts and have the position to detect the social problems and the needs of the local people (Brown and Rodriguez 2009). This is not just something that certain researchers think; it is also what 'researched communities' often think and expect. Through the project youth researchers gained academic self-confidence and self-esteem as being agents of positive change. They noted:

> It was good to be involved in finding out problems and [...] try to be part of the solution.

> It made me feel like I was doing something important, like I had a purpose, was doing something good, and it felt good talking about my research process to my family.

Second, in addition to personal confidence, their empathy for others was also enhanced:

> It really opened my eyes to different struggles people are going through.

> I learned not to judge people so quick, and to get to know them and I want to be able to help people that feel like that, that we can't do it [go to college or fulfil career aspirations]. Before I didn't really think about it. Now it makes me want to help them.

Third, one of the young men noted that the project had served a purpose during a vulnerable period, saying 'We needed it because we were ... in bad positions' emotionally, and noting that the twenty-one-year-old college student had been a 'role model' and that he 'made us want to succeed'. A further important factor that drew the youth researchers into the project and was related to survival was that they were paid. This underscored how poverty and obligations to others can exclude young people from learning about and participation in peacebuilding, when they need to make calculations about prioritising their time:

> I probably wouldn't have done it without being paid. Now that I know it is a chance that I can help the community, now it doesn't matter if I am paid or not. I would keep doing it. But it would be hard to find others to do it without paying them.

> [S]ome of the teenagers we interviewed, I know them from the streets and got to know through the interviews about their education and lives and that they actually do have aspirations and dreams. I got to learn whether they really care about education or don't. A lot were in the same boat as me. Education wasn't the most important thing in their life because sometimes it's not the most important thing in my life. They have family and they are helping them out. I have to, full disclosure, help with bills. I can't get no money from school,

but if I am out here working, it helps the family get food for tonight and that's most important.

Though obviously small-scale, the PAR Plus approach we used addressed structural violence by providing economic support and experiential education opportunities. Cultural or symbolic violence was addressed through self-esteem-building and relationships of respect and trust across difference. Participation in the project may also have provided a diversion, preventing fights and contact with law enforcement, addressing direct violence as well. At the beginning and just after the project ended, the young men were involved in fights at school and at the MLK Center. The end of the research project marked a break in their work with the college researcher who was graduating, and the fight that followed might suggest that there had been a diversionary aspect in their relationship. But it is hard to definitively make this claim given the multiple influences involved. Nevertheless, in addition to educational and psychological benefits and the economic benefit of being paid a wage, there was an additional benefit for one of the participants in being able to use the collaboration as a youth researcher as evidence of productive work in a probation hearing resulting from charges related to a prior school fight. Thus, it had some tangible and immediate positive impacts in the lives of the youth involved.

Expanding the circle of influence, the youth researchers presented their findings and recommendations to youth centre and school personnel, to some of their parents and to groups of university students and faculty at two conferences. The action plan of recommendations that the youth researchers developed also included further listening to the needs of young people in the community and not just focusing on 'one' aspect of a person's life in helping prepare youth for college and career. Based on the interview responses and their own experience, the youth researchers recommended more career counselling and guidance about making the transition from school to work, finding stable employment as well as financial counselling. These recommendations were implemented through programming at the community centre. Second chances for education after contact with the criminal-legal system were also highlighted as necessary. All three of the youth researchers continued to pursue their education and all three completed their GEDs through the community centre. The findings highlighted the importance of youth and community centres as spaces where youth who are unable or unwilling to return to school can continue their education and where psychological counselling and legal advice can be accessed. They also highlighted the need both for larger structural changes and for relational forms of peacebuilding in community, to liberate people from poverty and violence and from related shame and self-blame.

Speaking in such public community and academic spaces, the youth researchers said they enjoyed working with the Peace Lab because 'they don't judge us' and 'they care about us', and thus illuminated the importance of the relational Plus aspect of the PAR Plus project. Speaking in such spaces also allowed the youth to 'enter discourses of power' (Irizarry and Brown 2014, 65) and challenge stereotypes and adult complacency. For example, at an academic conference at Kent State, Ohio, the young men volunteered to speak as part of a fish-bowl dialogue on 'When Government Kills'. Joining much older professors and community members on the stage, Jaimarsin pointed out that 'state violence could mean a lot of things: there's the violence of poverty, and the cultural violence of racism'. Responding to one older white man who loudly said he was tired of hearing criticism of the government and that the problem was youth were 'killing each other', Karaijus calmly responded: 'Five of our friends were killed in 2015 … You are the older generation. What should we do?' He didn't get an answer from the stage but after the event both young men volunteered for and completed training on nonviolence and also participated in training their peers in nonviolence for a time.

Three years after the project ended, all of the formerly teenage Black and biracial participants are working in low-paying jobs to support themselves and help support their families. Two are parents, one has lost a parent, two have lost a sibling, none has yet continued on to university, and one is awaiting sentencing related to charges incurred as a result of shooting back at another youth who fired at him with an automatic weapon in a public place. The commitment to nonviolence is not easy to maintain in a very insecure context. The Latino university student researcher went on to a funded graduate-school study related to children's law. The white university professor involved in the project remains in her position and continues to develop youth-led action research opportunities. Thus the longer-term benefits of this initiative were uneven and the ability to contribute to peacebuilding knowledge skewed towards those already in third-level education and experiencing racial and class privilege.

Conclusions

Viewed through the lens of peacebuilding, the lives of BIPOC youth in the United States come into view as precarious terrain, shaped by direct, structural and cultural violence. So too 'peacebuilding' was brought under scrutiny and re-viewed through the gaze of those young people, bathed in the light of their own knowledge and experience, and sustainable peace takes form as a just society of practical thriving in close community.

So illuminated, we can get a better picture of what peacebuilding with, for and by youth entails in this and in other contexts.

First, the BIPOC young people in this study showed themselves as already involved in peacebuilding: enacting peace in their daily lives by supporting family economically and emotionally, seeking out nonviolence training, resisting efforts to stigmatise and exclude them from the academy and proposing solutions to social problems they identified and have lived. Second, the young BIPOC co-authors of this chapter designed a PAR project that opened up for viewing the lack of peace in their own lives and that of their peers. They highlighted what peace meant to them – access to education, job security and career success – and showed that this peace was prevented by poverty, gendered experiences of violence and ensnaring contact with a criminal-legal system shaped by systemic racism. Their research and their own experience showed that out-of-school young people need flexible, financially supported, multiple chances to continue their education alongside family obligations, at their own pace, and despite mistakes that bring them in contact with the law. They underscore the importance of listening to BIPOC young people and responding holistically to their stated needs and aspirations.

Creating alternative spaces for youth knowledge production is necessary but not sufficient, however. As the youth involved in producing the knowledge presented in this chapter have experienced, the emancipative impacts of such efforts may only be temporary without larger structural changes. There is a lack of infrastructure to support BIPOC and other marginalised young people's contributions to peacebuilding in the US. Vocational peacebuilding career tracks, and living-wage scholarships and fellowships that encourage research by BIPOC youth about peacebuilding in their local settings may be helpful. Combined with skills training in writing policy recommendations and advocacy, and sustained intergenerational mentorship and partnerships to promote networking, longer-term capacity for effecting larger-scale changes could be built. The lack of infrastructure for peacebuilding in the US is related to normative ideas of what 'peacebuilding' is and who it is for (namely an overseas endeavour for humanitarian and/or strategic objectives). These ideas do not seem to be challenged as yet by the US implementation of the global Youth, Peace and Security agenda (see Fett, Chapter 3). The 'racial silence within peace studies' (Azarmandi 2018) is a contributing factor as well. Ultimately, then, the chapter tasks us to critically reflect on how more inclusive and policy-relevant research about peace can be designed.

Complex insecurity for BIPOC youth in the United States involves the violence of state and non-state actors and deeply embedded historical trauma and social inequalities in a unique configuration. Peacebuilding may eventually involve top-down systematic truth-telling, national healing and reparation: the work of a perhaps future, but as yet politically unimaginable, American peace process. But, as Chapters 4 and 8 by Martuscelli and Mollica have shown, that would not guarantee the meaningful inclusion of diverse young people's ideas about peace. This leads to a general lesson about the need for continuing work around changing normative beliefs about youth capabilities and interests which are often shaped by systemic racism, as in this case, and also by other factors such as level of educational attainment. Addressing BIPOC and other in-school and out-of-school young people as experts in their own lives, as producers of knowledge about peace, and as already active agents of peace, is necessary to support just and sustainable peace. Furthermore, intergenerational solidarity that is dedicated to collaboratively and creatively reimagining ways out of systemic injustice, and repairing its harmful legacies in local spaces, continue to be vital work towards peace (see also Lederach and de Leon and Bighorn, Chapters 9 and 14).

References

Anderson, Meredith, B.L. 2018. *A Seat at the Table: African American Youth's Perceptions of K-12 Education*. Washington, DC: UNCF.

Annamma, Subini Ancy. 2017. *The Pedagogy of Pathologization: Dis/abled Girls of Color in the School-prison Nexus*. New York: Routledge.

Azarmandi, Mahdis. 2018. 'The Racial Silence within Peace Studies.' *Peace Review* 30 (1): 69–77, https://doi.org/10.1080/10402659.2017.1418659.

Bailey, Martha J., and Susan M. Dynarski. 2011. *Gains and Gaps: Changing Inequality in U.S. College Entry and Completion*. Working Paper 17633. National Bureau of Economic Research. https://www.nber.org/papers/w17633. Accessed 1 December 2023.

Bensimon, Estela Mara, Donald E. Polkinghorne, Georgia L. Bauman and Edlyn Vallejo. 2004. 'Doing Research that Makes a Difference.' *The Journal of Higher Education* 75 (1): 104–26.

Brown, Tara, and Louie F. Rodriguez (2009) 'Issue Editor Notes.' Special Issue: Youth In Participatory Action Research. *New Directions for Youth Development* 123: 1–9.

Cooper, Elizabeth. 2005. 'What Do We Know about Out-of-school Youth? How Participatory Action Research Can Work for Refugees in Camps.' *Compare: A Journal of Comparative Education* 35 (4): 463–77.

Darder, Antonia. 2017. *Reinventing Paulo Freire. A Pedagogy of Love*. New York: Routledge.

Duncheon, Julia C. 2018. 'Making Sense of College Readiness in a Low-Performing Urban High School: Perspectives of High-achieving First Generation Youth.' *Urban Education* 56 (8): 1360–87.

Freire, Paulo. 2021. *Education for Critical Consciousness*. Translated by Myra Bergman Ramos. London: Bloomsbury Academic.

Irizarry, Jason G., and Tara M. Brown. 2014. 'Humanizing Research in Dehumanizing Spaces: the Challenges and Opportunities of Conducting Participatory Action Research with Youth in chools. In *Humanizing Research: Decolonizing Qualitative Inquiry with Youth and Communities*, edited by Django Paris and Maisha T. Winn, pp. 62–80. London: Sage.

Kaye, Sylvie, and Geoff Harris, eds. 2017. *Building Peace via Action: African Case Studies*. Addis Ababa: University for Peace Africa Programme.

Kena, Grace, Lauren Musu-Gillette, Jennifer Robinson, Xiaolei Wang, Amy Rathbun, Jijun Zhang, Sidney Wilkinson-Flicker, Amy Barmer and Erin Dunlop Velez. 2015. *The Condition of Education 2015* (NCES 2015–144). Washington, DC: US Department of Education, National Center for Education Statistics. http://nces.ed.gov/pubsearch. Accessed 4 May 2021.

Lancaster, Illana, Sahlim C. Amambia, Felix Bivens, Munira Hamisi, Oliva Ogada, Gregory O. Okumu, Nicholas Songora and Rehema Zaid. 2018. 'Participatory Action Research for Advancing Youth Peacebuilding Work in Kenya.' In *Peaceworks*. Washington, DC: United States Institute of Peace.

Luthe, Allison. 2018. Personal communication. Indianapolis, Indiana.

Lupton, Robert A. 2011. *Toxic Charity: How Churches and Charities Hurt Those They Help, and How to Reverse It*. New York: Harper Collins.

McEvoy-Levy, Siobhán, with Cole Byram, Jaimarsin Lewis, Karaijus Perry, Trinity Perry, Julio Trujillo and Mikayla Whittemore. 2020. 'Between Borders: Pop Cultural Heroes and Plural Childhoods in IR.' In *Discovering Childhood in International Relations*, edited by Marshall Beier, pp. 179–98. New York: Palgrave Macmillan.

Nelson, Nici, and Susan Wright, eds. 1995. *Power and Participatory Development. Theory and Practice*. Rugby: Intermediate Technology Publications.

Smith, Linda Tuhiwai. 1999. *Decolonizing Methodologies: Research and Indigenous Peoples*. London: Zed Books.

Torre, Maria, and Michelle Fine. 2006. 'Researching and Resisting: Democratic Policy Research by and for Youth.' In *Beyond Resistance! Youth Activism and Community Change*, edited by Shawn Ginwright, Pedro Noguera and Julio Camarottta, pp. 269–85. New York: Routledge.

11

Young women and peacebuilding in Asia and the Pacific

Katrina Lee-Koo and Lesley Pruitt

Young women bring their lived experiences, priorities and skills to peacebuilding. Yet their needs, and their leadership, are often overlooked within their broader communities. There are a number of reasons for this including age- and gender-based discrimination, which often result in young women's agency and leadership skills not being recognised or deemed irrelevant to broader peacebuilding efforts. On the other hand, when young women are considered, it is too often assumed that their views and needs are captured by general efforts to support women, and/or young people's participation in peacebuilding. There is little recognition of the unique ways in which they experience conflict and crisis, and the unique contributions they make to peacebuilding efforts.

Young women's leadership in peacebuilding is often marginalised due to assumptions made around their gender and age. Gender is central to understanding young women's position in peacebuilding. Research has shown that gender equality enhances the likelihood of peace, and women's participation in peace processes increases the chances of a robust, inclusive peace (Hudson et al. 2012; Krause et al. 2018). Yet in formal peace processes women's contributions and concerns are often not seen as integral. While there has been concerted effort to increase women's participation in formal peace processes, women's leadership for peace is often exercised in different ways and forms, outside typically male-dominated formal decision-making forums (Cook-Huffman and Snyder 2018). Moreover, the most visible peace efforts often focus on preventing a return to widespread public sphere violence, and thus obscure other concerns – such as gender-based violence – which may increase in the so-called post-conflict period. This marginalisation ignores the fact that such concerns are not distractions from the goal of peace but rather themselves central to an inclusive peace (Cook-Huffman and Snyder 2018).

Intersections of gender *and age* are also significant for young women. As young men are often seen as the key cohort involved in violence, they tend to receive greater attention in peacebuilding efforts aimed at stopping post-accord violence. As this collection is testament, momentum has been growing for including youth in peacebuilding; yet, as consultations with youth have revealed, young women's leadership is often marginalised, over-looked and unrecognised in peacebuilding efforts (Altiok 2017). Research has documented how youth peacebuilding programmes often focus upon young men, while the programmes and advocacy to support women's rights or gender equality after conflict tend to focus upon older women (Pruitt 2015). Of course there are no doubt examples around the world of young women finding advantages in connecting with women's peacebuilding networks and with youth peacebuilding efforts that include young men. Our aim is not to discount such efforts but rather to highlight the less often examined, but no less important, work young women are doing alongside other young women.

In investigating these considerations, we focus on Asia and the Pacific, drawing on thirty fieldwork interviews conducted between 2016 and 2019 with young women (loosely defined as being eighteen to thirty years old) from conflict-affected countries in the region (India, Myanmar, Papua New Guinea and Bougainville, Sri Lanka, Solomon Islands) who had participated in a leadership training run by and for young women through the World YWCA.

Our research documents some of the many vibrant ways young women are redefining and practising leadership for peace and social justice through-out the conflict-affected region. This leadership, we argue, is pivotal to sustainable peacebuilding, including through enhancing gender equality and women's human rights and ensuring young people's contributions. Likewise the leadership of young women in post-conflict communities needs to be better understood and supported. In this chapter we demonstrate how the young women we interviewed adopted creative ways to support one another and lead within their communities in spaces that are aligned with, but none the less independent from peacebuilding efforts focused on or including young men and older women. We conceptualise this as responding to, resisting and challenging their common exclusion.

The chapter is structured as follows. First, we consider how young people have conceptualised and articulated peace and security in regional consulta-tions. In the sections that follow, we draw on fieldwork research to consider young women's experiences of conflict, their approach to peace leadership and the barriers to young women's peacebuilding. In the conclusion we look briefly at ways that young women can be supported to lead.

Youth, peace and security in Asia and the Pacific

Before the landmark adoption of United Nations Security Council Resolution (UNSCR) 2250 on Youth Peace and Security in 2015 young people in the region had articulated their thoughts regarding peace and security. Here they highlighted an interconnection between peace and gender equality in their peace leadership. For example, in 2014 the ASEAN (Association of Southeast Asian Nations) Youth Forum (AYF) adopted the Yangon Youth Statement, which demonstrated a commitment to building peace. It starts: 'We, the young people of ASEAN, aspire for the promotion of non-discrimination, equality, peace, protection, sustainability, and inclusive development of the ASEAN community', and goes on to outline the demands the youth make to achieve their vision. The Statement calls on ASEAN leaders to take a range of supporting actions, including creating 'safe spaces for youth to meaningfully engage in peace-building efforts such as interfaith dialogues and cross-cultural exchanges at the community, national and regional levels specifically in conflict areas', initiating alternative peacebuilding efforts and peace education curriculums focused on youth, and creating and supporting 'peaceful dialogues with governments and various stakeholders' (AYF 2014, 1). In calling for youth participation that is 'meaningful', and inclusive of women, adolescent girls, LBGTIQ people and pregnant girls in particular, the Yangon Youth Statement situates attending to gendered inequalities as part of the broader platform for peace and sustainability in the region.

In 2017 the first regional consultation on the Youth, Peace and Security (YPS) agenda was held in Bangkok. Participants included thirty-nine young people from across the region aged fifteen to thirty (twenty female and nineteen male). Through the two days of consultations, participants discussed how they see peace – and their role in facilitating it – in the region. The event's report documented a conceptualisation of peace that focused upon the grassroots commitments of individuals, as well as the interconnectedness of peace and security with values of justice, freedom and equality (see Altiok 2017). Participants in the consultation also highlighted key challenges in the region, including the lack of national and regional YPS policy frameworks. In particular they noted that while UNSCR 2250 on YPS offers a global framework for youth participation in peace and security, it does not offer the direct support needed for advancing youth leadership on peace and security locally. Moreover, participants suggested that, given the liminal state of youth and the lengthy time required for policy change, they would likely have 'aged out of the youth category by the time their governments start concretely implementing' the YPS agenda (Altiok 2017, 8). This makes youth representation in policy particularly challenging. These challenges could also be compounded by the mistrust governments often display around young people's appeals for social change, which may also delay action taken to address youth concerns.

Moreover, youth participants said further partnership development is required, including engaging family elders and the education and training sectors to educate for peace (Altiok 2017).

Finally, the consultation noted that advancing gender equality is essential for peacebuilding. Participants agreed 'that peace and security discussions in relation to young men and women should not overlook the importance of economic and environmental security, *gender equality* and basic human needs'. Participants stressed that, when they talk about peace and security, they mean 'eradicating social and economic inequalities, providing public services for all social groups, maintaining national social and health security systems, and *achieving gender equality and the empowerment of women*' (Altiok 2017, 6, emphasis added). Building on earlier declarations by youth, such as the Yangon Statement described above, this regional YPS consultation reiterated peacebuilders' understanding of gender equality and peace as deeply interconnected.

Young women's unique experiences of conflict

While gender justice has been a central concern for building sustainable peace, further attention is needed to adequately understand young women's specific roles and needs. After all, to build inclusive peace, peace processes must take the experiences of conflict-affected communities seriously. This includes recognising that young women's experiences of conflict can be unique and different from those of older women and young men. Failure to recognise this could result in a narrowly focused 'negative peace' in which violence remains widespread in many forms. Yet, in the scholarly and sector research available on women's experiences of conflict, studies dedicated to young women are rare. Instead, young women's experiences are routinely lost – or inadequately captured – in the overlapping categories of 'women', 'women and girls', 'youth' and 'children'.

Engaging with young women in conflict-affected communities around the region, we asked them what issues were of most concern for them. Their answers suggested that young women's key concerns, while nuanced and contextual, also showed specificity common to their gender and age group. Their priorities reflected young women's particular experiences and positionality in their societies. In Sri Lanka, for instance, young women identified services around accessing knowledge about consensual marriage and the right to make decisions about childbearing as key concerns shaping their sense of security. In Nepal young women said family violence and access to education were their dominant concerns, while in Myanmar human trafficking, HIV among young women, gender-based violence

(GBV) and high maternal mortality rates were major threats to young women's sense of security. Finally, in Papua New Guinea young women were concerned about violence against young women, high rates of early marriage and pregnancy, and low levels of political participation by all women. All of these concerns are critical to ensuring inclusive sustainable peace. Furthermore, they align with findings from other studies highlighting young women's unique perspectives and experiences on aspects of peace and security (see Frida 2015; Brimacombe 2018, 150–5; UN 2018).

Demonstrating the importance of including these issues as part of the peacebuilding agenda, research conducted by Valerie Hudson et al. (2012) found that countries which had higher rates of gender equality and inclusion were less likely to experience conflict. In making this assessment the researchers drew upon gender-equality indicators which included a number of the issues the young women we interviewed raised, such as trafficking and gender-based violence. Research elsewhere demonstrates that these issues are all exacerbated by conflict. Investigations undertaken by the NGO 'Girls Not Brides' found that child, early and forced marriage (CEFM) increases in times of crisis and conflict; this is poignantly illustrated by the finding that, of the ten countries with the highest rates of CEFM, nine are conflict-affected. Early marriage generates higher sexual and reproductive health needs, particularly around maternal health care and family planning (Girls Not Brides 2018). Similarly, extensive research has linked conflict and crisis with high rates of family- and gender-based violence (see UNFPA 2014). While older women will also experience these issues, the drivers, patterns and outcomes will be different for young women. For example, research on the Colombian conflict has documented that some young women joined armed groups to access educational opportunities, a key concern for young people generally, and that DDR programmes in Colombia have tended to focus on experiences of men and thus failed to meet women's and girls' needs (Bouvier 2016, 11–24).

Similarly, young women's experiences of conflict often differ substantially from the experiences of young men. When forcibly or voluntarily recruited, young women may be more likely to perform different roles from young men, including experiencing forced marriage and sexual slavery. This will result in different post-conflict needs, around health care, demobilisation and reintegration (see Girls Not Brides 2018). Young women may also find that their care and unpaid labour burden increases during times of conflict, with young women more likely to be expected to take on caring, cleaning, cooking and other home-based duties in times of crisis. Conflict may also bring gendered patterns to opportunities for continuing education in times in crisis (see, for example Ghazarian, Gordon and Lee-Koo 2019). These examples offer only a brief snapshot of the ways that age and gender intersect to shape the experiences of young women in times of conflict and crisis. However, young women's leadership is central in advocating around concerns that disproportionately affect them, as well as broader community concerns.

Young women's approach to leading for peace in Asia and the Pacific

We found that young women's leadership in peace and social justice initiatives challenged the dominant models of leadership operating in most of the world today. This is partly because they have developed accessible, relevant ways of leading in informal spaces in their community. But it is also partly because they have been excluded from traditional forms and sites of peacebuilding and community leadership. When asked whom their community saw as leaders, the young women we interviewed consistently responded that – regardless of their country or culture – it was men. Men in elite roles, such as in religious, military, community or village, or political roles were seen as the only 'real' leaders within their communities, particularly in areas where the conflict was reasonably recent. A young woman from Nepal replied: 'We live in a patriarchal society … where the leaders are the male only.' Across the region leadership tends to be seen as linked with adult men, vertical power hierarchies, masculine attributes and public sphere activities, all of which marginalise the participation of young women (Pruitt and Lee-Koo 2020, 26–7).

Despite being faced with this constraining context, young women did not resign themselves to exclusion but instead promoted their peacebuilding agendas through different leadership models, animated by distinct values. While Asia and the Pacific is a diverse region, we found a number of similar core leadership commitments among young women leaders. When asked what values are most relevant to their idea of leadership, young women told us that having confidence – in themselves and others – is one of the most important elements of being a leader. For many young women throughout the region, self-confidence is not a value that has been encouraged or comes easily. Instead it is often hard-fought and requires frequent defence against those who believe that young women should not have a voice in public, in community or even in family spaces. One young woman from Myanmar stated: 'When I was born, nobody expected me to become a leader.' In addition young women told us that values such as respect, humility, responsibility, motivation, passion, honesty and non-discriminatory attitudes were essential to their approach to leadership. A young woman from Papua New Guinea stated:

> I wasn't born a leader but I had to learn, I had to go through the process step by step to develop myself to become a young woman leader. So, leadership for me is trying to open yourself up, trying to have an open mind and trying to have an open heart and trying to accept things that come your way ... When you are a leader you have to be someone that serves people.

However, it was not just different values that set young women's leadership in the region apart from dominant models of leadership. We also found that young women's activism for peace blurs the boundaries of where peacebuilding takes place. Throughout our research we found that young women saw their leadership on matters of peace and security as starting in the private sphere such as the home, or in informal spaces such as in community or friendship-based groups. Young women discussed gendered stereotypes and discrimination in their homes, schools and churches as infringing upon their peace and security and therefore saw these as the places to begin their peacebuilding work.

Obstacles to peace the young women identified – such as early marriage, denial of education and violence – are often prevalent within these private spaces. A young woman from Papua New Guinea noted the importance of 'targeting young women [for support]', mentioning 'the vulnerability of young women, especially those who are out of school, most of the time they just engage in marriage and they have kids. They don't access their rights and the opportunities they have.' While young women are not always able, or supported, to defend themselves against such challenges, many were proud of the ways that they were able to seek support services (where available), build a peer-network of support, speak to family members about their concerns and change attitudes and practices. As one young woman from Bougainville explained: '[A]s a young person I feel that I have a big responsibility to go back to my village and to do something ... I would like to go back home and talk to our village elders so that they can allow time for me to talk to the people in the village about three things that I feel that I should talk about. That is, gender-based violence, peace and security, and drugs and alcohol, because this is what I see happening in our communities.

Young women also noted that their leadership is integral to the success of formal peacebuilding processes. Peace processes and post-conflict states can instigate legislative changes and governance frameworks around problems like early marriage and violence against women; however, they must be matched by cultural and attitudinal changes within the local communities. The young women we interviewed provided numerous examples of their own informal or private-sphere activities challenging attitudes towards gender inequality and social justice in their families, schools or churches. For example a young woman from Nepal spoke of her activism around HIV AIDS. She said that following her attendance at a YWCA leadership course she returned to her community and asked: 'What do you know about HIV AIDS?' When she was able to educate them on relevant issues, she reported that 'they are so surprised that I can speak so nicely about HIV AIDS [and] human empowerment'. Similarly, a young woman from Bangladesh cited her own leadership as pivotal in convincing senior family members of the negative impacts that an arranged marriage would have on her, despite the practice having been illegal in that country for decades.

Moreover, the young women we interviewed talked about the importance of building collaborative, horizontal peer-networks to advance their peace and social justice work. Unlike the vertical power structures that often define leadership models (see Lee-Koo and Pruitt 2020, 7–25), we found that across Asia and the Pacific young women preferred to work collaboratively as a group of leaders. For example, a young woman leader from Nepal described leadership to us in this way: 'Leadership means [the] ability to lead, but at the same time, when you're leading, you have to take the opinion of others … Just because you [are] a leader doesn't mean that your ideas and your decisions are always right. You have to take into consideration the opinion and views of others … as a leader, we have to [be] considering and taking other's ideas too.' These young women rely heavily upon their networks for input, knowledge sharing, emotional and practical support, and validation of their decisions and approaches (Lee-Koo and Pruitt 2020, 19–20). In this sense their leadership was not authenticated through a formal structure, process or title, all of which were often unavailable to young women anyway. Instead young women self-created spaces for their peacebuilding work, adopting a collaborative and participatory approach (Lee-Koo and Pruitt 2020, 20). Similarly, in her research looking at young Pacific women's participation in the Pacific Feminist Forum in 2016, Alver (2020, 70) found that 'rather than waiting for spaces to open up to be heard, and to be "invited" in to existing spaces, young women are creating their own spaces to lead and support other young women'.

Overall, young women in this research identified gender discrimination and stereotypes that exist in their everyday life as hindering their peace and security, and provided examples of the ways they engage in private sphere or informal activities to challenge gender inequalities. In doing so they echo statements by young people engaged in YPS consultations in the region, which have highlighted that young people identify peace and security as something 'individual' (Altiok 2017, 5) and that families are important partners in securing young people's place in implementing the peace and security agenda (Altiok 2017, 6).

Barriers to young women's peacebuilding in Asia and the Pacific

However, several barriers remain across the region to young women's peace-building work, particularly in formal peacebuilding spaces. Significantly we found that both gender and age bias limited support for, and recognition of, young women's peacebuilding efforts. In short the young women reported that they were not taken seriously as peacebuilders, nor were the issues they were advocating for and the work they were doing seen by the broader community as relevant to the core business of peace. This finding builds on existing evidence (e.g. Bolten, Chapter 5; Pruitt 2015, 9) documenting how young women and the concerns they hold have been deemed not serious or integral aspects of building peace and addressing conflict. Our research participants explained how the marginalisation of young women and their concerns from peacebuilding operated on a number of levels.

First, young women were seen to lack legitimacy in the business of peace. Across the region peace processes continue to be dominated by patriarchal and militarist cultures (Monash GPS, 2019). Even where women had been actively involved in their countries' peace processes, these roles were informal, and often marginalised. For example George (2016, 168) argues that the Bougainville peace process is often highlighted for the work of women peacebuilders to build positive outcomes but, at the same time, 'these "positive" outcomes [are] accompanied by shadows in the form of leadership activity that is unrecognised and [that] silences certain gendered aspects of women's conflict activity that persist'.

Second, *young* women were often seen as lacking legitimacy to contribute to peacebuilding efforts. This speaks to an intergenerational challenge in peacebuilding, particularly in Asia and the Pacific where there has been a generational shift in many peace processes. For instance the main conflicts ended in Bougainville in 1998, and in Nepal, the Solomon Islands, Aceh, Timor Leste and Sri Lanka throughout the first decade of the twenty-first century. The communities are starting to see a generational shift between those who fought in or lived through the conflict and those who have only faint, or no, memory of the conflict. This is important to consider. After all, young people involved in research analysing intergenerational peacebuilding in Aceh, Indonesia, reported limited knowledge about the Acehnese conflict, including women's experiences of it, and likewise said they felt uninterested in post-conflict efforts to advance gender equality and reconciliation; they also reported feeling marginalised from the peace process and therefore disconnected from it (Djohar and Pruitt 2021). Despite this the young women and young men involved showed their commitment to peacebuilding by joining in a creative writing peacebuilding programme in which they demonstrated curiosity and a willingness to engage in intergenerational dialogue to gain historical understanding of the conflict. They did this by studying the conflict's history, including the roles young people and women played, and directly connecting with women conflict survivors. The youth thus gained understanding of older generations and developed their own leadership on peacebuilding and gender-justice (Djohar and Pruitt 2021). Moreover, this example highlights that 'Gender should not be conflated with young women when it comes to youth, peace and security research', and, while our chapter here focuses on young women, we also acknowledge that 'failures to account for gender or to reflect critically on gendered stereotypes also harm young men' (Djohar and Pruitt 2021).

Furthermore, our research has found evidence that intergenerational relations can also shape attitudes towards participation in the peace process. One research participant from Papua New Guinea reported that when she spoke in a forum in favour of post-conflict reconciliation she was told by an older woman to 'sit down' and later chastised for speaking about things 'she knew nothing about'. Likewise research in Bougainville, Papua New Guinea, has reported that divisions between younger and older women around culture, expectations and education can sometimes hinder trust (Eves and Koredong 2015). In their exploration of intergenerational leadership in civil society and social justice sectors, Spark, Thomas and Brimacombe (2020) have similarly argued that many older women act in ways that create barriers to younger women's leadership. In their research in Papua New Guinea they noted that older women who had overcome significant gender-based barriers to gain a voice in civil society were reluctant to make space for young women's inclusion. This was particularly the case where younger women had different agendas and approaches from them (Spark, Thomas and Brimacombe 2020, 87–8). This, Spark, Thomas and Brimacombe argue, has created a division where younger women chose to 'go around' rather than 'work with' older women in their community in social justice work. The discrediting of young women as leaders in peacebuilding is also evident in Myanmar. Olivius and Hëdstrom (2020) have argued that, while in exile in Thailand, young Burmese women have had the freedom to engage in broad-ranging peace activities, including peace education and leadership training. However, once they returned to Myanmar, they experienced having their leadership constrained and rejected, significantly by patriarchal norms.

Third, when young women have been involved in peacebuilding, they report that they often experience a discrediting of their work as not real 'peace work'. This might include activities designed to promote gender equality and young women's human rights (such as programmes to raise awareness around GBV, trafficking, building leadership skills or sexual and reproductive health rights) or efforts to encourage post-conflict reconciliation and social justice. As discussed earlier, young people have demonstrated a strong commitment to inclusive peace approaches. These approaches, as outlined in the region's YPS Progress Report, identified the need for a holistic peace which recognises the interconnectedness of equality, justice and peace throughout the community. However, this has not been widely reflected in peace processes where both gender equality and justice work are seen as something that can wait until later, if they are to be addressed at all. Over the past two decades scholars have noted that women's everyday peace work remains unacknowledged in formal peace processes (Porter 2007; Mazurana and McKay 2002). More recent research has shown that there persists a lack of political will in supporting the implementation of gender equality as part of peace processes (Monash GPS 2019). Instead, much of this work is done at the grassroots level by women's civil society. This is the work of caring, rebuilding communities, promoting reconciliation, gender equality and non-violence (Mazurana and McKay 2002, 75). However, as Shepherd notes (2016), as women have become more active and vocal in peacebuilding, shifts are starting to appear in some governance circles, like the UN Peacebuilding Commission, where steps have been made towards recognising the value and impact of more inclusive visions of peace. However, tensions around what constitutes peace, and what issues are central to peace, remain, with *young* women's agendas being especially marginalised.

Conclusion: Enabling young women's peace leadership in Asia and the Pacific

Young women are significant actors in efforts to achieve sustained and intergenerational peace throughout the region. Yet in too many instances 'little has been done to ensure young women have a seat at the table' in terms of high-level, formal peace processes (Pruitt 2014, 488) or to ensure that their informal leadership for peacebuilding is recognised and supported as integral to sustainable peace. In this sense both the scope and the nature of dominant approaches to peacebuilding need to be challenged, and young women's leadership needs to be better recognised and supported.

In order to enhance young women's contributions to and leadership on peacebuilding, a number of ways forward can be pursued. First, advocacy for a broader understanding of peace is central. As the region's YPS Progress Report noted, 'to a great extent peace is about achieving social justice' (Altiok 2017, 6). Research that demonstrates the importance of social justice to peace will continue to evidence the value of the agenda that many young women peacebuilders put forward. Second, the creation of safe spaces for young women from across the region to speak about peace is important in building networks and developing young women's confidence to lead on peace and social justice issues. Third, community-based and externally supported leadership training assists in developing the skills and knowledge that young women rely upon to take on leadership roles. Finally, there needs to be a commitment to strong, intergenerational and gender-inclusive leadership. For peace to truly take hold, it needs to be sustained – equally – across generations.

References

Altiok, Ali. 2017. *Youth, Peace and Security in Asia and the Pacific: a Regional Consultation*. https://www.youth4peace.info/system/files/2017-11/2017.08.07%20-%20Report%20-%20Asia%20and%20the%20Pacific%20Regional%20Consultation%20on%20Youth%2C%20Peace%20%26%20Security.pdf. Accessed 1 December 2023.

Alver, Jane. 2020. "Building Inclusive Young Women's Leadership in the Pacific. In *Young Women and Leadership*, edited by Katrina Lee-Koo and Lesley Pruitt, pp. 63–78. London: Routledge.

AYF (ASEAN Youth Forum). 2014. *Yangon Youth Statement*. https://aseanyouthforum.org/wp-content/uploads/2019/03/AYF-Yangon-Declaration.pdf. Accessed 30 June 2020.

Bouvier, Virginia M. 2016. *Gender and the Role of Women in Colombia's Peace Process*. Washington, DC: United States Institute of Peace.

Brimacombe, Tait. 2018. 'Pacific Policy Pathways: Young Women Online and Offline.' In *Transformations of Gender in Melanesia*, edited by Martha MacIntyre and Ceridwen Spark, pp. 141–62. Canberra: ANU Press.

Cook-Huffman, Celia, and Anna Snyder. 2018. 'Women, Leadership, and Building Peace.' In *Peace Leadership: The Quest for Connectedness*, edited by Stan Amaladas and Sean Byrne, pp. 30–45. New York: Routledge.

Djohar, Zubaidah, and Lesley J. Pruitt. 2021. 'Creating an Intergenerational Feminist Peace? Global Research and a Case Study from Aceh, Indonesia.' In *Handbook of Feminist Peace Research*, edited by Tarja Väyrynen, Élise Féron, Swati Parashar and Catia Confortini, pp. 333–42. New York: Routledge.

Eves, Richard, and Isabelle Koredong. 2015. 'Bougainville Young Women's Leadership Research. Research Paper. Melbourne: International Women's Development Agency.

Frida. 2015. 'My Body, My Life, My Choice: Challenging Forced Marriage.' *Frida Special Impact Report, 2014–15*. https://www.yumpu.com/en/document/read/54892762/body-my-life-my-choice-my-forced-marriage-challenging. Accessed 19 August 2020.

George, Nicole. 2016. 'Light, Heat and Shadows: Women's Reflections on Peacebuilding in Post-conflict Bougainville.' *Peacebuilding* 4 (2): 166–79. https//:doi.10.1080/21647259.2016.1192241.

Ghazarian, Zareh, Eleanor Gordon and Katrina Lee-Koo. 2019. *Adolescent Girls in Crisis: Voices from Beirut*. https://plan-international.org/publications/adolescent-girls-crisis-beirut. Acessed 18 August 2020.

Girls Not Brides. 2018. *Child Marriage in Humanitarian Settings*. https://www.girls notbrides.org/learning-resources/child-marriage-and-humanitarian-contexts/. Accessed 1 December 2023.

Hudson, Valerie M., Bonnie Ballif-Spanvill, Mary Caprioli and Chad Emmett. 2012. *Sex and World Peace*. New York: Columbia University Press.

Krause, Jana, Werner Krause and Piia Bränfors. 2018. 'Women's Participation in Peace Negotiations and the Durability of Peace.' *International Interactions* 44 (6): 985–1016.

Lee-Koo, Katrina, and Lesley J. Pruitt. 2020. 'Building a Theory of Young Women's Leadership.' In *Young Women and Leadership*, edited by Katrina Lee-Koo and Lesley J. Pruitt, pp. 7–25. London: Routledge.

Mazurana, Dyan, and Susan McKay. 2002. *Raising Women's Voices for Peacebuilding*. London: International Alert.

Monash GPS. 2019. 'Towards Inclusive Peace.' https://www.monash.edu/__data/assets/pdf_file/0003/2088129/MONASH_inclusivepeace_workshop_ART.pdf. Accessed 29 June 2020.

Olivius, Elisabeth, and Jenny Hedström. 2020. 'Young Women's Leadership in Conflict: Crossing Borders in Myanmar.' In *Young Women and Leadership*, edited by Katrina Lee-Koo and Lesley J. Pruitt, pp. 45–62. London: Routledge.

Porter, Elisabeth. 2007. *Peacebuilding: Women in International Perspective*. London: Routledge.

Pruitt, Lesley J. 2014. 'The Women, Peace and Security Agenda: Australia and the Agency of Girls.' *Australian Journal of Political Science* 49 (3): 486–98.

Pruitt, Lesley J. 2015. 'Gendering the Study of Children and Youth in Peacebuilding.' *Peacebuilding* 3 (2): 157–70. https://doi.10.1080/21647259.2015.1052630.

Pruitt, Lesley J., and Katrina Lee-Koo. 2020. 'Critical Components for Advancing Young Women's Leadership.' In *Young Women and Leadership*, edited by Katrina Lee-Koo and Lesley J. Pruitt, pp. 26–44. London: Routledge.

Shepherd, Laura. 2016. 'Victims of Violence or Agents of Change? Representations of Women in UN Peacebuilding Discourses.' *Peacebuilding* 4 (2): 121–35.

Spark, Ceridwen, Barbra Thomas and Tait Brimacombe. 2020. '"There's Space for Both": Young Women and Intergenerational Leadership in Papua New Guinea.' In *Young Women and Leadership*, edited by Katrina Lee-Koo and Lesley J. Pruitt, pp. 79–98. London: Routledge.

UN (United Nations). 2018. *World Youth Report*. https://www.un.org/development/desa/youth/wp-content/uploads/sites/21/2018/12/WorldYouthReport-2030Agenda.pdf. Accessed 29 June 2020.

UNFPA (United Nations Population Fund). 2014. *Gender Based Violence in Humanitarian Settings*. https://www.unfpa.org/resources/gender-based-violence-humanitarian-settings. Accessed 18 August 2020.

12

How the international community can walk alongside local peacebuilders: lessons from South Sudan

Emmily Koiti, Bush Buse Laki and Chara Nyaura

This chapter shares stories and examples of authentic pathways taken by young peacebuilders in South Sudan to shine light on the importance of flexible accompaniment to local peacebuilding efforts. The narratives are followed by a set of recommendations that provide donors, international NGOs and outside peacebuilding practitioners insights into how to best support local peacebuilding initiatives. First, it is critical for donors and INGOS to devise a flexible funding approach to support local initiatives for ten years or more and to walk alongside the local peacebuilders and their initiatives to achieve the desired goals. Second, donors, international peacebuilding practitioners and local initiatives should create a strong ecosystem where they become one community of partners who interact with each other in a specific environment to achieve the desired goal. Third, local peacebuilders should maintain the courage of their convictions and stick to what is working locally rather than what is told to them by outsiders. Finally, local peacebuilders should connect with what is around them in terms of relationships and resources before seeking outside support.

Many peacebuilding projects and training initiatives talk of changing and measuring changes in attitudes, behaviours, values and narratives. But it is everyday things that indicate when peace exists, for example, being able to travel from one location to another with freedom of movement and freedom of expression, or sitting down to share a cup of tea with someone we have been told is 'the enemy'. As John Paul Lederach says, the key to envisioning and responding to social conflict is rooted in the quality of relationships that you create (2003, 13). We believe relationships are the key to peaceful coexistence. Supporting young people to engage in building new and deep relationships has a bearing on long-term peace and healing (Ayindo 2011).[1] In other words the process of nurturing a human being into a safe and responsible citizen through creating relationships with those who may not be just like them contributes to peacebuilding and produces potential peacebuilders out of everyday people.

The first section discusses the difficulty that young peacebuilders face in South Sudan, and how one of the important starting points is to learn to model the kind of new behaviour one expects to see from others. We then discuss some examples of how we attempted to reach other marginalised populations and create a larger shared imagination for what a peaceful South Sudan can look like. Finally, we share lessons on how international NGOs and donors can model behaviours that can spread to others like them in how they decide to walk alongside young peacebuilders.

Where we come from, no one listens

In South Sudan everyone, especially outsiders, seems to have solutions to our problems. But no one ever listens to what we young South Sudanese want. In our experience we are ignored by our elders, our leaders and those who come to 'help' address South Sudan's many problems. So often young people become dependent on outsiders for the answers and for the money and resources to take any idea forward. We become 'askers rather than doers' (Anderson, Brown and Jean 2012). However, young people in South Sudan are often the most affected by the repeating cycles of violence, poor health and lack of access to basic services that can allow us even a little space to think about the future. We see things that others do not. Other NGOs and donors should be encouraged to be a part of our journey and support what is working for us and what is owned by us. There is a nurturing process that can replace the neocolonial (Langan 2018) and external peacebuilding processes that pervade much of the work in South Sudan that is supported by outside NGOs and donors. But before they can listen to us, we must listen to ourselves and know what we are bringing to the table.

Learning to listen to ourselves

Sixty-Four Children from One Mother (64–1M); such a simple name to call our group of young South Sudanese from multiple ethnic groups, locations and vocations. There are sixty-four tribes that may act differently, but we are all from One Mother – South Sudan. We never thought of what relationships really mean in peacebuilding until we met this larger group of other young people who are passionate about changing the narrative of war to one of peace in our communities and country.

We are the voices that need to be heard throughout the peacebuilding world, but, before we could use our voices, we had to find our individual and collective voices. Fortunately we were connected to Nomfundo Walaza and Chris Spies, South African peacebuilders who created the Unyoke Foundation as a space to reflect on personal and collective journeys (www. unyoke.org). They helped us look carefully at past patterns and challenges and encouraged conversations with us to envision our future role in peacebuilding. They call this the 'Unyoke process'. Together Nomfundo and Chris created a space where people could disconnect or 'unyoke' from their daily frustrations and hardships, connect with colleagues in a similar emotional space and reimagine what is possible together. The 'Unyokes' were an immersive experience of transformation, inspiration, joy and pain. Together we shared past traumas, personal stories and the story of how South Sudan came to be this way. We thought through how we can write the next chapter of the story as one of a peaceful South Sudan. We connected not through log frames and theories of change but through tears and our own voices. We were seeking to transform our country towards a healthy, flourishing and accountable society. We also had conversations that contributed to mapping these dynamics and challenges in our country and understanding how to overcome them.

The conversations we had in the 'Unyoke' spaces were different from what we had encountered with other NGOs and people from outside South Sudan. Most of the time in those meetings we sit at long tables in air-conditioned hotel conference rooms, while someone (usually a white person) talks to us about building our capacity. There is often little space for our own voices to inform this process. There is often little attention given to what capacity we already have inside us and through the relationships that we have with other people. The lessons we learned from the Unyoke circle did not come from a lecture or capacity-building training with an external expert. They came from a literal circle, where everyone brought their true selves forward and built our collective ability to trust and deepen relationships with people who were supposed to be our enemies. We uncovered what many of us knew but never said out loud – creating a peaceful South Sudan is all about relationships, relationships with ourselves and with those around us.

Nomfundo, Chris and other friends walking alongside us have helped in finding what lies within us to achieve what we want to see. Paolo Freire called this 'conscientisation' – an awareness of self in context that requires new ways of knowing and thinking for both the oppressed and oppressor (Freire 1985, 185). This is not to say we were 'oppressed' but rather we have been on the weaker side of power dynamics that exist between the outside organisations that have funding and the local peacebuilders who do not. Action is fundamental in conscientisation because it is the process of changing reality. As a result, we as 64–1M seek to change our reality and the way we show up through repeated actions that 'model cooperative behavior' (Axelrod 2006, 334). Axelrod describes how co-operation can rarely emerge in a homogeneous population. On the basis of a study of the Prisoner's Dilemma, they explain that if you have a small number of isolated individuals who are co-operating, non-cooperators will eventually overrun them. He argues that the only way to change this is to put a cluster of innovators together who adopt co-operative behaviour, and they will eventually influence others through their behaviour.

The strength of our relationships builds self-confidence and the ability to believe in ourselves again. However, it is hard work. We have competing ideas about how we model co-operative behaviour. We create our own ways to ensure we do the work we say we want to do. Sometimes we fail. But there is a commitment to action that has slowly created a culture of accountability. We apply the lessons we learned in that Unyoke circle to listen to each other and to unfold what we want to do, what we have between us that can allow us to act on, and whom else we can bring into the work.

It is interesting how weaving together relationships sometimes feels like working with magic. Our collective experience – working deliberately, publicly together, connecting 64–1M with their individual stories, to keep their creativity flowing, to have ownership of their ideas and to share the journey of learning together – has created a new atmosphere of working with funders, donors and partners equally. These relationships led us to develop more open-mindedness to ideas that build on our collective strength and draw on practices that are known to our fellow citizens. Seemingly simple things like tea, dancing and talking with those who are also ignored all point us toward peaceful coexistence and changing the narratives about what young people can do.

Listening to the ignored

Since independence in 2011 over fifty thousand people are estimated to be amputees in South Sudan (ICRC 2012). Many of these are the results of severe injuries from armed conflict. The use of landmines was common during the pre-independence armed conflict between the North and South, and they continue to be used today. Documentation on amputees in the country has remained limited, and advocacy that mainstreams their issues in national discourse on peacebuilding is almost ignored. People with disabilities are not given serious consideration. The effects of amputation are far-reaching and varied, with no two cases being exactly the same, but the emotional and psychological effects are devastating. Affected individuals go through these challenges and yet their dilemmas are not documented and relied on in policy development. Additionally, they are not effectively represented in decision-making processes regarding national development.

It is against this background that we decided to create a platform to support people who suffer from limb loss by documenting their narratives and advocating for their rights, a project that highlights that youth peacebuilding concerns are not limited to the situation of young people per se. We shed light on the effects of amputation in people's lives, whether they resulted from armed conflict or not. This initiative models the behaviour we want to see, where every person's story matters no matter where they are from or who they are. This is the behaviour that for us indicates what peace can look like in the life of an amputee. The initiative aims at amplifying the voices of amputees as a special group of people with different abilities in a bid to enable them to influence the peacemaking initiative in South Sudan. The idea was inspired by our stories and by the realisation of how people who are differently abled can make a positive impact on peace in our country. Disability knows no age or ethnic boundary in South Sudan.

We initially did a survey to find out statistics for amputees by visiting offices concerned and talking to some of the amputees. After this survey we realised that a lot more needed to be done than was taking place at the time, and we thought our idea was worth committing to. First, we started by identifying amputees to participate in the initiative, which was mostly done through recommendations from our colleagues, friends and family members. We used our current relationships to find and engage amputees. Second, we followed up from the contact list and organised meetings to directly interact with the amputees. Some of them were hesitant to commit, but most of them gained the confidence to participate from seeing and hearing from Chara (one of the authors of this chapter), who is also an amputee. They believed the space was safe for them to participate and their stories would be safe as well. There are a lot of burning issues in the hearts of amputees, including feeling discriminated against, denial of their inalienable rights and stigmatisation by society. Amputees believe this initiative will help them advocate for their rights, create awareness and allow them to express their capabilities in peacebuilding.

We did a three-day mini 'Unyoking' process. Thirteen amputees, both male and female, from different South Sudanese tribes participated in the meeting. The meeting was for the amputees to have a safe space where they were away from the usual formal meeting spaces, to create a community by inviting participants to tell their stories freely, and to learn from each other's stories in the simplest way possible. It was for the amputees to experience the 'Unyoke experience' and to introduce the amputees to the idea of producing a book together and to get their consensus. The idea of the book became a way to think about how they would work together to share their story in a tangible published work. A book signified something that could record and capture experiences that are more often than not ignored in daily South Sudanese life. In the end, taking part in this experience of sharing together meant that they found it easier to relate their stories on talk radio stations and in other groups of people who had little exposure to people with disabilities.

Initially we had a huge challenge identifying female amputees. However, through our growing relationships, we were able to find a contact they trusted. He connected us to most of the amputees we are currently working with, both female and male, which allowed us to work on this issue in spite of the lack of exposure for it in national and international peacebuilding circles. Networking also gave us an opportunity to establish relationships with individuals and institutions like the International Committee of the Red Cross (ICRC) in South Sudan, South Sudan Wheelchair Basketball Association (SSWA), Giada Military Hospital administration, radio stations, authors, videographers and others. Since this modest beginning, our network has grown to over 112 amputees. Through reaching out to a group that was previously marginalised socially because they were perceived to be vulnerable, helpless, drunkards, unproductive or troublemakers, we were able to achieve many things due to the power of focusing on weaving a web of relationships, rather than fixating on a result.

We are inspired to build a bigger spider web, which is essentially a larger collection of relationships, by spreading the positive vision of peace in a unique and self-driven process. We did this ourselves, not because an outside organisation or donor wanted it done, but because we saw it was needed. In this way the contribution of amputees to peacebuilding initiatives and processes will include the building of effective relationships, and expansion to networks for sustainable peace.

Listening together: when tea is more than tea

Sometimes things that seem simple to outsiders are the key to uncovering deeper truths and relationships within a community. In 2018 the initiative 'Take Tea Together' (TTT) emerged from the same diverse group of civically engaged young South Sudanese who took part in the first Unyoke retreats. While one group did the amputee work described above, another came up with the idea of using the cultural importance of tea to bring people together physically and socially. The culture of taking tea in the markets and in the shades of community trees in South Sudan has been instrumental in promoting discussions about crucial issues pertaining to the economy, politics and cultures. Many people around South Sudan gain access to information in different spheres of life from tea places. Women, particularly widows, use tea vending to sustain themselves and their families. While tea has always been important in South Sudan, in the years after war broke out in 2013, taking tea in the markets, street corners and under trees became a code word for people plotting against their neighbours or spreading rumours, according to Buse, one of the founders of the Take Tea Together initiative. The four planners wanted to use tea as a way to bring people together and slowly began to reclaim what taking tea could mean for peacebuilding, creating a path for a new beginning to weave a network of united, informed and civically engaged young people in South Sudan.

TTT forums are usually conducted in an open and strategically positioned place close to the market area of Gurei in Juba where many people can have access to and potentially join the discussions and entertainment in the shade of the 'Gurei Peace Tree'. What started as four young people is now planned by a volunteer group of seventy-five people. The volunteers also play an instrumental role in mobilising community members through a megaphone, posters, radio and social media, which have enabled us to reach thousands of people per gathering in Gurei.

The first TTT forum attracted about two hundred people from the community. It focused on entertainment by comedians and musicians and listening to speeches from government leaders and civil society activists. We did not imagine that one day we would have a TTT where everybody sits at a roundtable to participate in discussions about issues of tribalism and peaceful coexistence. However, every time we conduct an event, we realise there is something to improve in the next forum. Some of the great ideas come from our volunteers and participants during our evaluation meetings where we reflect and share lessons and challenges learned. Planning, reasoning and deciding together with our volunteers and key participants demonstrate a true spirit of ownership of the idea.

These tea sessions foster an atmosphere of meditation, restoration and reconciliation. TTT participants usually decide on the topics that need to be discussed, including how to make the community safer, healthier and peaceful. They focus on promoting the economic empowerment of youth and women, addressing hate speech, tribalism, cattle raiding and violence, increasing the role of youth in nation-building, and advocating for policies with an aim to always keep a dialogue that resolves issues in a non-violent way.

A critical component of this work is to deepen the trust between youth peacebuilders and build our confidence as individuals and in our strength as a group modelling co-operative behaviour in an environment of rampant violence. As a result we have a greater level of trust and confidence to inspire our people to become agents of peace and development in their communities. For example, in 2019, a group of young peacebuilders was able to mobilise youth from the Protection of Civilians site (PoC) in Juba to participate in TTT events organised in the host community. One member from the Nuer ethnic community that joined the event testified that it was her first time emerging from the PoC since the outbreak of the conflicts to join a TTT roundtable discussion with members from the Dinka community. She explained, 'At first I was hesitant to open up for discussions because my brothers and sisters were killed by people from the Dinka ethnicity and I never wanted to sit with them … it took courage to release my bitterness because it was hurting and affecting my health. This provides the space to allow us to dialogue and address our internal problems.'

We work to extend the effectiveness of TTT in several ways. We have conducted talk shows over the radio, the South Sudan Television, and also follow-up visits to our participants in their homes to get feedback and strengthen our relationships. Many people appreciated the creative initiative and requested the TTT idea to be replicated across the country to provide spaces for dialogues that will help address the numerous challenges of cattle raiding, negative tribalism, tribal conflicts and revenge in communities. They also recommended a women's TTT to address issues of sexual and gender-based violence (SGBV), another important arena for us to expand into.

We believe that, had we been part of an international NGO, TTT would never have happened. In fact, several INGOs have made very generous offers to fund TTT. However, their demands for policies, a physical office and insistence that we become a registered NGO made it a challenge for us to acquire funding and have full control over our idea. It is hard to blame them, as even our accompaniers at the Unyoke Foundation were unsure of that idea at first. When we shared our idea, they said they were unsure what impact the gatherings would have. However, they did something different from other outsiders. They said, 'This is your idea and your work, and our role is to follow where you lead. So, lead us.' This attitude of support that places us at the centre is critical to how the INGOs and academics should work with local peacebuilders like us. We firmly believe that we are effective because we are from the areas where we work.

Accompaniment as a pathway to engaging young peacebuilders

Outside peacebuilders and experts walk alongside us through accompaniment: the ultimate role of the accompaniers, who are mainly from South

Africa, the US and Portugal, is to provide accompaniment, for which we use the metaphor of *scaffolding*. This metaphor tells us that it is the engineers that build the house but not the scaffold, which is temporarily there to support the engineers in their work of constructing a decent house for accommodation and comfort. This scaffold will be removed once the house is completed.

Ultimately, INGOs and donors should focus on scaffolding that nurtures and accompanies young peacebuilders in order to best actualise peace. The prospects for peace are determined by investment in both the budding and seasoned local peacebuilder. For example the members of the TTT Initiative received some flexible funds (which INGOs call 'General Operating Support') in 2018 from the Unyoke Foundation to try the first few TTT gatherings. The funding was small but it was flexible and allowed us time to learn and adapt our work. The organisers also received contributions from the members and some well-wishers in South Sudan through in-kind support for the initiative. The funds and the in-kind support were used to expand on the TTT idea to engage more than a thousand youths and community members.

Part of the money which community members contributed was invested in a shop business in Gudele market in Juba to create job opportunities for TTT volunteers. It is with this that we began learning that young leaders and peacebuilders could do so much if international partners offer flexible resources to them. Donors should relax their strict policies to allow local initiatives like movements, groups and associations that are not structured like NGOs to have more readily available access to funding and enable them to implement activities in an independent manner. It is also vital to always bear in mind that bureaucracies of the international systems should not hinder flexible support for small community initiatives. This is key in accompanying peacebuilders to allow them to create the change they desperately yearn to see. It is the lack of such flexible support for peacebuilders that makes many establish local organisations with haste when they hardly have the capacity or time to effectively manage and sustain them. They rush to get any amount of money from outside funds before stopping to see if outside money is the answer. It also postpones progress when passionate peacebuilders have to wait for the resources as dictated by bureaucracies.

South Sudan is routinely known as one of the most expensive places to operate an NGO, due to high operating costs.[2] Our total lack of infrastructure, horrible roads, risk of armed attacks and rampant corruption make even the apparently simple act of visiting someone in another town a costly and risky endeavour. Funding local approaches means that less money is spent with a higher chance for impact. For example the TTT approach is cost-effective compared to dialogue forums conducted by INGOs, which are often done in hotels and require quite a lot of money. A dialogue organised in a hotel by an NGO for thirty to fifty people may cost $30,000 or more, but this same amount of money can be used by TTT to conduct thirty to fifty dialogues in the shades of community peace trees, which can potentially create a bigger change.

A critical reminder for any academic or INGO is that our work is not a 'project' and our participants are not 'beneficiaries'. This is our life and our community. We will be here long after INGOs have left. TTT forums are there to stay so long as sugar and water continue to exist and that makes us unique in ensuring that dialogues continue in the community and that the local people have the ownership of the idea. We plan and decide together on what should be done and how it should be done. We know how to work in South Sudan without spending the money that INGOs spend.

Listen to locals: there is a better way for INGOs and donors to show up

It is important to name some of the shortcomings of how international peacebuilding organisations, experts and donors address local issues. From our perspective, INGOs want local peacebuilding initiatives to look like them and use their abstract theoretical approaches. Donors and INGOs have strict policies that local peacebuilding initiatives must follow in order to have access to funding and other kinds of support. While meant to ensure accountability, this sends the message that we cannot be trusted to create our own accountability. We have to do it 'their way'. This discourages innovation in doing things differently that fit the local context and pressures local initiatives to copy and paste what INGOs and other outside peacebuilding practitioners are doing. Youth associations, social movements and women's associations are examples of civil society that are not structured like NGOs, but they make a great contribution in society. The definition of legitimacy (often seen as being registered and structured like a Western organisation) as set out by the transnational funders has hindered our ability to organise in movements and coalitions over issues. The competition over resources takes precedence over achieving tangible results that benefit citizens.[3]

We would like to remind readers that peacebuilding is not a project. This implies that peacebuilding is not a short-term endeavour that must be achieved within a stipulated period of time. Peacebuilding must be a continuous process to strengthen relationships and address conflicts that emerge in life. Young people in South Sudan constitute more than 72 per cent of the country's population, and their energy, time and aspirations place them in a better position to shoulder the responsibility of achieving lasting peace in the young nation. NGOs and donors would be wise to support the work of young peacebuilders who, through ownership of their own work, can leverage their relationships to transform violent conflict.

Conclusions: recommendations on listening and acting together

International partners and local peacebuilders all have a role to play in successful peacebuilding. First, it is critical for donors and INGOs to devise a flexible funding approach to support local initiatives for at least ten years or more and walk alongside the local peacebuilding initiatives to achieve the desired goals. This can help to shift the current policies of many INGOs and encourage donors to reimagine and relax some of their strict funding policies and conditionality. The relaxation of strict policies can allow local initiatives like movements, groups and associations that are not structured like NGOs to have easy access to funding and enable them to implement activities in an independent manner. It is also vital to always bear in mind that flexible support for implementation of small community initiatives should not be hindered by bureaucracies of the international system. This is key in accompanying peacebuilders to create the change they yearn to see.

Second, donors, international peacebuilding practitioners and local initiatives should create a strong ecosystem where they become one community of partners who interact with each other in a specific environment to achieve the desired goal. Policy- and decision-makers should establish deliberate programmes meant to uplift young peacebuilders, especially women. It is this investment that sets fertile soils for budding great leaders and peacebuilders. The programmes should be pragmatic enough to accompany leaders as they start off. They should embrace ambiguity and give things time to grow. This community should regularly dialogue and accompany each other toward the attainment of the goals. This kind of healthy relationship will prevent assumptions, help outsiders understand local contexts and avoid imposing unpractical theories or approaches on local initiatives. All peacebuilding practitioners need to see this community as a safe space for peacebuilders to connect, share experiences and retreat for respite and group self-care. Peacebuilders are human beings who can break down and burn out. They can benefit from spaces where they offload their burdens and refuel for future endeavours. It is also important to be mindful to allow peacebuilders to have the greatest autonomy over any safe space created.

Third, local initiatives should adhere to their principles and vision. Local peacebuilders should maintain their courage and stick to what is working locally rather than what is told to them by outside experts, which may not work well in the local context. They should encourage mutual relationships with partners that are funding them to respect their values and anchor peace in local realities and needs. They should not be afraid to reject funding that undermines their values and vision.

Lastly, peacebuilders should learn to tap into local resources to create more funds for sustainability. Local initiatives should not be dependent on external funding to address their own problems, but rather create investments in relationships to generate support for their activities. Look to see what is around you before seeking outside support, as the people who are most affected by the violence will be those most willing to invest, however little they have, in the peace.

Notes

1 The author points out that the task of peacebuilding and healing are a collective one. He says, 'We need to be a mobilized community, acting systemically, motivated by our new story' (Ayindo 2011, 69).
2 See https://www.cbc.ca/news/world/south-sudan-ngo-fees-1.4098091 (accessed 1 December 2023), and also 'A Rock and a Hard Place: Operational Challenges for Aid Organizations in South Sudan' (https://www.csrf-southsudan.org/reposi tory/rock-hard-place-operating-challenges-aid-organizations-south-sudan/, accessed 1 December 2023).
3 More of the risks and limitations of registering as a CSO in South Sudan can be found at https://blogs.lse.ac.uk/africaatlse/2020/02/17/international-development-frameworks-civil-society-western-ngos/. Accessed 1 December 2023.

References

Anderson, Mary B., Dayna Brown and Isabella Jean. 2012. *Time to Listen: Hearing People on the Receiving End of International Aid*. Cambridge, MA: CDA Collaborative Learning Projects.
Axelrod, Robert. 2006. *The Evolution of Cooperation*. Second Edition. New York: Basic Books.
Ayindo, Babu. 2011. *In Search of Healers: A Study on Cycles of Violence, Collective Trauma and Strategies for Healing and Peacebuilding in Kenya*. Nairobi: Coalition for Peace in Africa.
Freire, Paulo. 1985. *The Politics of Education: Culture, Power, and Liberation*. New York: Bergin and Garvey.
ICRC. 2012. *Growing Need for Care for South Sudan's Amputees*. International Committee of the Red Cross, Multimedia Newsroom, 7 September. https://www.icrcnewsroom.org/story/en/1389/growing-need-for-care-for-south-sudan-samputees#:~:text=As%20South%20Sudan%20turns%201,present%20and%20past%20armed%20conflicts. Accessed 20 July 2020.

Langan, Mark. 2018. *Neo-Colonialism and the Poverty of 'Development' in Africa.* Basingstoke: Palgrave Macmillan.

Lederach, John Paul. 2003. *The Little Book of Conflict Transformation.* New York: Good Books.

Unyoke Foundation. n.d. https://unyoke.org/. Accessed 19 April 2021.

13

Global Unites: a new generation of peacebuilders rising with resilience and courage from the ashes of conflict

Prashan De Visser on behalf of Global Unites

Sri Lanka

It was the 15th of October, 1997. I was seated in my grade seven science class. From our classroom we had a brilliant view of the city. As my teacher was conducting the lesson, the largest explosion we had ever heard ripped into our lives. We were shaken into silence and gripped by fear. In disbelief we watched the billowing smoke as it engulfed the horizon. We knew what this meant. Yet another suicide bomb by the Tamil terrorist group known as the Liberation Tamil Tigers of Eelam (LTTE). However, this time the attack seemed more powerful than before. Our suspicions were right – news started streaming in, school was declared closed, and details on the bombing of the World Trade Center in Colombo, Sri Lanka, poured in.[1] It was one of the bloodiest, most costly attacks from the terror group thus far.

The ride back home was long and dreadful. What was usually a 30-minute drive now took nearly four hours. Without cell phones we couldn't communicate with our families. All of us were anxious to know if our parents were safe or if they were anywhere near the bombing site. When I finally got home, I ran in to find no one there. My heart sank. Were my parents at the wrong place at the wrong time? My sister's school was located very close to ground zero as well. My neighbours quickly comforted me: 'Your parents went to pick you and your sister up. They were not sure if your school bus would get you.' So I waited. I knew my parents would also get stuck in traffic. I stayed alone at home, watching the news of the incident. Fear, anger, frustration and hopelessness overwhelmed me. Many hours later my parents returned with my sister. It was such a joyous reunion for us as a family. However, we knew that wasn't the case for many families who were torn apart forever. With a heavy heart my father informed us that the father of one of my friends had been killed in the suicide bomb attack. I was shocked and furious. Being caught in the midst of violence in the war zone in the North meant many families were ripped apart and never reunited again. Countless other suicide attacks and other violent incidents in the past resulted in traumatised communities, crippled the economy, and our potential as a nation slipped further from our hands each day.

Afghanistan

It was just five days after starting my bachelor's degree programme at the American University of Afghanistan in Kabul. I was only 16 and was all alone in a province far from home when my university was attacked.[2] In August 2016, when classes were finishing, militants drove two trucks full of bombs into the school while several other militants entered the campus and started shooting. I was in the middle of the university premises when all of a sudden I felt like my soul had left my body. All I heard was 'buzz'. I think a bomb explosion is only loud to those away from it. When you are the target, it deafens you, and all you can hear is a buzz. At least that was how I experienced it, and what alerted my paralysed body was the sky filled with fire and smoke and shrapnel flying all over my head. I couldn't move any part of my body. But I remember wondering, 'What just happened? What does this mean? What am I supposed to do?' Perhaps I was too young to make sense of such a situation or perhaps my mind was paralysed too. But, when I looked at the people around me running for their lives (not knowing where but trying to escape the bullets), I realised I was supposed to rescue myself. But I could not. There was no strength in my feet to move. Suddenly, I remembered my mother – the woman whose ambitions, and career, were taken away from her due to the strict regime of the Taliban; despite the odds she supported me and empowered me to become who she couldn't be, to become a hope for her and the women back at home in Kandahar. I started crying out loud, 'What will happen to her? People will blame her for my death. I can't die.' A security guard noticed me and came towards me. He grabbed my hand and started running until he got me to the basement where there were other students. Some had been shot, some had broken bones and all were hiding in fear. We spent nine hours there while the shooting continued. We waited for our death, wondering when they would come find us.

Democratic Republic of Congo[3]

My introduction to violence started early. When I was four years old, government soldiers invaded my village. I remember running and hiding under a table. They questioned every family. If we were missing any family members, they would assume that they had joined the rebels and were fighting against the government soldiers. Then the killing started. They killed family members of rebel soldiers. Many of my friends and neighbours were killed. We had to drag the bodies away from our field where we played soccer. This was the first time we were traumatised. The trauma continued throughout my life, but I refuse to let this be the end of the story. We will rebuild and transform our nation. We will refuse to let our children suffer in the same way we did.

A global movement for grassroots peacebuilders
from the Global South

These accounts from leaders of the Global Unites movements happened
in very different cultural landscapes, with varied historical contexts and
different impetuses for violence. Young people are the best hope for sustainable solutions and peace for our nations. This chapter will seek to
unpack this further. Young people are not simply victims of horrible cycles
of violence, their unique positioning and perspective can be part of the
solution to creating sustainable peace (McEvoy-Levy 2008).

   Global Unites emerged organically, first as Sri Lanka Unites and then
expanding to launch and expand new youth movements in countries like
Congo, Kenya, Uganda and other nations from the Global South. These
movements found a kindred spirit in one another and an ability to better
empathise with realities of engaging in the midst of violent conflict, poverty
and corruption. The movement set its foundation in the following pillars of
engagement:

• Youth led
• Conflict transformational approach
• Non-violence at all cost
• Grassroots movements with national reach

Local youth leaders would lead these movements, endorsed and supported
by local elders, as a coalition established and led by the Global South. They
would be structured in a manner where the local leadership was placed at
the centre of every intervention with a commitment to finding solutions
from within the nation. It would be led by a new generation who were
committing their lives to bring about transformation to their nations and
striving relentlessly to that end. Thus began a global movement that has
now spread to thirteen countries while creating a model for peacebuilding
and conflict transformation originating from the Global South.

   Today this approach continues to be refined by scholar practitioners in
these nations, and has also inspired movements in the West. USA Unites
has formally launched operations as a fully fledged movement seeking to
engage youth to be peacebuilders across race and socio-economic divisions
in their nation. More interest continues to flow in from across Europe as
nations are experiencing a rise in toxic nationalism and growing tension
among youth from majority and immigrant communities. This has created
a new frontier of movements, and approaches from the Global South are
now being contextualised in the West to find meaningful solutions to
ongoing conflict. This is an interesting inversion of global intervention,
where hierarchy based on affluence, privilege and access to power are no

longer a reason for intervention, but rather the merit of the model and uniqueness of the approach, yet holding locals at the pinnacle of leadership and response.

The other side of violent conflict

Why are these young men and women the best hope for their countries? What supports them in their peacebuilding work? Why are these grassroots, locally led movements the best hope for their nations? There are some key reasons. In the first part of this chapter we argue that young people have an existential stake in peace, an undeniable resolve for peace, an acute understanding of the context and threats to peace and a generational mandate to build peace now and in the future. In the second part of the chapter we draw on the Global Unites experience to highlight the importance of transnational coalitions and support systems that help sustain youth peacebuilding, and we explore how these alliances operate in the midst of overwhelming challenges while benefiting one another in this global network of grassroots peacebuilders. Finally we will reflect on the long-term accomplishments these movements are seeking to achieve, that will in turn signify tangible transformation.

The young people in Global Unites know what is at stake: their education, employment, families, freedom, democracy, nation and even their lives. These young men and women have experienced the brutality of war. They have watched the crippling impact of violence and instability on their own economy. They have seen the devastating impact it has had on their lives and their future. Their experiences have been an assault on their emotional health, their confidence and dignity as a people. These young people have everything to lose, thus they engage with unwavering commitment to bring about long-term change (De Visser 2015). They have a resolve and commitment that goes beyond a project cycle or the attention span of an INGO or a foreign government's resolve to respond to their crisis.

In countries where youth and civil society have left the critical work of peacebuilding in the hands of dominant and well-funded INGOs, foreign interventions or even their own government, they have come to face the awful realisation that these institutions were never in a position to bring about transformation. The lack of resolve, commitment and even the comprehension of what was at stake has led to mediocre, short-sighted, out of touch and surface initiatives and efforts.[4] Many of these initiatives fit neatly into log frames and perfect theories of change. However, they often did not take root among the masses. They were never organic and did not build resilience among communities to overcome the next cycle of violence.

Young peacebuilders and community leaders who initiate peacebuilding efforts in these countries know that their future is at stake. They know they need to convince and recruit their communities to engage and that they need to hold their authorities to account.

A young man involved with Afghanistan Unites wrote to the Global Unites leadership six months before US and allied forces along with all major INGOs in Afghanistan departed Kabul.

> If the peace process continues to fail, our work as a local movement becomes even more important. I suspect all the well funded international organizations will leave Afghanistan overnight. However, we need to push for our own local initiatives to engage, as we always see them as better models to do so. We never received funding and support for these approaches. Given the current trend, I am even more committed to our local leadership focused efforts. This is our only hope. At the end of the day, they will leave, find a better hunting ground for large scale INGO initiatives. We can't give up. This is our future, our people, and our nation. Hence, we will build from the bottom up.

Many international initiatives for peace and the organisations that lead them are often focused on the project timeline. They strive to ensure that deliverables are met, then move on to do whichever project the foundation or government agency has allocated funding for. These donor resources are crucial for the sustainability of their high cost-operations.[5] These expenses quite often include lucrative salaries, luxury vehicles, security expenses, prime real-estate offices, contributions to head-office administration in their home country, and international travel expenses for 'qualified' resource people, that run a pretty steep bill. Once an INGO has set up a base in the nation, it is caught in a trap of having to follow the funding at all cost to maintain high-spending operations and justify continued presence. These organisations often follow the funding that makes the enterprise possible, even if local voices do not agree, or at times, even despite what they may know to be ineffective. That is what is at stake in the minds of most international organisations. However, when a new cycle of violence emerges, when the security and comfort of an operation are threatened, they leave in record time.[6] Locals who trusted and sought to engage with them are left without an income and, at times, their lives are endangered because of their co-operation with international organisations. These are the realities in many of the nations where we have engaged. The patterns are not the exception but are fast becoming the norm. While we must appreciate the many international interventions that have sought to do no harm and continue to learn from the mistakes of the past, it is crucial to conduct an ongoing re-evaluation of how peacebuilding takes place.

Undeniable resolve

In Sri Lanka young people who joined the LTTE were willing to strap bombs around their waists[7] and sacrifice their lives for their cause. Every young cadre wore a cyanide capsule around their neck. If they were captured, they would take their own life, rather than be taken captive. They committed these atrocities because they were indoctrinated to believe that their violence and bravery would assure their community of a better life. We see this type of conditioning in many nations in the midst of war. Youth are willing to give their lives for a cause. That same commitment, resolve and passion remains untapped for the cause of peace, healing, justice and national development.

> I believed in violence. I didn't see any hope anywhere else. My parents were active freedom fighters in the LTTE. I was once willing to kill and even die for what I thought would bring justice, freedom, and opportunity for my narrow definition of 'my people'. Today, I am willing to die for a cause of a united Sri Lanka, a just and thriving nation for all Sri Lankans. I will never take my life or the life of another, but my entire life, my future, my ambition is to build a great, united, and prosperous nation. (Sri Lanka Unites member)

Young peacebuilders leading movements in their nations are well placed to tap into this outstanding resource among their peers. They can be convinced that the pursuit of a better life and future does not require embracing violence or sacrificing one's life. A change of perspective makes room for personal transformation (Lederach 2003). A former enemy, now an ally with similar aspirations for a collective future; once a contributor to the destruction of self and others, now a passionate advocate and contributor to development; from intolerance of the 'other' to collective innovation. These youth hold the key to national transformation. To unlock their potential we need local young role models and leaders to speak to the hearts of the masses.

Acute understanding of context and a heightened sense of the emerging threat to peace

In countries in the midst of violent conflict, recovering from violent conflict or at the risk of violent conflict, local youth are better placed to identify new threats to peace and trends to enhance effective interventions (Donais 2012). Just as most violent extremists or violent uprisings require the recruitment of young people, young peacebuilders who are naturally more connected to their peers are able to bring attention to these dangerous new developments. They are strategically placed to understand the tactics, narratives and communication of extremist and violent groups. They are also able to understand and, at times, even relate to the frustrations and grievances that seem to attract young people to these groups. In addition they are also well placed to identify regions and demographics that extremist groups are seeking to engage.

Most local peacebuilding organisations, without a meaningful seat at the table for young peacebuilders, are often left in the dark about these developments. Even if they do come to know of these risks, they don't have the capacity to infiltrate or counter these messages with positive alternatives. In order to overcome these challenges, a nation needs proactive initiatives led by young people at the grassroots. To effectively counter these efforts you need these young peacebuilders to expose the inaccuracies of false information, as well as revealing the dangers both of hate speech and of joining violent groups. They need to make their communities understand that these extremists will most likely not address the grievance or respond to the challenge. Instead they are more likely to take the nation further backwards. In addition youth can also play an important role in educating their peers on how history repeats itself, and how the efforts of these violent groups have only caused greater pain.

In Sri Lanka, just three years after the end of the civil war, Sri Lanka Unites (SLU) had already built a national network of young peacebuilders. The movement did not have structures in place to gain any major funding. However, the youth of the movement made merchandise, created partnerships with smaller businesses and attracted local donors who saw the strategic importance of the movement. Sri Lanka had seen too many cycles of violence and many unaddressed grievances from previous and ongoing conflicts to ignore looming cycles of violence. Hence the locally bootstrapped model was now becoming the largest network for peace in the island, and this network was led by youth who had committed to being ambassadors for peace, justice and reconciliation. In 2012 these SLU youth groups started flagging a new trend of anti-Muslim content on Facebook and other online platforms. In some cases the posts encouraged violence against the Muslim community. These messages were mainly in local languages and largely undetected by the Facebook screening process at the time. Despite the community standards set by Facebook[8] that did not permit hate speech, these groups were able to recruit thousands of people to follow their misinformation, embrace their hate and, worst of all, consider their calls for violence.

SLU youth identified the links of these groups and the most visceral posts, and also provided English translations and shared them with their Facebook contacts, indicating the threat. The youth of SLU went further, creating a counter online campaign: THINK! Asking youth to THINK and not believe anything without questioning its validity, agenda and value, they would also use the teachings of religious leaders that countered these messages by groups that were plagued with toxic nationalism and misrepresented religion for their personal and political agendas. The campaign was embraced by large numbers of moderates across the nation. It even helped many youth to stay away from these violent and divisive groups. SLU went on to organise conferences for leaders representing all twenty-five districts and continued to do so for nearly a decade, thereby creating a strong resistance to efforts of extremist groups.

These student leaders curated inter-religious conversation in their communities and worked to minimise the negative impact of extremist groups. Today SLU is a trusted official partner of Facebook in Sri Lanka. Facebook has also refined its approach to monitor hate speech in local languages. For almost a decade SLU has continued these initiatives to counter hate speech as one of its many initiatives. As new waves of hate speech spread, SLU increases training and dispatches volunteers to counter these messages on the ground.

> I didn't grow up with any prejudice towards the Muslim community. My school only had students from my community, Sinhala Buddhist. I didn't have any friends from the Muslim community. However, I started seeing post on Facebook that Muslims were trying to take over a country, they were trying to make women in my community infertile and they were conspiring to destroy our nation with terrorism. Since I had no friends or interactions with the Muslim communities, these constant messages on my newsfeed started creating fear, mistrust, hatred and even a desire for violence against them. I started sharing these anti-Muslim posts, soon I started sharing my own narratives of hate. I even joined a riot to destroy Muslim shops. It was at this point that a volunteer from Sri Lanka Unites started writing to me and engaged me in conversation online. They shared an alternate message, helping me question the validity and the danger of these assumptions. They introduced me to many Muslim friends and invited me to national conferences. My entire perspective and actions have changed over the years. Today I help other young men like me, to understand how to question content online, and encourage them to expand their friendship to communities outside their own. Today I create my own counter-hate content. It gives me such joy when posts I create for peace go viral. I have come full circle. (Sri Lanka Unites member)

During the past five years SLU has also created partnership with Myanmar Unites to refine each movement's effort to counter hate. Myanmar has experienced similar challenges on this same issue.[9] Nationalistic Buddhist extremist groups seemed to have some level of communication and learning with their counterparts in Sri Lanka.[10] It is fitting that peacebuilders in both these nations are creating organic alliances to counter these challenges.

These case studies show the incredible capacity of youth to respond proactively and holistically to prevent conflict. Because of their careful study of historic patterns, their commitment to sustainable peace and their proximity to their peers at risk of being radicalised, they are well placed to respond to these emerging challenges.

A generation's mandate and purpose and an intergenerational legacy

Another key reason for the importance of youth in peacebuilding and the unique value they have to offer is the fact that this becomes their generation's cause. Youth who understand the qualities they add as peacebuilders and nation-builders embrace this identity, and consider it their generation's mandate to break the cycles of violence and regain their nation's lost potential, while becoming the generation that builds a just and thriving nation (De Visser, 2015).

Decades of conflict and many years of broken structures cannot be overcome by one project cycle or even a decade of work. It requires a generation's focus and attention. SLU is now seeing youth who joined the movement 14 years ago, still engaged as volunteers, mentors and donors. In fact, donations from former students are one of the growing income streams of the movement. Their ability to have a strong work ethic and a vision for their nation, along with their ability to work across any ethnic or religious background, has served them well as they have thrived in their workplace. In addition some of these former students of the movement are now parents themselves. Many of them will be sending their children to join the nationwide 'Sri Lanka Unites Kids' programme. An inclusive Sri Lanka identity and a just nation for all are a core value for their lives and they want their children to embrace these same values. This is the type of generational impact that grassroots movements can have and need to have in order to achieve their goals of sustainable peace and transformation. Many students of our movement have gone on to serve in government offices, where they are committed to bring about justice and reconciliation, while many have joined local and international organisations to serve for sustainable peace at various levels. Some advocate for diversity and inclusion at their corporate workplace, some are human rights lawyers fighting for justice in our nation. In each case the exposure they received to this cause at a young age has given them an edge to be effective for the cause as adults and professionals. This is no longer an extracurricular activity, it is a positive habit. The desire to strive for peace, justice and reconciliation has now become an integral part of their character.

This is happening not only in Sri Lanka. Congo Unites recently celebrated seven years of operations in their nation. We are amazed that most of our regional leaders from the inception of the movement are still engaged and at the helm. Despite many of their own economic challenges and the heart-wrenching realities of the Congolese context, these young peacebuilders refuse to walk away.

In sum, youth who are convinced by a bold and dynamic vision tend to engage with a high level of commitment and zeal, and a level of commitment and passion that money cannot buy. The capacity for lifelong engagement that is needed to bring about sustainable change, along with their ability to recognise new threats, to adapt and creatively respond, their ownership due to their futures being at stake, all lead to a dynamic culmination of effective engagement. These youth are well placed and pivotal to address root causes, respond proactively and pave the way for sustainable peace.

Conclusion

Youth peacebuilders and their movements are indeed crucial for sustainable peace and national transformation. In fact, as this chapter advocates, they are the best hope for meaningful change. The emerging alliances of peacebuilders from the Global South, along with platforming new innovative approaches from these regions, can prove to be a missing link to the longevity, dignity and enhancement of the impact of youth peacebuilding movements. Yet their impact towards true national transformations in the long run remains to be seen. How would one know if these movements are able to move beyond the mediocre, superficial or short-term impact of interventions in their nations? How would one know if a new generation of peacebuilders have helped a country turn the corner from recurring cycles of violence? The following would be the ultimate test: can these youth peacebuilders have the capacity to minimise the impact or even break the cycles of violence? Can their leadership and active engagement in broader society enable investment of former energies wasted on violent conflict to now create tangible positive economic, social, and cultural outcomes? Can this generation of leaders and peacebuilders shift harmful worldviews and prejudice that threaten sustainable peace in their nations? Can they inspire the nation to strive towards a just and thriving society for all their citizens? Time will tell. A brand of peacebuilding established on a power hierarchy, based on affluence and greater access to power and privilege, cannot continue to dictate and dominate the peacebuilding world. The results and the stagnant progress do not warrant a free pass for business as usual.

Local peacebuilders, and especially young peacebuilders, can no longer be pawns or a mere symbolic presence of a peacebuilding effort. Hence a seismic shift of approach is required, and putting local peacebuilders – especially youth – to pioneer intervention is undoubtedly the need of the hour. The success of locally inspired and engineered models which are recognised and platformed will be a major contributing factor to verify their potential. In addition, locally led solutions will help these nations overcome the shame of loss of dignity caused by the trauma of violence and the desperate need for external help. Local young leaders transforming the grim realities of their nations, once written off as broke, bloody and bound to fail, will give them the confidence to continue to lead their nations to greater heights. Their success should be celebrated as their own resolve, resilience and resurgence. They transformed these grim realities, not because they were saved by saviours from the affluent 'developed' nations but by a generation who rose from the ashes of violent conflict, a generation that inspired hope and championed change despite the bleak and overwhelming realities they were born into.

Notes

1 France-presse (1997).
2 *American University Attack: At Least 12 Dead and 44 Injured in Afghanistan* (2016). https://www.theguardian.com/world/2016/aug/24/american-university-afghanistan-attacked-kabul. Accessed 30 September 2021.
3 *Out of the Darkness.* Perf. Congo Unites. 2014. DVD.
4 See Gilchrist n.d.
5 M. Davey, *Is the International NGO Humanitarian Effort Failing?* https://asiathinkers.com/international-ngo-humanitarian-effort-failing/. Accessed 30 September 2021.
6 Pikulicka-Wilczewska (2021).
7 Gunia (2019).
8 See Facebook Community standards for hate speech: https://transparency.fb.com/en-gb/policies/community-standards/hate-speech/. Accessed 1 Decemeber 2023.
9 *Facebook Admits Failures in Myanmar* – BBC News (2018). https://www.bbc.com/news/world-asia-46105934.amp?fbclid=IwAR2LB0dupmGpZciqWBE4G-pgRpd0ebkYOizfP3LQCE6iY2-A2ZmZp7zlUiQ. Accessed 30 September 2021.
10 Sirilal (2014).

References

Davey, M. n.d. *Is the International NGO Humanitarian Effort Failing?* https:// asiathinkers.com/international-ngo-humanitarian-effort-failing/. Accessed 30 September 2021.

Dc Visscr, P. 2015. *The Role of Youth in Transforming Conflict.* University of Notre Dame. https://curate.nd.edu/show/r207tm7314x. Accessed 1 December 2023.

Donais, Timothy. 2012. *Peacebuilding and Local Ownership.* New York: Routledge,

France-presse, A. (1997). '17 Die, 100 Wounded by Huge Bomb and Gunfire in Sri Lanka.' https://www.nytimes.com/1997/10/15/world/17-die-100-wounded-by-huge-bomb-and-gunfire-in-sri-lanka.html?fbclid=IwAR3X6cZbqPYXxbX5_V6gD0l zaibr4Lj4wrDfMyaMIHt7EcBKOTZtu_8iA_8. Accessed 30 September 2021.

Gilchrist, J. n.d. *Civil Society Conflict: The Negative Impact of International NGOs on Grassroots and Social Movements – Community Mobilization in Crisis.* https://cmic-mobilize.org/civil-society-conflict-the-negative-impact-of-international-ngos-on-grassroots-and-social-movements/. Accessed 30 September 2021.

Gunia, A. (2019). *The Birthplace of Suicide Bombing: Sri Lanka's Grim History.* https://time.com/5575956/sri-lanka-history-suicide-bombings-birthplace-invented/. Accessed 30 September 2021.

Lederach, J.P. 2003. *The Little Book of Conflict Transformation.* New York: Good Books.

McEvoy-Levy, Siobhán, ed. 2006. *Trouble Makers or Peace Makers?* Notre Dame: University of Notre Dame.

Pikulicka-Wilczewska, A. (2021). *International Employers Accused of Abandoning Afghan Staff.* https://www.aljazeera.com/news/2021/8/27/afghan-local-staff-left-behind-as-evacuation-deadline-looms. Accessed 30 September 2021.

Sirilal, R. (2014). *Radical Myanmar Monk Joins Hands with Sri Lankan Buddhist.* https://www.reuters.com/article/us-sri-lanka-buddhism-myanmar-idUSKCN0 HO0GD20140929?fbclid=IwAR1Z4_zSCpBzvhc3MCaMCNTxMdi9ofhj8y-cL7dzFTv5Ue8KVMNoqFz3tBUs. Accessed 30 September 2021.

14

Building a new lodge: Native youth and peacebuilding

Justin de Leon and Jordan Bighorn

Decade of Indigenous Peoples

The United Nations designated the years from 1995 to 2004 as the 'International Decade of the World's Indigenous Peoples'.[1] This also corresponds with Indigenous-oriented efforts during this period at the World Bank, the International Labour Organisation, Oxfam International, the Inter-American Development Bank and in the UK's Department for International Development, culminating in the UN's 2007 adoption of the Declaration of Rights of Indigenous Peoples (UNDRIP). It would be a reasonable conclusion to conclude this rise in focus on Indigenous peoples is a structural shift of international affairs, no doubt affecting international peacemaking practices and approaches. It is debatable, however, whether this represented a genuine interest in Indigenous knowledge and experience, or a merely rhetorical and donor-driven move to 'local participation'.[2] What is not debatable, however, is the difficulty in implementing 'indigenous' and 'traditional' dispute mechanisms within a Western peacemaking context, an environment with a strong 'standardizing tendency' (Mac Ginty 2008, 157). Aside from this debate, one could hope that this international focus, at least, forces a 'recognition by powerful international actors that peace can be plural rather than singular' (Mac Ginty 2008, 159).

In spite of the UN's proclamation of an Indigenous decade, peace studies as a field has largely ignored Native American and Indigenous peoples in North America.[3] The irony here is that Indigenous peoples of the North American continent have had a storied history of peace agreements and mediation, tracing back thousands of years: a history filled undoubtably with valuable insights to those interested in contemporary practices of peacebuilding. For example one of the clearest examples is the Haudenosaunee Confederacy, also known as the Iroquois League or the Great Law of Peace. The Great Law of Peace was an agreement between the then-adversarial Native peoples of the Mohawk, Onondaga, Oneida,

Cayuga, Seneca and Tuscarora for over 325 years, from 1450 to 1777. The Confederacy represented both a security regime with its own rules of peace and, because it was composed of democratic nations, a representation of Immanuel Kant's perpetual peace (Crawford 1994). Another example is the Dish With One Spoon Wampum, a 1701 peace agreement between the Anishinaabe and Haudenosaunee peoples. Beads made from wampum shells were crafted to mark memorable occasions and gifted under such circumstances such as peace agreements or conferences. Each agreement would be accompanied by a wampum belt that acted as a mnemonic com-memoration of peace (Tooker 1998). This is to illustrate that there is much to learn about peace studies by exploring understandings and experiences of Native peoples of North America.

This raises the question, if Native and Indigenous peoples in North America hold such experience in peacemaking, why have they been largely left out of substantive practice and knowledge-based peace studies research? Surely the answer to this paradox is not straightforward. In an attempt to unpack this question we can see that peace studies as a field has been crafted within a Western context that centres Westphalian understandings of the nation-state, liberal democracy and liberal peace. This settler colonial context within North America has been in operation for hundreds of years, with the aim at erasing Native peoples, practices and knowledges. Settler colonialism 'destroys to replace', acting as a structure of dispossession and violence and not a singular event (Wolfe 2006, 388). It creates what Patricia Hill Collins (2000) refers to as a 'matrix of domination' that not only leaves Native peoples vulnerable but also works to erase their knowledge and experiences (18). It is also necessary to bring to mind the appalling record of US treaty-keeping with Native peoples – the US broke over five hundred treaties in the period 1778 to 1871 alone (Toensing 2013). Deeper yet, there are significant ontological differences between Indigenous North American and Western worldviews. Indigenous thought and practices 'overtly oppose many of the values that the United States presumes: the legitimacy of majoritarian democracy, the primacy of sovereignty, the rule of law, and especially American exceptionalism' (Ferguson 2016, 1029). Native worldviews premised on spiritual perception and interconnectedness are, in many ways, incompatible with Western worldviews (Cordova 2007; de Leon 2020b).

Many heard the call 'I can't breathe' uttered by George Floyd while a police officer held his knee to the back of his neck. This call stands as a tragic example of racism and police brutality and an evocative symbol of the past, present and foreseeable future for black, Indigenous and peoples of colour (BIPOC) in the US. 'Ever since 401 years ago, the reason

we could never be who we wanted and dreamed of being is you kept
your knee on our neck,' stated Reverend Al Sharpton at a George Floyd
memorial service in 2020.[4] Black communities continue to face systematic dehumanisation, as do many other communities of colour in the US,
though in differing forms and intensity. For Native communities many of
the direct forms of violence – such as the hanging of thirty-eight Dakota
men (which stands as the largest public execution in US history) and the
slaughter of over three hundred Lakota men, women and children in the
Wounded Knee Massacre in South Dakota – have been abated, giving
way instead to more invisible (yet no less insidious) forms of injustice.
These forms of injustice include racialised criminalisation and incarceration (Ross 2016), legal vulnerabilities leaving Native women vulnerable to
sexual abuse (Deer 2015, Goeman 2015), economic and political marginalisation limiting community power to challenge extractive oil companies
from building pipelines (Estes 2019), disproportionate rates of children
being taken for outside adoptions (Sullivan 2011), limited or low-quality
healthcare and education, and little representation or misrepresentation in
popular culture and entertainment (Raheja 2011).

Though not direct enslavement or genocide of racialised bodies, Native
communities face not only a slew of injustices but also psychological
trauma that can impede the building of peaceful, flourishing communities. This is particularly the case for Native youth, who are burdened by
epidemic rates of suicide that measure to nearly three times higher than that
of the general population (Gray and McCullagh 2014). For many Native
peoples – specifically we draw from experiences with Lakota Sioux traditions of the Great Plains[5] – youth are seen to be closer to the spirit world
than adults. For instance, Black Elk once asserted, 'I who am an old man
am about to return *to* the Great Mysterious and a young child is a being
who has just come *from* the Great Mysterious; so it is that we are very close
together' (Brown and Cousins 2001, 14). Youth are imbued with unique
insights, powers and responsibilities.

This chapter reflects on the role of Native youth in a broad understanding of peacebuilding. It begins by describing what we see as an
emergent moment of reflection and response, and then it moves to
describe the need for building a new world, putting forward a framework
of seven poles (or foundations) in which to imagine such a space. This
new world, or a new lodge as we cast it, is one where we envision Native
youth playing a significant role in the building of peaceful and thriving
communities.

Moment of reflection and response

The impact of the Covid-19 pandemic, the murder of George Floyd, the increase of political right-wing extremism and the increasing prevalence of climate change-related ecological disasters have put many 'business-as-usual' practices on hold. Political, social and cultural dysfunctions are ever more so on display. Times of uncertainty and turmoil, however, also present moments of reflection. Where do we go from here? How can the field of peace studies make sense of and learn from these contemporary moments of disruption?

This is where we, as two scholar-practitioners who combined have worked with BIPOC youth for a better part of four decades, turn our attention to Native and Indigenous peoples in North America, and even more specifically to Native youth. In many Native communities youth play a special role for the community. Because they are closer to the spirit world, youth carry with them unique spiritual clarity and energy, as well as responsibilities.

The living principle of seven generations influences every aspect of community and family decision-making – always keeping in mind how your actions will impact seven generations ahead. It is knowing that seven generations ago your ancestors were praying for you and, in turn, you are praying for those seven generations down the line. This orientation of honouring youth and future generations can be seen through the role that young people have played in working for Native rights, visibility and healing. The descending of tens of thousands of people on to the Standing Rock Sioux Reservation in 2016 was, in fact, started by a group of Lakota youth who, with community support, began a cross-country run to Washington, DC, to bring attention to their community's fight against the construction of the Dakota Access Pipeline. This run went through dozens of communities and eventually led to what the whole world saw: a show of solidarity of Indigenous and non-Indigenous alike.

Young people (throughout the world) are looking for new ways to meet the unique challenges of today, though finding meaningful responses is proving elusive. A central challenge, captured by what Eve Tuck and K. Wayne Yang (2012) refer to as incommensurability, comes with envisioning and creating a different, decolonial future while having to reconcile the many paradoxes woven into the fibre of settler realities. This 'ethic of incommensurability' is an invitation to move into uncertainty, to recognise there is no single panacea and to view paradoxes as opportunities of solidarity.

Relevant literature on change

Native studies scholars have theorised social change within an oppressive system. Taiaiake Alfred (2005) questions whether it is possible to engage the state without reifying its mechanisms, calling, instead, for an Indigenous resurgence based on foregrounding Indigenous thought and experience. This rings similarity with Black feminist scholar Audre Lorde's asking whether the master's tools are capable of dismantling the master's house. 'What does it mean when the tools of a racist patriarchy are used to examine the fruits of that same patriarchy?' Lorde (1984) asks, asserting, 'It means that only the most narrow perimeters of change are possible and allowable' (1–2). The Indigenous resurgence intellectual paradigm forcefully asks the question of how does one work to transform the system without reinforcing the same mechanisms that led to that oppression in the first place? (Alfred 2005; Coulthard 2014). More specifically it looks at how to engage the state without reifying its mechanisms. Moving away from settler-state forms of conciliatory forms of recognition requires 'the resurgence of cultural practices that are attentive to the subjective and structural composition of settler-colonial power' (Coulthard 2014, 24).

In the field of peace studies John Paul Lederach (2005) points to this tension, asking, 'How do we transcend the cycles of violence that bewitch our human community while still living in them?' (172). The necessity to foster a 'moral imaginary' requires embracing complexity as well as the unknown. It requires both the recognition of the power of creativity and the need for a relational framework. The transcendence of violence and the deleterious qualities of the oppressor are captured in the concept of constructive resilience (Karlberg 2010). A response that neither 'succumb[s] in resignation nor to take on the characteristics of the oppressor', constructive resilience, as explored in the response shown forth by persecuted Baha'is of Iran, points to the possibility of individuals to transcend oppression through inner strength and 'principled action' (UHJ 2009; Karlberg 2010, 234).

From a women's studies and feminist theory perspective Lorde (1984) writes extensively about moving into uncertainty by redefining the productive power of difference, framing difference from fear to interconnectedness. Much like embracing the unknown, interconnectedness requires engagements with others who look and think differently from oneself. To the potentialities of difference Lorde (1984) asserts, 'Difference must be not merely tolerated, but seen as a fund of necessary polarities between which our creativity can spark like a dialectic', continuing, 'Only then does the necessity for interdependence become unthreatening' (2). It is through the acknowledgement and interdependency of various points of views that new ways of being are generated, as well as the requisite 'courage and sustenance to act where there are no charters' (Lorde 1984, 2).

Feminist international relations scholars have called for attention to the use of language to usher in social or political change. Phrases such as 'fighting for justice' or 'waging war' can have problematic outcomes. Waging war on something – be it drugs, terrorism, Covid or police brutality – is a common analogy for marshalling significant resources to meet a danger or issue. It is an emotive tool to communicate urgency. In practice, however, waging war has 'fueled sexism, racism, homophobia, autocracy, secrecy and xenophobia,' asserts Cynthia Enloe (2020), continuing, 'They will not protect the most vulnerable among us. They will not keep us all safe. They most certainly will not lay the groundwork for post-pandemic democracy.' War rhetoric depends on antagonism, division, and nationalism as fuel, while normalising violence, coercive power and adversarialism (Caso 2020).

We offer a distinct way of rising to this unique moment: one that not only builds off of Native and Indigenous experiences and knowledge but that takes advantage of the important powers of youth. Accordingly the following is both a *letter for* Native youth navigating hardship and a *framework of resilience* that could be useful for peacebuilders looking for new horizons that encompass Indigenous principles of reciprocity and spirituality. Internalising this dual utility, we recognise that there will be a fair amount that may be 'lost in translation', attempting to move from insights from traditional and cultural learnings, learnings that often resist verbal articulation in the first place, to intelligible Western frameworks of understanding. Rather than fully reconciling this tension, we offer a scaffolding for the imagination and interpretations of the readers. We hope to bring the spirit of those magical moments when sitting with elders, grandparents and uncles who were both brief in words and yet resoundingly profound. We turn our attention to the building of a new lodge as a way to affirm the requisite resilience needed to build a new world.

Building a new lodge

Establishing a new lodge is akin to identifying building blocks to a new world. It is a recreating of an entire worldview, a peaceful one in which we wish to live. Yes, these building blocks point to something new, but in another way they are a pathway of returning unto ourselves. In crafting a new lodge the spiritual and material concept of mirroring is useful. Understood as 'what is below on earth is like what is above in the star world', mirroring is a useful way to understand a lodge or tipi – as an earthly representation of spiritual principles (Goodman 1992, 15). The image of the tipi has come to represent Native people writ large and is etched into the American imaginary (Deloria 1999). If poles extended upwards, they would draw two inverted triangles, standing on their top points. This is the Lakota symbol *kapemni*, or twisting – the earth is the base triangle and an upside-down triangle for the stars – representing the connection between the earthly and the spiritual (Goodman 1992; de Leon 2020b).

The Lakota, known as the 'three-pole people', start tipi set-up with three poles, each systematically aligning with particular stars that represent foundational understandings of the Lakota world (de Leon 2020a). Former Lakota Tribal University professor Ronald Goodman (1992) explains its significance: '[Setting up a tipi] is nothing less than re-creating or replicating a world' (17). This recreation is premised on the orientation of poles, all of which represent spiritual and material principles – the first three poles represent the foundation of the world, while the next seven represent the seven sacred directions (east, north, south, west, above, below and internal), allowing for balance and orientation. These ten poles represent the laws of the world, while the final two poles acting as storm flaps are used for ventilation and represent breath and the ability for the spirit to exit and enter. These last two poles also represent the arms of the mother embracing the family and keeping them safe from danger. These poles also represented the cyclical nature of life. Along with the twelve months of a year, the encampment would also be formed in a circle, acting as a 'constant reminder for the inhabitants that life flowed in a circle and that they were unalterably connected to everything that was part of it' (Marshall 2001, 224). A new lodge represents a reconnecting of the earthly to the celestial, or to the Creator.

In building this lodge we offer foundational poles in a spirit of humility and curiosity. We offer them knowing that the hearts of the youth, and those of us who support them, are longing for more authentic and nourishing practices of being, new ways of being in relation. In addition these poles can be viewed as a framework for exploring the challenging and sometimes dangerous work of re-establishing identity, sovereignty and place in a modern global context. In effect these poles would, in our estimation, orient us (Native and non-Native alike) towards a more just and peaceful world.

The mechanism of the process and procedure of building this new lodge is *ceremony*. Ceremony allows for one to communicate with the Creator – visions, guidance and clarity all come from ceremony. Ultimately, however, even ceremony cannot fully bring that which is celestial and divine into the material world. There is a necessary 'loss' in that relationship – communication, operationalisation and practice all fall short of the celestial realities they are inspired by and hope to represent. Likewise we recognise the limitations of attempting to place spiritual and cultural principles into words for you, our audience. As such, the following should be seen not as a checklist or comprehensive list of guidance but rather as an invitation to explore various understandings of our world. They are doorways that invite creativity, physical engagement and further contemplation.

Pole 1: Point of a Circle

The first pole establishes a beginning in a relationship, it is the essential genesis in the rhythm and passage of time. It is a recognition that creation is eternal, in the midst of mortality, that time can be measured systematically but without parameter. It is the umbilical cord of a people in their relationship with the land.

The image of a point on the line of a circle allows for the coexistence of all of these things. It provides the foundation with which to nurture a worldview, to develop values, beliefs and teachings. It is the beginning of the timeline of the life cycle of an individual, community and ultimately a civilisation. For this reason the lodge is constructed as a circle, its architecture designed specifically to reflect the cyclical and spherical nature of the world. Its entry and exit point directly to the east in acknowledgement of the sun's 'entry point' on the celestial hemisphere. It is the same cyclical understanding of life that allows for the closeness of youth to the spirit world. Moreover a circle means no corners, no points of termination or altered courses, and, perhaps most importantly, no opportunity for exclusion or hierarchy of those who occupy the circle.

With this as the cornerstone of the structure, the potential for the construction of an environment of complex interaction(s) between thought, body and feeling yields the potential for the proper balance of conditions with which yield the capacity to reflect the light of creation.

Pole 2: Conditions of Creation

> The most sacred ceremony is the birth of a child. (Phil Lane, Sr, Dakota and Chickasaw)

Throughout all natural phenomena the timing and sequence of creation are synchronous with the constituent conditions of any given environment. The length of time and sequencing of the creation process are secondary. It is not the revolution of the earth around the sun versus the events throughout 365 days of a year in the life of an individual that matters, but rather the 'miracle' of life that is manifested the moment that the property of diversity meets the conditions of unity, elements meet form. Indeed it is a further representation of the point on a circle and the duality of specificity and perpetuity, of individualism versus universalism, point versus circle.

That Indigenous communities of North America operated within this sphere of understanding sheds light on the nature of the sacredness of the birth of a child. Dakota scholar Charles Eastman (1911, 28) explains:

> The Indian was a religious man from his mother's womb ... it was supposed by us that the mother's spiritual influence counted for most. Her attitude and secret meditations must be such as to instill into the receptive soul of the unborn child the love of the 'Great Mystery' and a sense of brotherhood with all creation.

If the ceremony of the birth was sacred, the medium by which the ceremony takes place must be divine in nature, pure in its purpose and selfless beyond measure. Is it any wonder, then, that humanity refers to the planet it calls home as Mother Earth? Born with the inherent capacity to endure both the conditions of creation and its aftermath (child and birth), a mother represents within herself the spirit animating the ceremony of creation.

This second pole represents the growth and development of a foetus within a mother's womb. It is no mere analogy. While each pregnancy tells a unique story of the human condition, it also represents an act that is symbolic of the most astronomical phenomena. All the forces and kingdoms of nature coalesce within the womb, the centre of gravity of a mother's body moves beyond a function of balance and becomes a force of attraction, pulling within itself infinitesimal particles of dust to form a body capable of reflecting life (planet and soul). Ábdu'l-Bahá (1921) explains:

> In the vegetable world, too, there is the power of growth, and that power of growth is the spirit. In the animal world there is the sense of feeling, but in the human world there is an all-embracing power. In all the preceding stages the power of reason is absent, but the soul existeth and revealeth itself. The sense of feeling understandeth not the soul, whereas the reasoning power of the mind proveth the existence thereof.

The subtlety between an effort to understand a 'Great Mystery' and submission to the reality of a 'Great Mystery' is an example of the human condition being both a result of creation and an active participant. In order to coexist in these juxtaposed states, a bridge must be erected in order to traverse back and forth between each state. Again the structure calls for a singular point on a circle, meaning that an individual cannot occupy two distinct points. The individual has, however, the capacity to bring these two points of being a result of creation and being an active participant in creation within a human body, facilitating a power of vision to both witness and study the nature of that 'Great Mystery'. Charles Eastman, Santee Dakota and the first Native to be certified in Western medicine, describes how the mother's gift instilled in her child (internal) can be explored only via relationship with all created things (external), lies within that bridge by which the child can traverse creation in both exploration of and exposure to the 'Great Mystery'.

Pole 3: Crying for a Vision – Humblechiya

For the Lakota, the powers granted in visions can be thought of as the ability to recognize and utilize the transformations of the natural world. Implicit to this belief system is a conception of interdependence that is more fundamental than mere interrelationship: the universe is one, and its varying life forms are different configurations of the universal animating power. (Raymond DeMallie 1984, 87)

The experience of a rite of passage is both universal and timeless. There are countless examples across cultures where young individuals subject themselves to a process by which they emerge as an adult, a full contributing member of the people. Often these events motioned to a turning point of a community, a transcendent moment when the individual returns with new insight(s), medicine(s) or vision.

Perhaps the most widely read account of such a vision, at least in a North American Indigenous context, is that of Black Elk. First published in 1932, *Black Elk Speaks* relates the experience of Black Elk as a nine-year-old boy who received a vision of beautiful magnanimity with a profound message of hope. It is also important to note that this experience was not shared anecdotally or for posterity. Speaking about his vision, Black Elk states, 'What happened after that until the summer I was nine years old is not a story' (Black Elk and Neihardt 2014/1932, 13).

This third pole represents an act of 'crying' for a vision, a supplication to the Creator. It refers to the state of being, behaviour and presentation of the individual in a way to be susceptible to receive spiritual communion. For the Lakota it is the ceremony of Humblechiya through which (and in perhaps direct reference to the condition of a newly born child) the individual would endeavour to strip themselves of attachment to material elements such as sustenance (fasting), shelter (exposed to nature) and self (meditation or prayer).

Pole 4: Ceremony of Performance

Ceremony has been a universal mechanism engaged across cultures throughout human history, acting as a bridge between the visible and invisible plane. It is not merely an event, ceremony is a process. It is a process that can come to represent a significant moment on the timeline of a community, people or civilisation. Ceremony provides a means in which the individual, as well as the community, is able to navigate between different worlds, the slipstream. It is a navigation between the known and unknown, material and immaterial, and the present and the future.

While Black Elk noted his curiosity, fascination and respect for what was communicated to him in his ceremony and vision (by the Six Grandfathers), he also acknowledged his fear of the power and presence of the Grandfathers, and, perhaps most critically, how he would in turn communicate what he witnessed to the people (Black Elk and Neihardt 2014/1932).

Ceremony requires a set of predetermined conditions before the process can begin. This can consist of prepared medicines such as sage and tobacco and/or established protocols such as the specific songs and prayers or use of the sacred pipe. These predetermined conditions constitute the material elements that facilitate the reception and validation of a spiritual experience. David Martinez (2009, 63) explains:

> In the Dakota way, as in many Indian traditions, a vision is more than a mere dream; it is a sacred experience in which any messages must be respected and any directives must be fulfilled, lest the recipient incur misfortune upon himself, his family, or his community.

Similar to the ceremony of bringing a child from the realm of the unseen into the material plane, this fourth pole represents the threshold between life once known and an unknown future full of potential.

Pole 5: Travelling Without Moving

Indigenous history has seen an onslaught brought on by colonial erasure and genocide. Creation stories, geographic sovereignty and historical narratives have been collected and preserved, with the purpose of human reunification. This can become problematic as it implies the dissolution of many hegemonic ways of knowing and being. This is to say, such an invitation to consider a future where human connection and relationships move beyond connection by land, technology or genetics can appear threatening and unintelligible.

For the countless others who have left their homelands in hope of realising the so-called American dream, the same path cannot be said to be as easily travelled for Native peoples. Native peoples of North America have been reduced to living on impoverished reservations, sufficiently shackled by oppressed economies and overruled by colonial legal and political configurations. It does raise the question: Why, after all the injustice and oppression, haven't Native peoples sought refuge in another country or land?

Rewinding five hundred years, Indigenous peoples were, in fact, the first to explore, migrate to and ultimately establish societies in North America. The arrival of Columbus ushered in the ensuing movement of the peoples of the world from the Eastern to the Western hemispheres. This in many ways represents an inevitable reunion, a coming back full circle, and thus setting the stage for the birth of a singular civilisation. Neil deGrasse Tyson (2018) explains:

> Our species is separate ... now, Columbus crosses the Atlantic and makes contact with humans. This is the first time that's happened in 10,000 years. We have rejoined two branches of the human species. We are now one common genetic group ... This was a hugely significant event, the rejoining of the branches of the human species.

The fifth pole represents an inner migration, the means by which movement can occur without the dramatic results of local geographic devastation (read: colonialism). While technology, media, scholarship and text can disseminate a worldview from one part of the planet to another, the ancestors of Indigenous North America draw from the historical context of having been the first to physically travel the furthest away from their point of origin. In effect they closed the circle to a termination point.

Pole 6: Consummated Transformation

Smudging is a ceremonial act of cleansing, of daily ablution, or to promote general well-being. Using medicines such as sage, sweetgrass or cedar, smudging is, in itself, an act that consumes materialism while inviting and revealing a transformed state. Picking, braiding and lighting sweetgrass is a ceremony unto itself – the primary focus on the rising smoke, gentle aroma and belief in the purpose and outcome of the smudge. Indeed it could be argued that the moment of transformation from one state to another is akin to the relationship of birth and death. Where a bowl of medicines might represent the grown foetus, the lighted braid might then represent its birth, where the previous form (bowl or womb) is no longer needed and the rising smoke (baby) can now exercise its new powers.

Herein lies the most critical pole in terms of the furthest most step of development from the originating point. The perfection of the braid of sweetgrass, with its beauty, symmetry, aroma and potential properties locked within, is ultimately barred from fulfilling its inner purpose unless it is subject to destructive fire. Burning away the outer layers, the braid falls to ash and no longer represents any aspect of its former self. Applying this analogy to the growing child, we see that all the previous poles provide new challenges for the child, providing new developmental experiences, opportunities and insight. At this sixth stage, however, all those properties must be subject to destructive fire – in whatever form that may take – in order for both the individual and the community to best benefit from the outcome.

Ceremonies such as the sundance, sweat lodge and vision quest all have elements and conditions which mirror this process of consummation and transformation, benefiting both the individual and the community.

Pole 7: Circle Complete

In the life of the Indian there was only one inevitable duty – the duty of prayer – the daily recognition of the Unseen and Eternal. (Charles Eastman 1911, 45)

There is much that can be speculated and suggested about the result of completing this process. On the one hand, the lodge is built and is transformed from discrete elements into a complex form capable of sustaining life. On the other hand, material civilisation is obsessed with self-preservation (i.e. the past), and cannot bear the invitation to consider life beyond its current form.

Suicide rates among Native youth are among the highest per capita on the planet (Gray and McCullagh 2014). Social scientists have offered a plethora of studies suggesting addiction, depression, violence and trauma as major contributors (which we acknowledge as having real impact on families and communities). Resulting efforts to address this tragedy are subsequently found in other material remedies which, ironically, often include other pharmaceuticals derived from natural materials. If, by Eastman's account, a core value of Indigenous life is to constantly interact with the spiritual world, then the process to re-engage the 'Unseen and Eternal' may require processes such as these poles suggest, offering a potential pathway to protect and insulate Native youth from such ideations and actions.

Concluding thoughts

The Haudenosaunee confederacy and the Dish With One Spoon Wampum treaties that took place on this land represent a recreation of Native and Indigenous worldviews. With those treaties they were turning over new ways of being in relation to one another. Peacebuilding and peace studies as a field have much to learn from these lessons of the past, the lessons of Indigenous peoples of this land.

We feel that this current moment of disruption offers a breaking point, a moment of reflection with many asking, 'What's next?' and 'What's possible?' Turning to Native teachings and Native youth provides a potential pathway, an opportunity to reconstruct new worldviews representative of spiritual realities of the unseen and eternal. The realities of day-to-day life, however, cannot be ignored. Racked with the plague of high suicide rates, Native youth need to be nourished, protected and supported. Native youth need to survive. The seven poles we outline – point of a circle, conditions of creation, crying for a vision, ceremony of performance, travelling without moving, consummated transformation and the circle complete – come to signify a spiritual foundation that could support Native youth in their journey of survival and rebuilding, while also providing framework for resilience for 'outside' peacebuilders interested in spiritual and Indigenous-informed approaches to sustainable peacebuilding. These poles offer a remapping that allows us to look to the path forward through the returning unto ourselves.

Notes

1 Special thanks to Helen Berents, Catherine Bolten and Siobhán McEvoy-Levy who envisioned this project and provided generous feedback and guidance, without which we would have never been able to move this contribution to its completion.
2 For more on the 'local turn' in peacebuilding, see Leonardsson and Rudd (2015).
3 A cursory look at peace studies publications focused on Indigeneity found zero book monograph, a handful of peer-review articles (Huber 1993, Walker 2004, Mac Ginty 2008, James 2016, Randazzo 2021), four chapters in edited volumes (Mac Ginty 2010, Brigg and Walker 2016, Cormier 2019, Walker 2019) and two unpublished dissertation (Cormier 2012, Schoeppner 2020). Certainly there could be more, though it is reasonable to conclude that there is not an influx of Indigenous focus in peace studies.
4 Talk given 4 June 2020.
5 Jordan Bighorn is from the Fort Peck Assiniboine and Sioux Tribes and Justin de Leon comes from an Indigenous region of the Philippines and has worked closely with Lakota communities.

References

Ábdu'l-Bahá. 1921. Tablet to Dr Auguste Forel. Translation from *The Baha'i World* XV: 37–43. https://www.bahai.org/library/authoritative-texts/abdul-baha/tablet-auguste-forel/1#690115704. Accessed 12 December 2023.

Alfred, Taiaiake. 2005. *Wasase: Indigenous Pathways of Action and Freedom.* Toronto: University of Toronto Press.

Black Elk and John G. Neihardt. 2014/1932. *Black Elk Speaks: The Complete Edition.* University of Nebraska Press.

Brigg, Morgan, and Polly O. Walker. 2016. 'Indigeneity and Peace.' In *The Palgrave Handbook of Disciplinary and Regional Approaches to Peace*, Edited by Oliver Richmond, Sandra Pogodda and Jasmin Ramović, chapter 19. London: Palgrave Macmillan.

Brown, Joseph E., and Emily Cousins. 2001. *Teaching Spirits: Understanding Native American Religious Traditions*. Oxford: Oxford University Press.

Caso, Frederica. 2020. 'Are We at War? The Rhetoric of War in the Coronavirus Pandemic.' *The Disorder of Things*, 10 April. https://thedisorderofthings.com/2020/04/10/are-we-at-war-the-rhetoric-of-war-in-the-coronavirus-pandemic/. Accessed 1 June 2023.

Collins, Patricia H. 2000. *Black Feminist Thought: Knowledge, Consciousness, and the Politics of Empowerment*. Abingdon: Routledge.

Cordova, Viola F. 2007. *How It Is: The Native American Philosophy of V.F. Cordova*. Tucson: University of Arizona Press.

Cormier, Paul N. 2012. 'Kinoo'amaadawaad Megwaa Doodamawaad – Thee Are Learning with Each Other while They Are Doing: the Indigenous Living Peace Methodology.' Unpublished Dissertation, University of Manitoba.

Cormier, Paul N. 2019. 'The Paradox of Complexity in Peace and Conflict Studies: Indigenous Culture, Identity, and Peacebuilding.' In *Routledge Companion to Peace and Conflict Studies*, edited by Sean Byrne, Thomas Matyok, Imani M. Scott and Jessica Senehi. Milton Park: Routledge.

Coulthard, Glen. 2014. *Red Skin, White Masks*. Minneapolis: University of Minnesota Press.

Crawford, Neta. 1994. 'A Security Regime among Democracies: Cooperation among Iroquois Nations.' *International Organization* 48 (3): 345–85.

Deer, Sarah. 2015. *The Beginning and End of Rape: Confronting Sexual Violence in Native America*. Minneapolis: University of Minnesota Press.

De Leon, Justin. 2020a. 'Process as Product: Native American Filmmaking and Storytelling.' In *Racialized Media: The Design, Delivery, and Decoding of Race and Ethnicity*, chapter 6. edited by M.W. Hughey and E. Gonzalez-Lesser. New York: New York University Press.

De Leon, Justin. 2020b. 'Lakota Experiences of (In)Security: Cosmology and Ontological Security.' *International Feminist Journal of Politics* 22 (1): 33–62.

Deloria, Phillip. 1999. *Playing Indian*. New Haven: Yale University Press.

DeMallie, Raymond J. 1984. *The Sixth Grandfather: Black Elk's Teachings Given to John G. Neihardt*. Lincoln: University of Nebraska Press.

Eastman, Charles. 1911. *The Soul of the Indian*. Alexandria: Library of Alexandria.

Enloe, Cynthia. 2020. 'COVID-19: "Waging War" Against a Virus is NOT What We Need to Be Doing.' Women's International League for Peace & Freedom, 23 March. Accessed 25 March 2020.

Estes, Nick. 2019. *Our History Is the Future: Standing Rock versus the Dakota Access Pipeline, and the Long Tradition of Indigenous Resistance*. London: Verso Books.

Ferguson, Kennan. 2016. 'Why Does Political Science Hate American Indians?' *American Political Science Association* 14 (4).

Goeman, Mishuana. 2013. *Mark My Words: Native Women Mapping Our Nations*. Minneapolis: University of Minnesota Press.

Goodman, Ronald. 1992. *Lakota Star Knowledge*. Mission: Sinte Gleska University.

Gray, Jacqueline S., and John A. McCullagh. 2014. 'Suicide in Indian Country: the Continuing Epidemic in Rural Native American Communities.' *Journal of Rural Mental Health* 38 (2): 79–86.

Huber, Marg. 1993. 'Mediation around the Medicine Wheel.' *Mediation Quarterly* 10 (4): 355–65.

James, Jesse. 2016. 'Scholarship as Activism in the Field of Native Studies: a Potential Model for Peace Studies.' *The International Journal of Conflict Engagement and Resolution* 4 (1): 90–103.

Karlberg, Michael. 2010. 'Constructive Resilience: The Baha'i Response to Oppression.' *Peace and Change* 35 (2): 222–57.

Lederach, John P. 2005. *The Moral Imagination: The Art and Soul of Building Peace.* Oxford: Oxford University Press.

Leonardsson, Hanna, and Gustav Rudd. 2015. 'The "Local Turn" in Peacebuilding.' *Third World Quarterly* 36 (5): 825–39.

Lorde, Audre. 1994. *Sister Outsider: Essays and Speeches.* New York: Crossing Press.

Mac Ginty, Roger. 2008. 'Indigenous Peace-Making versus the Liberal Peace.' *Cooperation and Conflict: Journal of the Nordic International Studies Association* 43 (2): 139–63.

Mac Ginty, Roger. 2010. 'Gilding the Lily? International Support for Indigenous and Traditional Peacebuilding.' In *Palgrave Advances in Peacebuilding: Critical Developments and Approaches*, edited by Oliver P. Richmond, pp. 347–66. London: Palgrave.

Marshall, Joseph M. III. 2001. *The Lakota Way: Stories and Lessons for Living.* New York: Viking Compass.

Martinez, David. 2009. *Dakota Philosopher: Charles Eastman and American Indian Thought.* St Paul: Minnesota Historical Society.

Raheja, Michelle H. 2011. *Reservation Reelism: Redfacing, Visual Sovereignty, and Representations of Native Americans in Film.* Lincoln: University of Nebraska Press.

Randazzo, Elisa. 2021. 'The Local, the "Indigenous" and the Limits of Rethinking Peacebuilding.' *Journal of Interverntion and Statebuilding* 15 (2): 141–60.

Ross, Luana. 2016. 'Settler Colonialism and the Legislating of Criminality.' *American Indian Culture and Research Journal* 40 (1): 1–18.

Schoeppner, Lydia. 2020. 'The Inuit Circumpolar Council – Agent of Peacemaking for Inuit in Nunavut and Greenland.' University of Manitoba, Unpublished Dissertation.

Sullivan, Laura. 2011. 'Incentives and Cultural Bias Fuel Foster System.' National Public Radio, 25 October. Special Series Native Foster Care: Lost Children, Shattered Families.

Toensing, Gale C. 2013. 'Honor the Treaties: UN Human Rights Chief's Message.' *Indian Country Today*, 23 August.

Tooker, Elisabeth. 1998. 'A Note on the Return of Eleven Wampum Belts to the Six Nations Iroquois Confederacy on Grand River, Canada.' *Ethnohistory* 45 (2): 219–36.

Tuck, Eve, and K. Wayne Yang. 2012. 'Decolonization Is Not a Metaphor.' *Decolonization: Indigeneity, Education and Society* 1 (1): 1–40.

Tyson, Neil deGrasse. 2018. 'Columbus Discovering American Was a Great Achievement.' Joe Rogan Show, 22 August.

Universal House of Justice. 2009. 'Letter to the Baha'is of Iran.' 23 June.
Walker, Polly O. 2004. 'Decolonizing Conflict Resolution: Addressing the Ontological Violence of Westernization.' *American Indian Quarterly* 28 (3): 527–49.
Walker, Polly O. 2019. 'Indigenous Ceremonial Peacemaking: the Restoration of Balance and Harmony.' In *Handbook of Research on Promoting Peace through Practice*, edited by Mohamed W. Lufty and Cris Toffolo, pp. 299–319. Hershey Academia & the Arts. IGI Global.
Wolfe, Patrick. 2006. 'Settler Colonialism and the Elimination of the Native.' *Journal of Genocide Research* 8 (4): 387–409.

Conclusions: Futures for, with and by young people

Helen Berents, Catherine E. Bolten and Siobhán McEvoy-Levy

The chapters in this volume reveal, through examples from around the world and across more than half a century, that youth, outside of their sustained contact with the state, are neither a monolithic group of people who share political aims, nor are they necessarily revolutionary or even radical. Rather it is the perpetual habit of states to define an otherwise amorphous life-stage as a category of identity that generates the narrative of youth as a potential problem – and as a potential solution – to the issues of violence and peace in the world. The contributors to this volume reveal the assumption across state leaderships that young people are not fully socially, emotionally or intellectually formed, and thus can be influenced and swayed by whatever source of power is applied to them. Their influenceability renders them simultaneously as potential threats and potential assets to the state. Youth, according to states, are either 'with us or against us', they are never simply citizens whose agendas may not be politically oriented to the state at all, and they are certainly never imagined to be politically conservative, or simply motivated by the same goals their parents had. This imaginary of the unformed, easily influenced, always potentially radical young person is the primary foundation of states' youth 'problems'.

At the same time the 'youth problem' is not necessarily solved by policies directed at all young people. States habitually focus on those individuals they believe to be the leaders or emergent leaders among the youth – whether their leadership is thought to be a positive or negative influence – assuming that young people look to other young people for guidance, rather than engaging in novel forms of knowledge creation and deliberation. Lawmakers have demonstrated a pattern of seeking those who make the statements, or appear to set the agendas, without necessarily taking into consideration that, for example, young people who appear to represent their fellows may be motivated by inclusive and non-hierarchical forms of organising, that their organisations may be gender- and identity-diverse, and that their goals – such as protection for amputees, or community spaces for girls – may not be recognisable to states. This tunnel vision, which relies on an ill-defined set of criteria for 'leadership' and misattributes many of the social structures and goals of young people, leaves the vast majority of young people at odds with or in direct opposition to the goals and motivations of the state. Young people who want to be part of peacebuilding in their countries are forced to conform to hierarchical, compartmentalised, rigid structures that not only fail to reflect their own values but often explicitly devalue their skills, ideas and potential contributions as young people. In short, young people who engage actively with the state, and youth peacebuilders especially, do not want to be condescended to, nor do they seek a source of parenting in their engagement with larger structures of peacebuilding. They seek a world otherwise, one that does not try to compartmentalise their identities and their possibilities into narrow structures that were not built for them.

As the chapters have shown, youth participation in institutions requires more than quotas or seeking ever more diverse representation: it requires the fashioning of new narratives, tools and perspectives on 'participation' and on youth. Including young people as stakeholders in the foundational texts of peace agreements, transitional justice mandates and global policy agendas is only a first step. As demonstrated in this volume, such textual inclusions can inscribe some categories of youth as deserving of inclusion and write others out. The violence of institutional inclusion is seen when such measures shore up structural inequalities and create narrow understandings of 'the peacebuilder' and of who has authority to speak about violence and peace. Moreover, if institutional inclusion approaches are set up to privilege youth who are already politically involved and whose chief goals are political careers, then transformative policies or challenges to the status quo are unlikely to emerge. Thus, while 'the violence of exclusion' (Simpson 2018) is already acknowledged, more critical attention should be paid to the potential 'violences of inclusion' also.

States, multilateral institutions and peacebuilding organisations often think about including young people as a means to an end: youth are instrumentalised to serve goals of state stability and counter-terrorism, to legitimise peace agreements and transitional justice mechanisms or to access donor funding and reinforce institutional credibility. The prioritisation of these other goals, rather than the rights and knowledge of diverse youth representatives, risks doing great harm to youth and their communities. The violence of inclusion is shown when youth and their peacebuilding contributions are at intervals politicised and then depoliticised to serve institutional interests at different times.

Young activists are bridging formal and informal civic and political spaces in confident and creative ways that refuse to sacrifice justice for participation. But young people's desire for inclusion and partnership is not unconditional or inevitable. New norms and practices for youth participation in peacebuilding institutions are evolving in the YPS era, and they require continual updating and self-reflection from all parties involved to preserve and renew their system-transforming aims. The participative structures and spaces that some young people initiate – such as multi-species and intergenerational practices of land-based care and solidarity or critical memorialisation of violence through street art – shape new forms of power, knowledge creation and peacebuilding praxis. It is decolonial by nature, not by purposeful design.

What contributions to this volume demonstrate is the diversity and complexity of young people's efforts to build peace and respond to violence and insecurity. Categorisations of youth that rely on stereotypes, or framings that limit recognition and inclusion to those who conform or fit the narratives of non-youth actors and institutions, miss the already-occurring activity and contributions of youth. Despite this, often with limited resources and enormous logistical challenges, youth are active peacebuilders in their communities, countries and beyond. As noted above, while these activities may not be legible to institutions or the state as peacebuilding activities, youth nevertheless persist in their efforts.

Youth are not homogeneous, and, while their heterogeneity poses challenges to states and institutions who approach youth with preconceived notions, it also is a key source of strength and possibility for youth peacebuilders. Intersectional approaches to youth peacebuilding pay attention to the ways gender, race, class, geographical diversity and age shape young people's experiences and contributions to peace. Young people's peace work is often incredibly fraught and risky, motivated by lived experiences of violence and exclusion, and being active and visible peacebuilders may further raise their profiles as potential targets of violence. As chapters in this volume demonstrate, youth peacebuilding work is also an act of world-building in response to those risks and violences; with their actions being relational, intergenerational, generative, and collective.

This volume does not argue that youth are inherently peaceful (just as they are not inherently violent or radical or risky), or that youth inevitably have new ideas to share simply by virtue of being young. We do not romanticise or essentialise young people's contributions and potential. However, we do argue that sustainable peacebuilding with, for and by youth must involve more research, action and advocacy that asks scholars and practitioners to take seriously and build from the following ideas:

- Move away from reflexively and unthinkingly framing youth as security threats, despite the fact that this framing remains powerful and dominant in influencing political agendas and in accessing funding streams.

This takes courage and continuous reflection and re-evaluation on the politically and socially constructed nature of youth 'problems'.

- Recognise the multiple forms of violence, insecurity and risk which are experienced by young people as forms of expertise and elements of their identities as peacebuilders, but not the sole source of their values, potential contributions or political commitments.
- Conceptualise (sustainable) peace in pluralistic ways which are grounded and informed by the intersectional spaces, ideas, politics and relationships which young people live within, shape and create.
- Admit and acknowledge that recognition and invitations (as well as expectations) to participate can create new problems for youth, which can be symbolic and ideological as well as practical. This requires further efforts and actions, by adult power-holders, to both remove barriers to participation of young people in peacebuilding institutions, processes and practices and to imagine and enact new, diverse forms of youth inclusion.
- Appreciate that the different issue-based concerns and commitments of youth are preconditions for sustainable peace and therefore a priori part of peacebuilding even if they do not fit existing frameworks – adjust the frameworks, not the activities of youth.
- Support youth to define and choose the tools and spaces of participation which could be spiritual, ecological, artistic, educational, entrepreneurial or some other combination of those as yet unimagined by adult peacebuilding scholars and practitioners.
- Collaborate with commitment, bravery and humbleness in seeking truly co-constituted pathways and engagements between youth and non-youth that centre trust, power-sharing and a willingness of non-youth actors to meet youth on their terms.
- Diversify who is recognised as a youth peacebuilder across race, class, gender, sexuality, geography and other identities and across phases of conflict including pre-, post- and post-post-conflict as well as in 'at peace' countries.
- Accompany and support – without directing the outcomes of – young people's intersectional peace work that ranges from the interpersonal to the collective, from the everyday to the organised, from the local to the global, from the intimate to the transnational, and from that which is commonly identified as 'peacebuilding' to activities that may seem to be outside the scope of peacebuilding according to existing schema and assumptions.

These are bold and challenging offerings to dominant academic and policy approaches which are resistant to new ways of doing things and sceptical of new actors. However, practitioners and scholars, both youth and non-youth, are already successfully undertaking these actions, and embodying these approaches. Existing work on local and hybrid forms of peacebuilding open space to account for youth peacebuilding. The struggles and perspectives of many of the youth peacebuilders in these chapters appear to endorse or at least engage hybrid peacebuilding – seeking engagement with organisations and institutions that value their praxis and take their leads. However, there are still unresolved paradoxes and tensions involved in bridging the local and the global, and/or the informal and institutional.

Calls for intergenerational dialogue, commitment to multigenerational shifting of values around youth capacity, and previously overlooked understandings of peacebuilding as multi-species or intergenerational healing or intersectional, offer new sites of opportunity but also new spaces for co-option and silencing. Institutional inertia and unwillingness to cede power or bridge differences pose significant obstacles to any advancement of sustainable and youth-led peacebuilding. The detailed accounts within this book suggest that, to have any chance of being relevant and accountable, the YPS agenda will require diverse and bold participation by dynamically evolving groups of young people that are not direct representatives of states. For this to be a success, youth will need to bring the non-traditional knowledge and manners of peacebuilding that are rooted in the practices of their peers in non-formal spaces of participation, and institutional and non-youth actors will need to bring a willingness to partner with youth to achieve shared common goals. This is a daunting task.

Young people's activities offer other ways of thinking about what peace means and where peacebuilding occurs. These other ways of thinking are not *new* but rather only newly noticed by peacebuilding actors too often set in their own pathways and practices. Close engagement with the complexity of experiences, expertise and contributions of youth, as demonstrated throughout this volume, opens new avenues of inquiry, new insights that challenge stale, limiting and damaging representations of youth, and new possibilities for partnership and collaborations across diverse populations. Youth peacebuilding does not only benefit youth; rather the inclusion and leadership of youth has the potential not only to support young people but to build more peaceful, inclusive and sustainable worlds for all.

Reference

Simpson, Graeme. 2018. *The Missing Peace: Independent Progress Study on Youth and Peace and Security.* United Nations. https://www.youth4peace.info/system/files/2018–10/youth-web-english.pdf. Accessed 5 May 2021.

Index

War on Terror 77
Women, Peace and Security Agenda
  (WPS)
  and Youth, Peace and Security 138,
    143–4

youth
  perceived as delinquent 11, 32, 36,
    40, 41, 43, 68, 148
  see also youth bulge
  future promise 8–9, 35, 40, 42, 109,
    113, 158, 160, 170, 177, 184, 219,
    245
  victims 92–3, 95, 97, 101, 159, 232

youth bulge 8–9, 30–31, 67–70,
  77–8
Youth and Community Centers
  role of 192–3, 199
youth participation *see* participation
Youth, Peace and Security (YPS) Act,
  US 67–8, 77–8
Youth, Peace and Security (YPS)
  Agenda 1–3, 67–8, 77–8, 85, 122,
    130, 137, 140, 205–7, 261
  development of 140, 141–142
youth–to–youth peacebuilding
  strategies 218–20, 222, 232

Printed in the USA
CPSIA information can be obtained
at www.ICGtesting.com
JSHW011338150724
66431JS00021B/154